BEING
PAKISTANI

Raza Ahmad Rumi is a Pakistani policy analyst, journalist and an author. Currently, he is the editor, *Daily Times* (Pakistan). He is Visiting Faculty at Cornell Institute for Public Affairs and has taught at Ithaca College and New York University. Rumi has been a fellow at United States Institute for Peace and National Endowment for Democracy. Earlier, he worked for the Asian Development Bank as a Governance Specialist and an officer in the Pakistan Administrative Service.

Rumi is the author of *Delhi by Heart: Impressions of a Pakistani Traveller, The Fractious Path: Pakistan's Democratic Transition and Identity* and *Faith and Conflict*. www.razarumi.com

Praise for *Being Pakistani: Society, Culture and the Arts*

As partition became inevitable, the incisive Urdu literary critic Muhammad Hasan Askari, raised the question: what would Pakistani culture be like? How would it be distinct from 'Indian' culture? Raza Rumi's book is a response to questions that reference a shared cultural past that resists fracture. Raza's book engages with the globalization of culture in ways that are both subtle and pertinent.

— **Mehr Afshan Farooqi**, Associate Professor, Department of Middle Eastern and South Asian Languages and Cultures, University of Virginia

Raza Rumi represents the intellect that defies identity and its lethal politics in the company of a few great classical minds that Pakistan is straining to forget. The mystic best represents his kind of political analyst: honest and non-partisan and therefore the target of the obscurantist. *Being Pakistani* enables us to understand cultural anxieties in a non-challenging, persuasive manner.

— **Khaled Ahmed**, Consulting editor, *Newsweek Pakistan*; Columnist, *Indian Express*

Riddled with one crisis after the other and perennially at crossroads in a relatively short span of time, Pakistan's turbulent years lend a sense of urgency to cultural questions, as much as and sometimes even more than socio-political issues. Writing from within the eye of the storm, Raza Rumi's lively and lucid essays never fail to be incisive and thought-provoking, a true product of this country and their time.

— **Asif Farrukhi**, Writer and Critic

BEING PAKISTANI

◆

SOCIETY, CULTURE
AND
THE ARTS

◆

RAZA RUMI

HarperCollins *Publishers* India

First published in India by
HarperCollins *Publishers* in 2018
A-75, Sector 57, Noida, Uttar Pradesh 201301, India
www.harpercollins.co.in

2 4 6 8 10 9 7 5 3 1

P-ISBN: 978-93-5277-605-4
E-ISBN: 978-93-5277-606-1

Typeset in 11/14 Bembo at
Manipal Digital Systems, Manipal

Printed and bound at
Thomson Press (India) Ltd

Contents

ARTS

PERSONAL ESSAY

Author's Note

~

Three decades ago, I asked Pakistan's celebrated writer and intellectual Enver Sajjad to define Pakistani culture for me. I vividly remember that restless summer evening and the erudite response which emphasized the pluralistic nature of Pakistan's myriad cultures. And the fact that Pakistan was way too diverse than I, as a schoolboy, understood. Pakistan's cultural landscape is a fascinating kaleidoscope that endures in stark contrast to the singular notion of one-religion, one-nation, one-culture that we learnt at school and heard on the radio and TV. *Being Pakistani* is a composite, layered and often contested idea.

The occasional writings in this volume reflect my attempts to understand the country of my birth and identity. Some of these essays were presented at conferences while others were written for specific publications. Despite the variations in style and tone, there are common threads: the richness, the contradictions and the power of cultural expression.

After 1947, Pakistan as a new nation-state had to carve out an identity separate from India. This was a peculiar struggle. While religion brought together the majority of the population, local cultures and languages and a shared past with India made the task more complicated. Artists, writers and intellectuals have continuously challenged the state narratives of nationhood. This book features profiles of Intizar Husain, Fahmida Riaz and Mustafa Zaidi among others, whose literary works have delved into such themes. Literature has also been a powerful instrument of political resistance through dictatorships; and more recently poets and writers have confronted extremism that afflicts contemporary Pakistan.

'Pakistani' identity and ecology include the River Indus, the cult of the feminine in folklore and the indistinguishable spirituality of Sufi Bulleh Shah and Bhakat Kabir. Its contemporary popular culture entails influences from Bollywood and Indian TV soaps. But there is also an emergence of a distinct Pakistani cultural sensibility. The works of artist Shahzia Sikander and others that revived miniature painting at the global level, artistic battles of Saira Wasim and (late) Asim Butt (featured in this collection) testify to how a meaningful Pakistani cultural idiom has evolved over the years. Pakistan's poets, writers, and artists have been producing alternative histories, yet to be properly documented.

Geopolitics and the dominant global security discourse have reduced Pakistan to 'terrorism' and military coups. Films, novels and global media images reaffirm such reductionist frames.

I hope this book will allow the readers to notice the intricate mosaic of Pakistani identity and vibrant cultural expressions.

DEVOTION

1

The Unholy Trinity of Love: Kabir, Bulleh and Lalon

~

Fifteenth-century India witnessed the coming of age of a process that started brewing with the arrival of the eternal travellers, the Central Asian Sufis, who arrived in India with the message of Islam and mystic love. When Sufi thought, an offshore spiritual undercurrent to the rise of Islam, met its local hosts, the results were terrific. There was no shortage of fundamentalists and communalists in that cultural landscape, and the gulf between alien rulers and the native subjects was a stark reality as well.

Nevertheless, hundreds of yogis, Sufis and poets of India navigated a synthesis of sorts. Very much a people's movement, the Bhakti movement articulated a powerful vision of tolerance, amity and co-existence which is still relevant today. This was many centuries before the suave, western-educated intelligentsia coined the 'people-to-people' contact campaigns. Yes, much has been lost in the tumultuous twentieth century and perhaps the histories and nation states rhetoric are also irreversible. But common ground remains. This article explores that common ground, which has been nurtured by the mystic poets from various parts of northern India, now comprising India, Pakistan and Bangladesh.

The powerful and soulful voices of Kabir, Bulleh Shah and Lalon Shah sing a shared tune: of love, rejection of formal identities based on caste, organized religion and class. In doing so, these mystics unleashed a process of inter-faith dialogue and understanding, and the triumph of humanism even in the most adverse political and economic circumstances.

As the following lines will show, their messages are so similar in tone and tenor that there seems to be a thread — like Kabir's weave or Bulleh's dance or Lalon's rustic songs — which was more prominent from the fifteenth to the nineteenth centuries, and continues even today. In a linear and non-linear sense of time, the messages of these poets have become embedded in popular psyche, language, rural rites and day-to-day existence; thereby shaping what we broadly understand as 'culture.'

In their rejection of Muslim and Hindu orthodoxies, these mystic poets are messengers of love, oblivious of caste hierarchies and indeed spurned by both the Mullahs and the Pundits, but loved by the people — the nameless and faceless millions who have found a meaning in their existence through them and have learnt to love their fellow human beings.

Kabir (1398–1448)

Do not go to the garden of flowers! O Friend! Go not there;
In your body is the garden of flowers.
Take your seat on the thousand petals of the lotus, And there
gaze on the Infinite Beauty.

TRANSLATION BY RABINDRANATH TAGORE

Kabir, born seventy-one years before Nanak, is the supreme, sublime and perhaps the simplest of voices from the Bhakti movement. His poems have been sung across the subcontinent now for nearly five centuries. And there are so many versions of his poetry that researchers continue to grapple with the challenge of sifting the 'original' Kabir from all that is attributed to his name. Does it matter? At the popular level, not really! Was he a Muslim or a Hindu? We do know that there are more than one tombs of Kabir where he is ostensibly buried. Similar confusion abounds over Kabir Samadhi. His name was evidently Muslim but his origins were shrouded by labels of all kinds. However, his internalization of the Indian spiritual tenet; and lore made him a complete Hindustani – beyond the barriers of religion, creed and identity politics which generates violence.

> *Don't go to the gardens outside, don't go: Your body itself*
> *contains a bower in bloom. There you can sit on a thousand-*
> *petalled lotus, And gaze upon the ultimate infinite form*[1].

A weaver by profession and therefore at the lower end of the socio-economic strata, Kabir also represented the woes of the rural folk who lived in 'thousands of villages' at the margins of central power and its intrigues. Kabir's songs were reformist in nature and influenced the ordinary villagers and lower castes and provided them the self-confidence to question Brahmins.

Rabindranath Tagore's translations introduced Kabir to the world outside India. His translations are lyrical and retain the essential simplicity inherent to his otherwise complex thought. Here is a powerful thought: God is the breath of all breath.

This is the fundamental pillar of Bhakti where worship and divine experience emanate from and are located in the self:

> *O servant, where dost thou seek Me?*
> *Lo! I am beside thee.*
> *I am neither in temple nor in mosque: I am neither in Kaaba nor in Kailash:*
> *Neither am I in rites and ceremonies, nor in Yoga and renunciation.*
> *If thou art a true seeker, thou shalt at once see Me: thou shalt Meet Me in a moment of time.*
> *Kabîr says, 'O Sadhu! God is the breath of all breath.'*

Echoing Rumi and his successor Bulleh Shah, Kabir sings:

> *I do not know what manner of God is mine.*

The Mullah cries aloud to Him:

> *And why? Is your Lord deaf? The subtle anklets that ring on the feet of an insect when it moves are heard by Him.*
> *Tell your beads, paint your forehead with the mark of your God, and wear matted locks long and showy: but a deadly weapon is in your heart, then how shall you have God?*

The deadly weapon (or the conceited self) in the hearts is what prevents the realization of the divine light and beauty. This is why Kabir tells us to look inwards as opposed to brandishing the external symbols and structures of formal religion and religiosity.

A few years ago, I came across Vinay Dharwadker's excellent translations[2]. They are imaginative and open up newer vistas of meaning layered in Kabir's ostensibly simple songs. However, it was the erudite introduction that added a newer dimension to my previous understanding of Kabir.

While exploring the underlying secularism of Kabir's verses, Dharwadker detects the extra dimension that, amazingly, is far beyond the known boundaries of secularism. He writes how between the sixteenth and eighteenth centuries, the followers of Kabir added to the discourse of spirituality and the primordial search for God:

'In this dissident conception of the secular, institutionalized religions – with their wealth, power, mediating structures and violent practices – determine what constitutes religion and what is legitimately "religious" in the human world. But the human world belongs wholly to the domain of Maya, so these institutions and their definitions of *dharma* or religion cannot reach beyond the limits of Maya to be God without attributes. Nirguna God stands outside the immense scaffolding of organized human religions and what they define as religious doctrine and practice, and since the "secular" is that which lies outside the scope of the "religious", God as such is entirely secular.'[3]

Therefore, the process of attaining mukti, liberation, from the trappings of religion to achieve a union with a God without attributes is a secular process.

'It is precisely such a secularism that makes both God and mukti completely accessible to anyone and everyone, regardless of caste, class, birth, gender, upbringing, status or rank, and that becomes indistinguishable from the deeply subversive egalitarianism and cosmopolitanism of the Kabir community.'[4]

The Kabir community comprises scores of followers, and later poets, who kept adding verse to the Kabir anthology and today it is all ascribed to the great sage. Let's hope this community grows and flourishes. My favourite translation from Dharwadker is:

> If Khuda inhabits the mosque,
> Then whose play-field is the rest of the world?
> If Rama lives in the idol at the pilgrim station,
> Then who controls the chaos outside?
> The East is Hari's domicile, they say,
> The West is Allah's dwelling place.
> Look into your heart, your very heart:
> That's where Karim-and-Rama reside.
> All the men and the women ever born,
> Are nothing but Your embodied forms:
> Kabir's a child of Allah-and-Rama
> They're his Guru-and-Pir.[5]

Bulleh Shah (1680–1757)

Bulleh Shah of Kasur in Central Punjab is another towering voice that provided a mystical message beyond caste, institutionalized religion and ideologies of power. Born in 1680 in a Syed family, he found a *murshid*, a spiritual master, in Shah Inayat who was an Arain, a lower caste. This enraged his family and they nearly disowned him. However, intoxicated with the love for his master, and driven by ideas of unity of existence and equality of humans, he rejected all notions of upper or lower caste and stuck to his humanism.

Bulleh's poetry reflected his rejection of the orthodox mullahs who had hijacked the message of Islam, the nexus between the clergy and the rulers, and all the trappings of formal religion that created a gulf between man and his Creator. A common theme of his poetry is the pursuit of self-knowledge that is essential for the mystical union with the Beloved.

Yes, yes, you have read thousands of books,
But you have never tried to read your own self.
You rush in, into your mandirs, into your mosques,
But you have never tried to enter your own heart.
Futile are all your battles with Satan,
For you have never tried to fight your own desires.

Bulleh Shah's murshid, Shah Inayat, belonged to the Qadiriyya Shattari School which was known for its close affinity with yoga and other meditative practices.

On the limitations of organized rituals, Bulleh Shah says:

Demolish the mosque, pull down the temple
Pull down everything in sight
But don't break a human heart
For that is where the Almighty lives

Echoing Kabir, Bulleh says:

If you can understand, then why all this commotion?
What's this fuss about calling Him Ram, Rahim or Moula?

About priests in general Bulleh Shah writes:

Mullah tay mashaalchi dohaan ikko chit
Loukan karday chananan, aap anhairae vich

Mullah and the torch-bearer, both from the same flock
Guiding others; themselves in the dark

The yearning for anonymity and connecting with the Beloved requires that there be no distractions, no castes and no illusions of attachment. Bulleh Shah's verse says it so directly and passionately. His famous poem, *Ik Nuktay Wich Gal Mukdee Aay*, is a culmination of all that he imbibed from the Bhakti-inspired milieu of the subcontinent and the people's everyday beliefs and coexistence at the subaltern level. The English translation by Muzzaffar Ghaffar[6] is my favourite:

> *Ik nuktay wich gal mukdee aay (On one point the matter ends)*
> *Catch the point, drop the academe*
> *Push away divisions which blaspheme*
> *Cast off hell, the grave, chastisement extreme*
> *Cleanse out the heart's every dream*
> *Into this house everything descends*
> *On one point the matter ends*
> *Some to jungles, to the seas go*
> *Some daily a single grain swallow*
> *Without perception tiredness they stow*
> *They return home emaciated, in imbroglio*
> *Just in prayer-rigours life expands*
> *On one point the matter ends.*

Nukta (literally meaning dot) is difficult to decipher. My personal interpretation has to do with the nukta of Being – like the letter *Alif* (the first of the Urdu/Persian/Arabic alphabet) that is Single and a whole. So we, the created, are not different from the Creator; and we, the lovers, are not separate from the Beloved. It is this unity of being and all interlinked forms of existence that converge on one little dot that has all the answers and comforts we spend our lifetimes attaining.

Perhaps the best reflection of Bulleh's irreverence is the poem where he likens dogs to the ideal Sufi:

They do not stop barking
And ultimately sleep on a dirty pile of waste
They are superior to you

They do not leave their master's door even
If they are beaten by shoes

Bulleh Shah! Perform good deeds
Otherwise dogs will supersede you
They are superior to you

In the footsteps of Kabir, this is what Bulleh sang in the rural environs of Punjab:

I am neither a Hindu nor a Muslim.
I sit in the spinning bee forsaking pride
I am neither a Sunni, nor a Shia.
I take to the path of amity for all

He concludes this poem with these lines:

I know not the path of vice and virtue.
O Bulleh! If in the heart dwells the Lord
One would renounce both Hindu and Muslim.

Since the deregulation of the media in 2002, Pakistan witnessed a *glasnost* (openness) that surprised even the most hard-boiled cynics in the country. Sufi pop plays on privately owned

electronic media which also churns out much that could not
be transmitted before. The famous band Junoon (and more
recently Coke Studio) and other exponents of the pop genre
have created this incredible fusion between the old and the
new, and have instantaneously popularized Sufi poetry to the
MTV generation that otherwise might not have discovered
this aspect of our heritage and its perennial cross currents.

In this milieu, the iconoclasm of Bulleh Shah is a fascinating
polarity – bringing out the 'other' discourse in full public
view. Pakistan's famous Ajoka Theatre's landmark production,
'Bullah' is another cultural milestone that continues to reinvent
and reintroduce Bulleh Shah within and beyond Pakistan.
In particular, the revival of Bulleh in India is partly linked
to Ajoka's various performances in the different Punjabi-
speaking states and other parts of India. Ajoka's handiwork
was a seminal attempt to trace the life and progression of
Bulleh Shah in a truly subaltern format. Almost in quick
succession, we heard Rabbi, who earned instant stardom with
his video 'Bullah Ki Jana Main Kaun'. Rabbi's voice has had a
timeless quality and its transportation of soulful verse into the
rock genre made the song an instant hit. The video director
weaved in a modern translation of the lyrics into the images,
thereby making Bulleh's poetry comprehensible to millions
worldwide. The translations appeared quite terrific in a caste-
ridden, geography-obsessed and conflict-laden South Asia.
Clubs across India and abroad played the song with a fervour
that may have surprised even Bulleh Shah himself!

Bulleh's revival, admittedly on a limited scale, is comparable
to the fascinating ascendancy of the thirteenth-century poet-
mystic Jalaluddin Rumi in the West, particularly the United
States. The US media outlets reported that Rumi ranked as

America's bestselling poet in 1997. While it is true that the likes of Deepak Chopra have transformed Rumi into a love-therapy icon, his popularity has nevertheless led to his full-scale launch in academia and journalism. In fact, one of the antidotes to Islamophobia in the US has been Rumi's songs of love – a glimmer of discernment in the largely Eurocentric (and somewhat xenophobic) world of mainstream Western media. The Internet hosts thousands of sites which translate, sell, offer and package Rumi for all kinds.

It is not a mere coincidence that this Bulleh–Rumi resurgence took place in two very different contexts. At a fundamental level, albeit for different reasons, the resistance to formalism and packaged consent found a voice:

Bulleh! to me, I am not known
Not a believer inside the mosque, am I
Nor a pagan disciple of false rites
Not the pure amongst the impure
Neither Moses, nor the Pharoah Bulleh!
To me, I am not known

And the desire to be free of all trappings of identity, convention and routine:

Not an Arab, nor Lahori
Neither Hindi, nor Nagauri
Hindu, Turk, nor Peshawari
Nor do I live in Nadaun
Bulleh! To me, I am not known.

TRANSLATED BY UMAIR RAJAI

Four centuries prior to Bulleh's outpouring, Rumi sang the story of abandon:

> *What is to be done, O Moslems? for I do not recognize myself.*
> *I am neither Christian, nor Jew, nor Gabr, nor Moslem.*
> *I am not of this world, nor of the next, nor of Paradise, nor of Hell*
> *I am not of Adam, nor of Eve, nor of Eden and Rizwan.*

The identity of the messages in these poems speaks a common language, that of existential anguish. Confronted by social conflict, wars and everyday struggles, ordinary humans relate to the subtext of a transcendent spiritual yearning, regardless of their backgrounds and nationalities. Three strands of mystical poetry are clear here: conflicts of identity wear people down; the illusions of adherence to creed at the end of the day does not solve anything, and overplay of the ritual and the formal is at the expense of inner peace. I will conclude my thoughts on Bulleh with an evidently inadequate translation by the author:

> *If God was found by bathing and cleansing*
> *He would have been found by frogs and fish*
>
> *If God was found by wandering in the jungles*
> *Stray animals would have found him*
>
> *O Bulleh, the Lord can only be found*
> *By loving hearts − true and pure.*

Lalon Shah (1772-1890)

> *Why must we go to temples and mosques to reach Him? Love*
> *all people and you will reach your*
> *Krishna or your Allah.*

If the western and central parts of India were fragrant with the songs of Kabir and Bulleh Shah and many others of their ilk, the Bauls of Bengal were challenging orthodoxies in the golden climes of rural Bengal. The Bauls are a community of low-class, illiterate, wandering singers whose wisdom is not based on formal schooling, but emanates from 'lived' contact with an intensely experienced life and close interaction with nature. Rabindranath Tagore introduced the world to the mystic songs of Lalon Shah. In a lecture delivered in London in the 1930s, Tagore stated he discovered that mystic 'man' from the songs of Lalon who was singing in the late nineteenth century – *ai manushe ase se mon* – the 'man' is within yourself.

Tagore compiled and published some of these songs in the monthly *Probashi* as *'Haramoni'* in 1920. Others followed suit. *'Haramoni'* of 1932 quoted Tagore: 'Hindus and Muslims have been united under the same sky – there is no barrier of caste or creed...'

It is well known that Tagore was inspired by East Bengal's countryside (Sealdah, now in Bangladesh), which found the man and the chiseled poet in him. The Baul thought processes and music found their way into his creative output and vision. This particular ethos was rebellious but preached love and self-knowledge without which the idea of God and religiosity was meaningless:

His play knows no end
no telling what shape He'll take, and when
How will you understand the Saain's Divine Play?

Water of the Ganga is called Holy.
But it's the same water filling
The puddle on the road we call dirty!
That is how the Saain shapes Himself
in size with the vessel He fills!

How will you understand the Saain's Divine Play?

He is the room and its occupant,
as well as the thief that steals from it!
He is His own Magistrate,
sentencing Himself to chains!

How will you understand the Saain's Divine Play?

Eternal streams flow out of the One.
You and I are nothing in it, nameless.
Lalon says, 'If only I knew "me,"
all riddles would be solved!'

How will you understand the Saain's Divine Play?

TRANSLATED BY SUDIPTO CHATTERJEE[7]

The mystical cult of Bauls emphasizes a peculiar spiritual discipline that brings together the animistic past and the organized religions of Buddhism, Hinduism and Islam. For instance, the lines below remind one of Bulleh Shah and Kabir.

He who is my soul-mate lives in my soul itself
Thus I see him everywhere
He exists within my eyes, he exists in the stream of light
So he is never lost
So he is visible for me here there and at all places wherever I
cast my eyes

TRANSLATED BY GAUTAM SENGUPTA[8]

Lalon, the best-known Baul, has articulated thoughts akin
to Sufism, calling for the purity of soul and emphasis on
humanism. Like Kabir, Lalon's origins are contested. Some say
he was a Hindu by birth but raised in a Muslim household.

Legend has it that as a child, Lalon contracted smallpox
during a journey and was so unwell that his companions
assumed he was dead and abandoned him. Fate took him to
a nearby village where a Muslim family from the weavers'
community saved him and helped him fully recover. Another
tradition records that a farmer named Malam found him in
the Kaliganga river, a tributary of the Ganga that would pass
through Kushtia. Malam and his wife Matijan found a near-
dead Lalon and brought him back to life.

That his spirit survived between soil and water has a
profound and symbolic meaning among Lalon's followers.
Thus, the origin of his birth is both known and unknown.
Between water, mud and close to death and yet Lalon lived on.

During his stay with the Muslim family, Lalon met Siraj
Sai, a local spiritual guide who left a permanent mark on
him. When, after his recovery, Lalon returned to his village,
he was castigated by his own community for cohabiting
with a Muslim family. This became the turning point in
Lalon's life. He went back to the Muslim family who later

became his disciples. Matijan is buried next to him as per his wish and he wanted the tomb to be known as Lalon–Matijan's tomb.

In his life and his death, like Kabir and Bulleh Shah, Lalon shunned all distinctions of caste and creed.

> *People ask, what is Lalon's caste*
> *Lalon says, my eyes fail to detect*
> *The signs of caste. Don't you see that*
> *Some wear garlands, some rosaries*
> *Around the neck? But does it make any*
> *Difference brother? O, tell me,*
> *What mark does one carry when*
> *One is born, or when one dies?*
> *A Muslim is marked by the sign*
> *Of circumcision; but how should*
> *You mark a woman? If a Brahmin male*
> *Is known by the thread he wears,*
> *How is a woman known? People of the world,*
> *O brother, talk of marks and signs,*
> *But Lalon says: I have only dissolved*
> *The raft of signs, the marks of caste*
> *In the deluge of the One!*

TRANSLATED BY AZFAR HUSSAIN[9]

Lalon was inspired by the Sufi thought that was taking root in West Bengal. Mystics such as Shah Sultan Rumi, Hazrat Shah Jalal, Shah Sultan Makkah and others had already spread the message of love. But Lalon was also inspired by the Bhakti Movement and teachings of enlightened Hindu yogis. Thus he wanted to stress freedom from the bonds of conventional religious frameworks. In a poem, 'A Strange Bird', using the metaphor that was also used by Tagore later, he sings:

> *Look, how a strange bird flits in and out of the cage!*
> *O brother, I wish I could bind it with my mind's fetters*
> *Have you seen a house of eight rooms with nine doors*
> *Closed and open, with windows in between, mirrored?*
> *O mind, you are a bird encaged! And of green sticks*
> *Is your cage made, but it will be broken one day*
> *Lalon says: Open the cage, look how the bird wings away!*

TRANSLATED BY AZFAR HUSSAIN[10]

It is believed that Lalon died at the age of 116 years. Prior to his death, he was singing a song that is now sung at night as a call for union. After his death, Hindus claimed Lalon as their own as did Muslims.

It is believed Lalon was not unaware about his family or his religion; but that he chose never to reveal his 'identity' is highly political. Lalon knew that histories and birth and belonging shaped the politics of identity; and perhaps he wanted to avoid that. The choice of name 'Lalon' was also instructive as it could belong to any religious community or either gender! Like Kabir, Bulleh and their predecessor Rumi, he rejected and buried his identity under the broader and larger identity of humanity.

Lalon was not a traditional Sufi, however. He did not call for a Being outside the given 'body' of human beings. Allah abided in the human form and the challenge was to 'know' and 'taste' oneself to find Him:

> *O Allah! who could decipher your endless play*
> *You are the Allah but calling for Allah yourself*[11]

Lalon, a poet and singer of inclusive disposition, composed songs in praise of Prophet Mohammed as well as Chaitanya and Nityananda. Like Kabir, he had no formal education and lived in extreme poverty. He continues to inspire the Bengali rural peasantry today. Lalon celebrates the freedom of body, soul, and even language, reiterating that music has no identity or caste.

Kabir, Bulleh Shah and Lalon are petals of a mystic lotus that blossomed in medieval India, imbibing the past and the present that gave a new vocabulary of spirituality and cultural coexistence to the people. Punjabis across India and Pakistan are united by the *kaafis* of Bulleh Shah and the Bengalis sing Lalon's songs across geographical divides. And Kabir and his hundreds of versions permeate our language, ethos and cultural attitudes. Maybe not in those palaces and power-mongering lanes that perpetrate violence or the seminaries of organized religion which preach ignorance. But in the hearts and everyday lives, in those tender precincts of the personal and ' communal'

It is therefore essential to rediscover this vibrant past of India, Pakistan and Bangladesh. While accepting that history has drawn borders, there is a need to look beneath the surface. Whether it is fighting communalism in India or extremism in Pakistan and Bangladesh, the Sufis, Bhaktas, mystics and Bauls have much to offer to make South Asia a safer and more prosperous part of the world community.

Published in *Third Frame*, Vol 1 no. 2, Summer, 2007 Jamia Millia Islamia, Delhi.

2

Devotion, Syncretism and Politics:
Myth and Legends of the Indus

❧

Indus – A Lifeline

Along its 1,800-mile course, the Indus joins cultures from the steppes of Central Asia to the arid plains of the South Asian subcontinent. It affects patterns of thought and behaviour, shapes expressions of culture and also provides inspiration for art. The hopes and aspirations of its people are reflected in stories and elaborate myths, transmitted through the consciousness of successive generations by bards and storytellers. While the focus of this is not the ancient culture of the Indus Valley, it is important to mention that the Indus Valley Civilization originated in the fertile plains of the Indus River, in the third and fourth millennium BC. This civilization, or the Harappan Culture, was coeval with the ancient civilizations of Egypt and Mesopotamia, and is recognized as the third major civilization in the history of humankind. Archaeological excavations in present-day Pakistan show that the people of this culture lived a life of refinement and opulence, with a well-developed civic system and prosperous trade links.[1]

The Indian Subcontinent derives its very name from the river Indus. In Sanskrit, the river was known as 'Sindhu'. The Persians gave it the form Hindu and through successive generations it finally came to be known as India, with various forms being derived from this root. The Indus region excited the imagination of the Europeans, with the lure reaching the West even in the time of Alexander the Great. Since then, exotic tales of this vast and seemingly enchanting land have spurred on the ambitions of many a great conqueror.[2]

Those living along the banks of the Indus know it by a multitude of names. To the Sindhis, it is known as 'Purali', the capricious river whose floods can make and destroy civilizations. The Sindhis also refer to it as 'Samundar' (sea), as a tribute to the sheer size of the river as it flows down to the Arabian Sea. Further up the course of the river, the Pashtuns refer to it as the 'Nilab' (blue water), 'Sher Darya' (Lion River) and 'Abbasin' (father of rivers). The mountain people of Baltistan know it as 'Gemtsuh' (the Great Flood), or 'Tsuh-Fo' (the Male River).

Mohanas, the boat people of the Indus valley, still live along its banks, near the shrine of Khwaja Khizr and in other areas as well. They traverse the mighty river on boats which have remained essentially similar in design to those depicted in the art of the Indus Valley Civilization thousands of years ago.[3]

Today, even as conflict and political tensions tear apart the unity of those who live along the Indus, their lives continue to be as linked to it as they were millennia ago. It remains, even today, a powerful unifier of India and Pakistan, for Pakistan would not survive without the might of the Indus and India would not be the progeny of the Sindhu Sagar.

Globalization and integration into the world economic system have transformed the Indus and the lives of those who live along its banks. The process of harnessing the waters of the mighty Indus to the yoke of profit, initiated by the British colonial rulers, was continued by a military-dominated Pakistani state. Today, an extensive network of dams, barrages and canals have been built along the course of the river, from Mangla in the north to Sukkur in the south. In the south, especially, the river has become dry. Its fresh waters have become saline in some places too. Where barrages have been built, many have adopted fishing as an occupation; agriculture in those areas no longer being an option.

Indus as a Source of Belief Systems

Though the last three Vedas proclaim the River Ganges to be one of the most important 'holy rivers in India,' the first sacred text ascribed this position to the Indus River.[4] Hymn XXV from 'Hymns of the Rig Veda,' describes the reverence and significance given to the *Sindhu*:

> *12. May we, unharmed, serve bountiful Visnu, the God who slayeth none: Self-moving Sindhu hear and be the first to mark.*[5]

Here the Sindhu is a witness to the acts performed by the people in the name of Vishnu. It is also seen as a protector for the people:

1. This stream Sarasvati with fostering current comes forth, our sure defence, our fort of iron.
As on a car, the flood flows on, surpassing in majesty and might all other rivers.[6]

Moreover, the Indus also represented a space that was geographically pure and unpolluted. In Hinduism, different physical spaces are categorized as pure and impure territories. Thus, crossing the river, especially into the far north-west of the country meant entering impure territory. This region was part of 'northern Punjab and the city of Taxila,' which was looked down upon as a marginal area where odd occurrences took place.[7] For this reason, the Indus was often referred to as *kalapani* (black water, a term traditionally used for the ocean), and those who crossed it suffered a loss with reference to their caste position.

As a result of the role attributed to the river, the Indus was also a main component of the everyday-beliefs of the people. It was used as a reference to carry out various actions such as bringing health to those who were sick:

2: Here these two winds are blowing far as Sindhu from a distant land. May one breathe energy to thee, the other blow thy fault away.[8]

The river was also given due importance when using charms against jealousy:

1. Brought hitherward from Sindhu, from a folk of every mingled race, fetched from afar, thou are I deem, a balm that cureth jealousy.

2. As one with water quencheth fire, so calm this lover's jealousy, like heat of fire that burneth here, or flame that rageth through the wood.[9]

According to Griffith, as seen from a hymn in Hymns of the Rig Veda, the river may also have been referred to as a mechanism to gain strength before a battle fought on the shore of the Indus. In this particular hymn, Sindhu's strength, beauty and influence have been focused upon, and it represents an undefeatable symbol:

1. The singer, O ye Waters, in Vivasvan's place, shall tell your grandeur forth that is beyond compare. The Rivers have come forward triply, seven and seven. Sindhu in might surpasses all the streams that flow. 2. Varuna cut the channels for they forward course, O Sindhu, when thou rannest on to win the race. Thou speedest o'er precipitous ridges of the earth, when thou art Lord and Leader of these moving floods. 3. His roar is lifted up to heaven above the earth: he puts forth endless vigour with a flash of light. Like floods of rain that fall in thunder from the cloud, so Sindhu rushes on bellowing like a bull. 4. Like mothers to their calves, like milch-kine with their milk, so, Sindhu, unto thee the roaring rivers run. Thou leadest as a warrior king thine army's wings what time thou comest in the van of these swift streams. 5. Favour ye this my laud, O Ganga, Yamuna, O Saturdi, Parusni and Sarasvati: with Asikni, Vitasta, O Marudvrdha, O Arjikiya with Susoma hear my call. 6. Flashing and whitely-gleaming in her mightiness, she moves along her ample volumes through the realms, Most active of the active, Sindhu unrestrained, like a dappled mare, beautiful, fair to see. 7. Rich in good

*steeds is Sindhu, rich in cars and robes, rich in gold, nobly-
fashioned, rich in ample wealth. Blest Silamavati and young
Urnavati invest themselves with raiment rich in store of sweets.
8. Sindhu hath yoked her car, light-rolling, drawn by steeds,
and with that car shall she win booty in this fight. So have I
praised its power, might and unrestrained, of independent glory,
roaring as it runs.*[10]

In modern day Pakistan, the Indus continues to hold certain
significance in the lives of many people. The only difference
being that this significance is now interlinked with Islamic
religious beliefs. Albinia narrates an event near Sufi saint
Khwaja Khizr's shrine where she sees a woman drop the
Qur'an in the middle of the river where the water is thought
to be in its purest form. She carries out this action as she
believes that she will receive a blessing and her sick child will
become healthy again. To Albinia's skeptical comments on her
actions, the woman replies that she should know better as she
is educated.[11]

Despite a radical transformation in the social environment
of the subcontinent, one can see how the belief systems
associated with the river have persisted in various forms and
remain a significant part of the current social reality in India
and Pakistan.

Indus Legends and Folklore

The story of Sohni–Mahiwal is a well-known legend in the
region associated with the subcontinent. Sohni, a potter's
daughter, is forced to marry her cousin. However, her heart
remains with Mehar, 'a merchant who took up buffalo-

herding and pipe-playing to woo her.'[12] Every day, after nightfall, Sohni crosses the Indus to see him. The love story continues until her sister-in-law finds out and substitutes the baked clay pot Sohni uses to cross with river, with an unbaked pot. Sohni meets her tragic end in the Indus which then shifts from facilitator to obstacle in the love-story. Sindhi Sufi poet Shah Latif mentions this very moment in his poem:

> *Pot in hand, trust in God, she enters the waves;*
> *Her leg in the dogfish's mouth, her head in the shark's,*
> *Bangles twisted, hair drifting through the water, Fishes, big and*
> *small, crowd around her Crocodiles waiting to devour her.*[13]

Sohni thus meets the destructive end associated with carrying forth a lover's ambitions. However, she is no longer tied to the 'material body' and 'is united in death with the beloved'.[14]

Sassui figures as another protagonist in Shah Latif's stories. Here too, the Indus plays a pivotal role. Sassui, a Hindu orphan, was found in the Indus by a Muslim washerman who raised her as his own child. Sassui later falls in love with Punhu, a Baloch noble, who acts as if he is from a modest background in order to court her. Punhu's privileged family resents this transgression and ensure that the two remain separated. Sassui's journey into the vast expanse of the Balochistan desert to search for Punhu denotes her separation from the Indus lands – her precious belonging – and this becomes a metaphor for the impact of two separations: from love and from belonging. This makes Sassui an ideal in the mystic sense, for her path is what yogis and fakirs have ventured to follow through centuries. She symbolizes the difficulties associated with undertaking 'the quest for God.'[15]

Folk romances were used as a method of imparting mystical education, particularly by Qazi Qadan (d.1551), Abdul Karim of Bulri and Mian Shah Inayat (d. circa 1700), amongst other Sufi saints.[16]

Xuanzang, the Chinese Buddhist monk, who travelled 10,000 miles from China to India to see Buddhism in Swat, also wrote about the power of the Indus as part of his famous pilgrim chronicles. On his return from China, after his boat toppled over and he lost his botanical collections and sutras, Xuanzang wrote:

> *The River Sin-tu [Indus] is pure and clear as a mirror...*
> *Poisonous dragons and dangerous spirits live beneath its*
> *waters.*
> *If a man tries to cross the river carrying valuable gems, rare*
> *flowers and fruits, or above all, relics of Buddha, the boat is*
> *engulfed by waves.*
>
> XUANZANG, C. 645 CE[17]

This belief had been propagated by the local king who told the monk, 'Whoever attempts to cross the river with seeds of flower is subject to similar fortunes.'[18] Thus, one begins to have an idea of the grandeur and force associated with the river.

The Indus is a major component of the story of Allor as well. At one point, Allor was the capital of a kingdom situated on the riverside. This story revolves around Allor's Hindu prince, Dillu Rao and a Muslim merchant, Saiful Mulk. All river merchants who came to Allor had to give half of their cargo as toll to Dillu Rao. However, once he ordered Saiful Mulk to provide him with the toll as well as an attractive handmaiden named Badiul Jamal. It is said that Mulk requested he be given eight days to fulfil the demands. Simultaneously, however, he managed to 'raise a mighty dam on the river upstream from Allor.' As a result, the river was steered away from the influence of the wicked prince.[19]

Qureshi states beautifully that in all these stories, what is important is 'not the particular moral of the story, but the common feature it has with all other stories of this region: the river. The river dominates the folklore of this region, whether as an artery for commerce, a grave for loves or a balmy surface for boats to float on. Even in the tales of the desert, of the rock hills of Balochistan, water – or its antithesis, sand – are protagonists in each plotline.'[20]

The Indus, Sufism and Syncretism in Sindh

Every wave is filled with rubies, water perfumed with musk,
From the river waft airs of ambergris.

SHAH ABDUL LATIF (1689–1752)[21]

From the ancient Vedic times to stories told by Sufi saints, the Indus continues to play a central role in legends and folklore. Even today, the shrine of Uderolal, a composite Hindu–Muslim place of worship and the cult of Lal Shahbaz Qalandar are rooted and nurtured by the Indus and its magic. Until the nineteenth century, it was thought by both Muslims and Hindus that the ebb and flow of the Indus depended on Lal Shahbaz Qalandar's liking. He is also referred to as Jhule Lal, one of the Hindu names for the god of water and as Raja Bharati by the Hindus.

Current beliefs and practices still reflect continuity with the past. Sehwan Sharif, the site of Lal Shahbaz Qalandar's tomb, was also the location of a prominent Shiva centre. It is said that the name Sehwanistan has been derived from Sivistan, the city of Shiva. Moreover, there is a striking similarity between the dressing of contemporary faqirs and shivite yogis as both dress in 'torn clothes with matted hair'.[22]

In Uderolal lies the tomb of a saint referred to as Shaikh Tahir by the Muslims and as Jhulelal or Uderolal by the Hindus. Both refer to him as the Zindapir, Living Saint. Uderolal is one of the places where the Indus is still worshipped by Hindus and Muslims and is also worshipped in another part of Sindh, near the town of Sukkur.

Shrines of Sufi saints are situated along the riverside in Sindh. It is believed that 1,25,000 holy men are buried 'in the yellow sandstone necropolis at Thaata' alone.[23] All year round, a great number of people continue to visit the tombs as a way to show their respect and receive blessings. Just like Lal Shahbaz Qalandar, Khwaja Khizr is also referred to as Zindapir and 'pani ka badshah', or water king. The devotees still believe he lives under the water and the river flows the way that he commands. As recently as the late nineteenth century, Hindus and Muslims would also worshipp side-by-side at Zindapir's shrine in Sukkur. Moreover, many of the saints are said to have performed miracles in the region through their powers over the Indus.

Such meta-religious beliefs and practices can also be understood with reference to Shah Abdul Latif's *Risalo*, a sacred Sindhi book. It is given equal reverence by both Hindus and Muslims, and contains excerpts from the Quran, 'the traditions of Muhammad, Persian mystical poetry and indigenous Sindhi folk literature'.[24]

It does not focus on any one form of authority and also includes doctrines from various sects of Islam. On the whole, it represents the similarity in spiritual beliefs related to Hinduism and Islam as practiced in the region. Moreover, it is still a symbol of this peaceful co-existence between followers of the two religions. In the home of the custodian of Latif's shrine, in Sindh today, the Qur'an and the Risalo are covered with a piece of cloth and 'laid like babies – like the Baby Krishna – in a cradle'. Thus the syncretism present in the region is evidently visible.[25] Similarly, Latif's folklore, most often, represents the heroine as 'the soul on her spiritual quest', where she is often from a caste lower than the hero's. According to Qureshi, this is done in order to show that 'a fuller spiritual experience can be enjoyed by taking on a feminine consciousness...it is in keeping with the Indian mystical concept of the *virahini* – the pining woman separated from her husband.'[26]

A majority of the Hindus in Sindh consist of Nanakpathis, those who follow Guru Nanak. There is the absence of a clear-cut distinction between Sikhism and Hinduism in the province. According to Alibina, 'during the 1881 and 1891 censuses, Nanakpanthis could not decide whether they were "Hindu" or "Sikh" and gave different answers each time.'[27] This syncretism can further be seen as the Ismailis who settled in the region in the ninth century CE (in particular, the Satpanthi community and their text *Dasa Avatara*) believe that the Prophet Muhammad, or his son-in-law Ali, was the tenth avatar of the Hindu god Vishnu.[28]

As noted above, Uderolal is also the saint of the water worshippers. Sindh continues the ancient water worship practices, some evidence of which has been discovered in the ruins of Mohenjo-Daro. Close to Sehwan, Laki Shah is a small place where visitors gather to purify their bodies and souls by bathing in the springs. Similarly, in the localities of Mol Sharif, near Thano Bula Khan and Lahoot, water provides the sacred arena for worship. This is not different from the Ganges as a revered river.

The composite culture that evolved over the centuries of amalgamation of various spiritual practices continues to date. This consensus of sorts was truncated by the events of the early twentieth century when Muslim identity and corresponding claims to nationhood resulted in the political demand for Pakistan. Sindh and its myriad subcultures became a victim to the higher games of politics, power-seeking and economic interests of local leadership.

Indus Saga Since 1947[29]

The partition of the subcontinent in 1947 brought with it new shape to the politics and cultures of the Indus region. The physical shape took over the mythological one, as the new state of Pakistan was dependent on the Indus as a major source of water and livelihoods.

The post-Partition issues centered on how to divide the waters of the Indus basin -- a previously 'cohesive and unitary network of irrigation'. This was eventually decided with the Indus Water Treaty that was signed in 1960. The fact that it took thirteen years to reach an agreement reflects the difficult nature of the task. Essentially, this difficulty arose because the source rivers were located in Indian territory. As noted in the archive at Stimson Center, USA: 'The waters of the Indus basin begin in the Himalayan mountains of Indian held Kashmir. They flow from the hills through the arid states of Punjab and Sind, converging in Pakistan and emptying into the Arabian Sea south of Karachi.'

Pakistan was insecure in terms of the availability of continued water supply from the Indus as this was its primary source of irrigation for its agricultural land. Pakistan claimed that it was entitled to all of the Indus's tributaries. However, this was unacceptable to India which later demanded that the Western tributaries be given to Pakistan and the Eastern tributaries to India.

Initially after Independence, the Inter-Dominion Accord of 4 May 1948 determined how the waters were to be divided. Under this accord, India had to ensure sufficient water supply to Pakistan in return for a payment from the Pakistani government. Negotiations for a permanent solution continued soon afterwards, however no agreement could be made. India also refused to take the issue to the International Court of Justice as it claimed that the problem 'required a bilateral solution'.[30] Tensions were high by 1951 as negotiations were no longer taking place. However, both sides knew it was essential for talks to continue as there could be no lasting peace without them.

In 1951, David Lilienthal, former chairman of the Tennessee Valley Authority and of the US Atomic Energy Commission visited both India and Pakistan. With a background provided by the US's State Department, he aimed to understand and give his opinion about the conflict between India and Pakistan as well as ways to work around them. Lilienthal suggested that the antagonism between India and Pakistan could be reduced and cooperation could be ensured in the long run if both countries worked together on an Indus Development Programme. Through this programme, they would aim to increase water productivity in both countries.

He also suggested that the World Bank assist both countries in reaching an agreement and also finance the plan.

His ideas were subsequently taken up by the World Bank, and eventually by Pakistan and India as well. India agreed to the World Bank's involvement as they claimed it would only 'work as a conduit for agreement'.[31] Eugene R. Black, the president of the Bank at that time, consequently formed a working party of Pakistani, Indian and World Bank engineers in the hopes of working out a 'functional' solution without worrying about political concerns. However, a solely functional and technical solution could not solve the problem since both sides refused to compromise over their initial positions. It then became evident that political concerns could not be sidelined to reach an agreement.

In 1954, overstepping its previous role, the World Bank offered a proposal which supported giving India the three eastern tributaries and Pakistan the three Western ones. It proposed the construction of canals and storage dams to 'divert waters from the western rivers and replace the eastern river supply lost by Pakistan'.[32]

This was unacceptable to Pakistan and negotiations came to a stalemate at this point. However, both sides could no longer ignore the issue and were forced to resume talks by December 1954. It was decided that the World Bank proposal was now to be used as a basis for negotiation instead of settlement.

The talks continued for the next six years. The Indus Water Treaty was signed in 1960 after it was agreed that the United States and United Kingdom would finance the construction of canals and storage facilities to divert the water to Pakistan. As part of the Treaty, the Permanent Indus Commission was also set up in order to arbitrate any possible disputes over the water in the future, and to ensure communication between the two countries over this matter.

After much effort and compromise, the agreement was in place and has continued to be this way over the last sixty-odd years. This agreement is indicative of the fact that peace between the two countries is possible in the long run, and agreements can be reached -- especially when the cost of not doing so is higher for both countries.

Saving Indus

Whilst the Indus as a major supplier of water and life to Pakistan is a paramount reality, preserving the Indus folklore is also a major challenge. Indus legends are a lived reality of the communities which reside along its majestic banks. In addition to this, their livelihoods are threatened due to environmental degradation and the forces of globalization where commercial greed is the key driver for change and 'progress'. Mangroves are vanishing and the boat-communities are struggling to survive. This is where culture and environment acquire a powerful synthesis for they are equally important to preserve and conserve life patterns.

The World Wildlife Fund states that the Indus eco-region is one of the forty biologically richest in the world. The Indus eco-region is situated in a semi-arid environment; it harbours riverine forests along the Indus River, and mangrove forests in the coastal areas while desert ecosystems occupy the periphery of the region. Currently, about 50 per cent of the gross area of riverine forests is inundated during high floods. As a result, the riverine forest area is shrinking alarmingly fast while less salt-tolerant species have almost disappeared.[33] It is estimated that this situation may further be compounded by the construction of new dams and barrages.

As a result, livelihoods and cultural practices are under rapid transformation and this has a direct impact on the way folklore is getting diminished in the wake of ecological neglect, population explosion and policy environment. Indus communities engaged in traditional livelihoods of agriculture, fisheries and livestock rearing have been forced to give up their traditional professions. The Mohanas, fisher folks, have been displaced and driven towards alternative livelihoods. Over two million Mohanas have been impacted across Sindh. This has been termed as a major loss to 'the cultural diversity of Sindh'.[34]

As noted above, water holds an especially significant position in the cultural existence of the Sindhi people. It has been a source of literature, mystical beliefs and a composite way of life that is threatened now. This state of affairs is equally relevant to the communities that live along the Indus in the Southern parts of the Punjab province.

Reclaiming the Indus folklore along with environmental conservation is a powerful way of saving the shared heritage of India and Pakistan. The Indus is an all-encompassing metaphor of securing long-term peace in the region, documenting and preserving cultural heritage and maintaining the sublime literary standards set by the followers. India cannot be without the Indus and Pakistan cannot function as a viable ecological zone without it either.

What could be a better agenda for the two countries to agree upon and take their cooperation forward beyond the constructed walls of acrimonies and bitterness?

Presented at Folklore Festival organized by the Foundation of SAARC Writers and Literature, Chandigarh, 2009.

3

Through a Screen, Darkly

On weekdays she watched The Bold and the Beautiful *and* Santa Barbara, *where brittle blondes with lipstick and hairstyles rigid with spray seduced androids and defended their sexual empires. Baby Kochamma loved their shiny clothes and the smart, bitchy repartee. During the day disconnected snatches of it came back to her and made her chuckle.*[1]

(*God of Small Things:* ARUNDHATI ROY)

The Pakistani cable operators, following the cyclical escalation of imagined hatreds, discontinued the transmission of Indian satellite channels in 2002. India-Pakistan standoff at the borders following the 2001 attacks on Lok Sabha added layers to the martial tunes. The absence of Indian TV soaps, fodder for the entertainment-hungry populace, was widely mourned. Once, not long ago, the axiomatic edge of Pakistan's TV serials was widely acknowledged. But not anymore. This is the age of the market, of selling dreams and drama, of converting the stereotype into a saleable commodity and citing it on the cultural stock exchange.

The popularity of Hindi language soaps is not limited to Pakistan alone. I have witnessed squatters at Dhaka's decrepit Bihari camp glued to their coloured TV sets in what can be described as Bangladesh's largest no man's tract. Here, Biharis lack citizenship, are denied humanity and that elusive yearning called hope. Yet, Star Plus is beamed 24/7 in their tiny, leaking one-room family units.

On my last visit to Bhutan, the little fairy kingdom isolated from the world until recently, the most striking impression was the kingdom's entry into the mainstream South Asian cultural world – thanks to satellite technology and a wave of openness. Little shops, often home-based enterprises, functioned amidst the blaring background sounds of Ekta Kapoor's melodramatic productions.[2] Indian soaps have made inroads even into Afghanistan, newly 'liberated' under the occupation of Western forces led by the United States. They were wildly popular until the Afghanistan government set out to ban these serials, terming them as inimical to Afghani values. Interestingly, its tribal society with its glorious history of family relationships found the Kapoor *parivar* mantra offensive!

While in India, the soaring viewership of Star Plus and Zee TV serials with their in-your-face family mantra is all too well known. The hype is also a constructed story of success and market acquisition. On the face of it, the commodification of entertainment is a global phenomenon. So what's wrong with it, one may ask, given that most of us in South Asia want to integrate into the global economy and its uniform cultural variants. Junk food, designer brands, pop music and corporate media ethos are all 'signs' – visible and audible – of progress. Of having arrived and found ourselves.

The extraordinary story of Ekta Kapoor's TV production from near oblivion to glories of unprecedented commercial success[3] and fame is awe inspiring and almost an urban model of what self-attainment can mean. It is a small wonder that Kapoor bagged the Ernst&Young (E&Y) Startup Entrepreneur of the Year award in 2001. Crowned as one of Asia's most powerful communicators, Kapoor was inducted into the 'Hall of Fame' by the Indian Telly Awards and was also crowned 'Young Global Leader' by the Forum of Young Global Leaders (affiliated to the World Economic Forum) in the year 2006. Her website proudly notes:

> The serials produced by her company Balaji Telefilms are a smashing hit with the masses and dominate all the major TV channels in India. Ekta's serials have not only captured the imagination of the masses but also their soul.

Such soaps light up the lives of housewives across South Asia. If we ignore the wild exaggerations of her plots (cinematic license perhaps to grab attention), the women in Ekta Kapoor's soaps, however, live the lives of ordinary South Asian housewives. Have these soaps given them an ego boost? A sort of satisfaction that the mundane lives they live are not that mundane after all. The characters are inspired from their conventional lives, transformed into objectified glamour. This accounts for their phenomenal appeal, apparent viewer loyalty and high ratings.

There was a time when I liked watching Ekta Kapoor's soaps. The plots, the conflicts, and the families resembled daily dramas of our relatives (sic) but now we know what it is — all nonsense. There's nothing in her serials. Absolutely nothing. We just watch them ... because we have nothing better to do.

(PUSHPA SINGH, HOUSEWIFE)[4]

The overwhelming viewership of this soap-world has understandably invited criticism from various quarters. Traditionalists think that by aping Bollywood, family values are endangered, progressives find the domestication of women problematic, rationalists are irked by an overdose of miracles, the non-Brahmin world feels that it only projects one segment of Indian reality while the nation-statists find the Indian cultural onslaught hegemonic. There is perhaps truth in all these reactions as they emanate from particular, grounded angles. For instance, an archetypal conservative reaction in Delhi noted:

Balaji is destroying India's image! They show ****t packaged as drama specially Kyun ki... The characters do not respect their elders ... marry and remarry ... for money they can do anything (sic) even disrespecting relationships when brothers kill their brothers, mothers marry their old flames ... how come big companies sponsor such serials? How come Star Plus maintains no ethics? Don't we all have some responsibility towards society? These serials make India dirty ... we have great family values but these serials are a threat to the society (sic).[5]

Prior to understanding such reactions, I was struck by a brazen statement made by Ekta Kapoor herself on a popular TV show where celebrities walk in to have coffee with a young market-savvy film director whose light-hearted, silly banter is sold as entertainment. While on this show, Ekta shrugged her shoulders and advised those who did not like her TV soaps not to watch them or switch to news channels instead. This was akin to stating that the content and style of her shows will continue and thumbing her nose at her detractors.

Essentially, this is a dangerous argument; a veiled arrogance rooted in a smug knowledge of the power she holds over the TV 'market'. Given that her loyal clientele is so hooked to the magic of her *shubh* 'K' productions sanctioned by the gods and astrologers, critical remarks do not matter to her any more.

Yet the truth is not as simplistic as Kapoor seems to believe. By engineering an oversupply of regressive domestic dramas and almost flooding the market – a phenomenon curiously similar to Chinese goods sold worldwide – this demand is generated or to use a Chomskyite term, 'manufactured'. Thus, the middle-class demand and supply cylce become self-fulfilling prophecies.[6]

I do not wish to rant on the beaten-to-death theme of the villainous corporate media but would venture to highlight the underlying, entrenched, socio-cultural patterns common to South Asia, a sort of primordial shared heritage. Arguably the popularity, appeal or demand – however one looks at this – can be better explained by the embedded societal dysfunctions that the Balaji-Ekta brand of television soaps employ to spin entertainment.

Encashing the decades long permutations of Bollywood melodrama and catchy themes of love, honour, revenge and the family, the K-series (and several others attempting to ape the authentic) plays up, cajoles and transmutes patriarchy to the hilt. The hysterical emphasis on women's role in the household -- especially the venerated kitchen -- as the model of womanhood is a subscription to the centuries old song of patriarchy. Women who break out of this trap, or seize power, are vamps often dressed as mini draculas with a dress code that depicts them as whores compared to the temple-toting homely Sitas.

In fact, the trumpeting of right-wing versions of the historical role and persona of the great Sita is an easy to sell and instantly consumable ploy. The various tribulations which female characters play in the name of *Agni Pariksha* are greatly misogynistic. Suffice it to say that the good old epic Ramayana is twisted and converted into a recurring interpretative context: property (the kingdom), invisible but powerful father (Dashratha -- Rama's father), scheming women (Kaikeyi who forces Dashratha to send her step-son Rama into exile so that her own son can capture the kingdom) and docile woman (Sita) are the lines that script writers overuse with nauseating repetition. Following Goebbels, this particularistic version becomes the over-arching truth suiting patriarchy and validating its passionate guardian, the clergy, in full measure.

Feminist critics have long had problems with the Ramayana. For instance, one analyst has stated: 'Valmiki's *Ramayana* has been wrongly ascribed canonical status, giving rise to a sort of patriarchal, literate, pan-Indian elitism, which in recent times has been scorned.'[7] Indian feminist writers[8] have strongly critiqued the male-centered interpretation of India's great epic. As with mythologies, the continuous evolution of narratives embeds the biases and hopes of their interpreters.[9] The myriad interpretations of The *Ramayana* differ with the linear, uniform vision which portrays Rama as the strong male and Sita as the subordinate, obedient wife. The 'repudiation of the sensuous and the cultivation of the masculine' is, therefore, a political project rooted in patriarchal reinvention of India's militaristic past.[10]

In the Balaji TV soaps, the treatment of property relations between the household characters, men and women, and overvaluing of the ownership not only serves patriarchal definitions of property but, in a modern sense, legitimizes accumulation of capital, vulgar consumerism and a one-dimensional understanding of empowerment. The good women – such as the BJP ticket holder, Tulsi, from *Kyunki Saas Bhi Kabhi Bahu Thi* (KSBKBT)[11], the gullible Kasturi or such other self-sacrificing species – are almost always pitted against evil and vile women responsible for their plight. The men disappear or become secondary characters and thus the reality-reversal renders the 'system' invisible, or at worst, benign.

This is a world where a father's reign is undisputed, despite the loud histrionics of women and their activism within the family arenas of honour. Who said that the kitchen-sink drama has faded? The household and the implicit position of men as its masters is celebrated. The Oedipal mother-son dynamic, the second-most overrated virtue after virginity in South Asia, is paramount at the expense of healthy, self-respecting and equitable relationships.

Why should this be a concern, one may question. After all, it is all fictional and not *that* different from other popular media such as the cinema. This rhetorical concern, at best, is lame since the idiot box is an everyday, integral, home-based phenomenon as opposed to the extraneous cinema halls. Not to mention that Bollywood is struggling to break free of the typecast even though daunted by conservatism of the distributors and the imagined markets, compounded by the shortage of trained screenplay writers.

The centrality of the *saas-bahu* tension, therefore, is located in the power matrix where the *saas* finally attains chunky crumbs of patriarchal power and is willing to reap the subjugation gains. Women are dependent on men for financial and emotional security and the over-play of marriage is portrayed as the *raison d'être* of the creation of women. The solution to all existential and other problems is marriage. Rarely does a woman take control of her own life. The interludes of women heading households culminate in the re-entry of the male leader – often proclaimed dead and alive in the span of one single serial.

❧

Rooted in violence as a means of control, misogyny is intertwined with the way the human race and its defined relationships have evolved within the domain of patriarchy and male control of resources, including women's sexuality. Much of all this is well known and documented in the global and South Asian context. As students of history, we were told that the British banned customs such as sati and female infanticide and enacted laws to that effect. The colonial push for modernity – fractured and self-serving though it may have been – became a vigorous agent of change. However, deep-seated cultural mores take a longer span than rules imposed from the above. This is why violence against women remained, and still remains, a reality all over South Asia. The dangers of a popular TV culture is that it can reinforce these embedded trends even where the law calls for an end to these inhuman practices.

In *Karam Apna Apna*, the heroine Gauri, from a middle-class background, is willfully married to a man whose wife according to astrological predictions is destined to die. As events unfold and the mischievous conspiracy is exposed, Gauri accepts this as her fate and prepares to die. Miracles save her but her *pariksha* is not over. Her husband also dies. And later her mother-in-law is murdered as part of a family conspiracy by the classic vamp–aunt and Gauri, charged with the murder, is later pushed over the cliff. She re-appears to avenge the murder, suffer violence and humiliation at the hands of her *devar* only to re-marry him. So the saga continues and the good woman has to prove her innocence at the altar of misogyny.

This is a recurring theme, a tryst with a destiny that holds misogyny at its core. The suffering and humiliation of women is legitimately sanctioned by the myth of *sanskar*, an imagined value system distorted to bolster patriarchal relations where a *pativrata* (loyalty to one's husband) wife shines like an ominous planet in individual lives. Bani of *Kasam Se*, Kasturi, Tulsi of KSBKBT, Nimmo of *Kya Hoga Nimmo Ka* and other icons recognized and celebrated of late through another corporate gimmick of Star Parivaar Awards, are all fated to live with and accept misogyny in their lives. The middle-class patriarchal morality is viewed as 'normalcy' and any deviation is castigated. While the television personas redefine the discourses of women's liberation by giving them visibility, they eventually end up reinforcing the prejudices of upper-caste males. There is considerable space for the adoption of Western culture, however 'dangerous', by Indian men.

Indian-ness and the celebration of its values are filtered through the lens of elite upper-caste Hinduism. And if one were to analyse the unwitting subtext in the non-scripts of soaps, this would appear the best way to live. In corporate media, Indian women are implicitly appropriated and maintained. Thus, the modern woman's depiction and her societal roles were, and continue to be, set by men. Quite appropriately, the advertisements for a washing machine interspersed between prime time soaps scream: 'You and Videocon, the perfect homemakers'.

A Delhi-based teacher, Shalini Pattabiraman, who also blogs, reacted to the overplay of Tulsi's character in print media thus[12]:

> *Why does the woman in us split and become two contrasting people ... Sex, gender, religion, education, profession, caste, place, people, name, brand, lifestyle – all these categories exhibit a clear lack of tolerance or an individual's right to personal space or freedom in terms of self expression ... If educated, independent young women who are leaders in their profession and in a position to make a difference in society begin to respond to such regression by not raising a voice what will be the outcome ... If they allow the split or allow it to coexist with their other self, what might just happen? That thought worries me.*

❧

'Paanch sau crore ki property meray haath kaisay lagaygi?' (How will I get my hands on property worth 500 crores?) is a

constant refrain in our ever-changing lives, or at least that is
what most soaps make us yearn for. The ultimate happiness
is linked to power, property and greed. In Dhaka, my elderly
friend Ahmed complained that he was shocked when his
daughter asked him where the papers were for their up-market
Dhanmondi apartment. When Ahmed told her that theirs was
a rented apartment she was most dismayed and wanted to
know her expected quantum of inheritance. Ahmed said that
this was all a result of his wife and daughters' incessant soap-
watching. 'Our value-systems, especially that of inculcating a
materialism-free mindset in our children, have obviously been
trampled and TV has accelerated it,' he rued.

So, I asked why they watch it and Ahmed's wife responded:
'Well, most channels show these family dramas, and increasingly
they all churn out similar stuff. It is so easy: the episodes are
repeated several times, summarized on the weekends and it is
just in your house, flexible, accessible and ... glitzy. My teenage
daughters love the Bollywood dance numbers and I'd rather
they watch TV with me rather than on their own...'

What Ahmed's wife did not mention and several others
have pointed out is that this glossy, dream soap-world provides
a fuelled version of the middle class aspirations for success.

Arundhati Roy in an interview made a point that India's
growing middle class is reared on a diet of radical consumerism
and aggressive greed. Unlike the advanced Western countries,
which fed on colonies and their resources and slave labour, '...
we [Indians] [13] have to colonise ourselves, our own nether parts. We've
begun to eat our own limbs.'

In the television world, poverty is a curse: not as a reflection
of any exploitation but as a marker of 'envy' undermining
humanity. All the romanticized and glamourized families are

big business houses. The poorer families are in awe of them and aspire to be like them. Of course, there are the occasional outbursts of the inherent superiority of middle-class values. The rich families reluctantly accept daughters-in-law from lesser backgrounds and make sure that this is time and again reiterated in the scripts. The formula is simple: the richer the family, the bigger the favour to lesser families by marrying their daughters; and greater the sense of gratitude of poor girls' families.

The advertising campaign of *Karam Apna Apna* depicted an elderly lady wishing happiness to the ill-fated Gauri by praying that she marries into a wealthy business family. There are exceptions when the poor make it big, a la Bollywood, but these are often through deceit or a means of revenge. Nowhere is the class stratification and immutable rich-poor gap so cleverly maintained, though admittedly under the garb of melodrama and rich family's inner dynamics. In line with globalization trends, huge wealth is presented as a 'fabulous spectator sport'[14] and eminently enviable. This accords it a dangerous legitimacy for the winner of globalized wealth accumulation takes it all. Indeed it projects that there is no ingrained injustice in this wealth-gaining system. Moreover, such wealth is not victimless as if there is no exploitation anywhere but a divinely sanctioned law that bestows success on the 'big company' *parivars*.

In the televised post-surreal version of urban India, a pernicious objectification of the youth takes place incessantly and with great ease. The young are hardly ever depicted as real beings with real issues. 'Pretty Young Things' – known as

PYTs in popular media – is an image that corporate media is required to brandish for its profit-ends. This objectification of the youth on TV serials articulates a clear message to them: spend your time, energy (and money) on cultivating a sexually attractive image. Just stroll along any young peoples' hangout and you will realize that this is a message that the spin doctors of the advertising world promote for their own profit.

It is assumed that the young viewers are only interested in the 'sexy' claptrap where bare-chested hunks contemplate power or scantily clad babes feed into the ultimate fear of a wayward daughter. The danger here is that such stereotyping can desensitize society towards its youth. But this trend is far more imperceptible than gender stereotyping. Corporate conformity places a premium on being 'cool', 'happening' and being a good consumer come what may. The term 'sexy' therefore is not limited to looks but to attitudes, beliefs and identities. Thus, Manthan and Bhoomi of KSBKBT are tattooed, tanned sex objects who trounce the oppressive familial bonds and indulge in mindless pursuits for pleasure. The young Tanu in *Kahani Ghar Ghar Ki* is another cool girl who is pitted against the boring sari-clad parivaar women. Tanu does not want to be independent or find herself so to speak but she is portrayed as brainless, vapid and easily vulnerable to the machinations of her mother-turned-into-a-vengeful-member of the big happy family. *Karam Apna Apna* follows a similar pattern in depicting its youthful characters.

Conformity is the desirable path, say these soaps. This is the apolitical and consumerist environment that is then reflected in 'page 3' of the print media. With a following in millions, each of these soaps has countless Internet 'social'[15] forums where the young stars are adulated, worshipped and promoted as role models. Individuality can only be attained if you are insane or vile -- 'mad or bad' to put it simply. Thus Ishaan, of *Kahani Ghar Ghar Ki*, is only interesting when he is a rebellious vile son of the family or when he is pretending to be insane. His recovery leads him straight into the folds of conformity and predictable patriarchy.

The young Kasturi can only be relatively free when pretending to be insane. In her 'normal' life, she cannot expose the evil, speak the truth and be herself, out of fear and social conformity -- values inspired by the subordinate Sita. She bears all the cruelties of her mother-in-law because the latter is her husband's mother. And the mother-in-law, a power-hungry witch, repeatedly announces that she had done a favour by producing a hunky son who in turn bestowed another favour to the poorer Kasturi by falling in love with her. And this is the garbled and twisted world that is shaping the minds of a younger generation all over the subcontinent!

A world where miracles occur on a daily basis is a dangerous one. In such an environment, human effort becomes redundant and secondary, creating inaction and fuelling conformity. The overwhelming rangoli pattern and the holy tulsi plant of KSBKBT, and the fluttering lamp of *Kahani Ghar Ghar Ki* are iconic symbols which weave a subliminal message: superstition, totem and transmutated fears sell, and in the process legitimize the ignominy of the past. When cancer patients recover through poojas at home, the dead come to life and temples intervene in daily struggles, the landscape becomes ethically and politically murky. In transitional polities, such high-profile depictions are inimical to the evolution of a modern, dynamic society. And pray, why promote a specific brand of totems? How about the tribal, the animistic and multiple religious symbols for an inclusive, entertainment–worldview?

The truth is that the miracle and plastic surgery masala is oddly mixed, leaving behind cultural dross that a society as a whole has to deal with. I am reminded of a reaction from a Lahore aunt who told me: 'Initially the *saas-bahu* sagas start off well but then with time too much conspiracy happens, too much of superstition and incredible stuff and characters circulate (reappearing after ten years with a plastic surgery) which makes it droll, confusing and irrational...'

As I made further inquiries into the Ramayana mythology, academics in Delhi informed me that there are almost 300 'versions' of the Ramayana and that all of them are open to interpretation. To my surprise, as I attempted to check the Valmiki version, some of it became clearer: Sita did not undergo the *agnipariksha* (trial by fire) at Rama's command. Her indulgence in the act was to invoke the gods themselves to come to her aid, and Dashratha makes it clear when he appears at the gods' command to seek pardon for his exalted son. Towards the end of the epic, I discovered further that Sita specifically rejects both a second *agnipariksha* and Rama himself.[16] The scriptwriters for TV soaps need to hear Sita loudly and clearly when she proclaims that she is returning to her mother, leaving Rama and his beloved Ayodhya![17] I wonder if Ekta's Sitas would be willing to do so.

Another glaring omission is the existence of any Muslim character, a fact even more skewed than the percentage employed in the Indian civil service. Lest I am accused of overstating Muslim invisibility, one can easily detect the Bollywoodization of the local cultures and languages.[18] Beyond the Hindustani, the packaged Punjabi and supposedly comic Bhojpuri, the idiom remains uniform and linear, reducing reality and re-bottling the old wine of prejudice. The local gets subsumed and, therefore, the religious practices of even the myriad groups in the imagined monolithic Hinduism are rendered invisible or at best marginal.

Last year, the interiors of a plush home in Lahore owned by an old acquaintance looked oddly familiar. The lady of the house proudly walked us through the refurbished interiors (after a new dose of wealth). The walls had different colours adorned with art-deco stuff and then rather coyly informed us that some of the inspiration was the way homes were done in Mumbai. When I, rather excitedly, asked her about her visits to Mumbai, I learnt to my disappointment that her inspiration came from the Indian TV soaps she regularly watched.

Noticeable for its linearity, a culturally confusing aesthetic thus enters the public domain. The Balaji sets – loud, colourful and stacked with dreamy kitsch – are repetitive and use an identical locale for different situations. To make things worse, there is an obvious emphasis on display – of wealth, style and taste, if one may venture to call it that.

Zeenat D, while searching for an apartment for her son in a middle-class apartment block in Delhi, was struck by the multicoloured walls and garish colours of the ones she was shown. The contractor revealed that the Star Plus wall hues were 'in' and this is why he was preparing the flats in that style for this made them more acceptable.[19]

Mariah Carey's apartment in New York, the homes of Pakistan's successful classes and posh apartments in Gulshan,

Dhaka, are all designed and decorated with a closely similar, yuppie-ized zeal and taste. There is a global taste reinforced by brands, swanky interior outlets they creep their way into the Mumbai TV aesthetic sensibilities. Are we set to consume kitsch at homes after a dissatisfying and indigestible fast food meal?

The extravagant parties of the tele-visual *Richistans* also project a prototype aesthetic that other than the occasional marigolds and temple settings is disconnected with 5,000 years of the Indian subcontinent's cultural reality. Parties in Lahore, Dhaka, Delhi and Karachi ape and reproduce this aesthetic of vulgar display, of choreographed Bollywood numbers and reinforce every stereotype on vegetarianism (or its converse), alcohol (or hypocrisy in Muslim countries about it), propriety (or lack thereof) and the primal male fantasies (projected as innately female).

❧

It's important to understand that the corporate media doesn't just support the neo-liberal project. It is the neo-liberal project. This is not a moral position it has chosen to take, it's structural. It's intrinsic to the economics of how the mass media works.

ARUNDHATI ROY[20]

Most people I questioned on what is so endearing about the TV soaps did not give any satisfactory replies. There are coy, confused references to the glamour and everyday-ness of the TV serials. This was quite intriguing for the obvious contradictions and a kind of helplessness implied, 'We like what we get'. From these individual perceptions and in the absence of credible data and extensive research, it is difficult to draw any definitive conclusions.

While India and South Asia struggle to fight their legacies of colonialism and caste and class-related inequities, the mass media, especially the electronic media boom, have facilitated an unprecedented opening up of societies, leading to greater degrees of public accountability. However, as globalized interests poach markets for profits, the media becomes an eminently attractive space for capital movement and of replicating its established proximity to power in the advanced countries.

Are we destined to follow that? Is that the only route available for media development and citizen empowerment? This is a serious question that is now looming on the political and societal horizons across the South. In this wider context, the perpetuation of regressive trends and attitudes can be effective agents of dumbing-down public consciousness, of ingraining the imperatives of consumerism and in celebrating profit as the new god.

From the cultural perspective, ignoring the rich, fascinating and interpretative stories constituting Hindu mythology, the televisual experience clings to particularistic, standard versions. In other words, such versions are visibly 'inspired' by clergy sanctioned worldviews. In this sense, patriarchy and misogyny, as deep-rooted socio-cultural trends, get massive airtime – all in the name of entertainment. India's endless and variegated pool of ingenious, indigenous stories and experiences spanning 5,000 years are reduced to the lowest level and distorted to the point of caricature. Sadly, other soap-makers inspired by the success of Ekta Kapoor are shy to break free from their complacent dark enclosed wells and continue to gaze at the same view of the infinite sky.

Under the convenient guise of 'this is what people want', and inventive market demand assessment[21], creativity has thus been crippled. Does this signal the death of imagination? Or is it simply the larger corporate media project to manufacture consents, tastes and aesthetics without questioning power, exploitation and violence? One would think that the Indian middle classes, in whose name such programming is created, deserve better.

The last thing we need is the linearization of societies, emotion and values. A world where the market decides aesthetics and manufactures culture has a perverse – some would argue, a pernicious – effect on the present and the future. Absence of self-regulation, untrammelled lust for profits needs to be questioned and challenged. Therefore, the all-pervasiveness of TV soaps provides a fitting agenda for advocacy around issues of media responsibility and accountability. How else would we change the present or begin to overcome the past?

Published in *India International Centre Quarterly*, Vol. 35, No. 1, 2008, pp. 96–114.

4

The Cult of the Feminine: Kali and the Sindh Province of Pakistan

❧

Pakistan's Sindh province – the fulcrum of the Indus Valley Civilization (IVC) – also known as the land of the Sufis, has retained its centuries' old belief and worship practices. Since the advent of Islam in the eighth century, the emergence of an Islamicate, the ancient and well-grounded beliefs and deities acquired a new dimension representing themselves in the mystical poetry and folktales associated with the major Sufis. The tumultuous events of 1947 and the gradual but massive exodus of the Sindhi Hindus and the Sikhs from the province have not affected the historical patterns of cult-worship in this region.

Interestingly, the ascendancy of the feminine is also reflected in the Sufi poetry of the medieval eras, especially in the works of Shah Abdul Latif Bhittai, whose mystical thought represents a culmination of Sufism in Sindh. This essay will review these trends and identify more recent feminine cults that start with Marvi of Malir to the struggles of the peasantry represented by Mai Bakhtawar in the early twentieth century.

More recently, the start of the twenty-first century presents us with yet another invocation of the representation of the feminine as the quintessential figure of resistance and strength in Sindhi culture, with the 'martyrdom' and 'sacrifice' of Pakistan's twice-elected prime minister, Benazir Bhutto. This is seen as a continuation of the way feminine legends are constructed and revered in this region.

History of Sindh

The name Sindh is derived from 'Sindhu', an archaic title for the River Indus. Sindh has been the home of many ancient civilizations, and recent findings in archaeology have furnished a corpus of information about the ways and lifestyle of the area's civilization. Neatly constructed pavements, intricate drainage systems and splendid handicrafts point to the adroit craftsmanship of the people living in that era. There exists evidence that Indus cotton was being converted into cloth with excess cotton being exported to ancient Egypt through shipping lanes. This at a time when many other civilizations across the globe were beginning to explore and learn about the benefits of applying such sophistication in fabric production.

Sindh became a part of the Persian Achaemenid Empire in sixth century BCE. After a gap of almost 200 years, an army led by Alexander the Great invaded Sindh in the fourth century BCE. The Greco-Bactrian era followed in which different Greek rulers controlled the region with barely any interruptions. It was also the time when many living in the Indo-Greek kingdom converted to Buddhism. Later on, Scythian tribes invaded India through this area in the late hundreds BCE, with Sindh also a part of the Tocharian Kushan and the Gupta Empires at one time or another.[1]

Sindh gained an independent status under the Rái Dynasty in 478 AD. The Rais were replaced by the Chach, the founder of the Brahman Dynasty, around 632 CE. During the reigns of caliphs Umar and Uthman, Muslim armies and expeditions reached the western bank of River Indus approaching from Makran, though never having crossed the mighty river due to the geographical conditions on the other side which were determined to be strategically unfavourable. Ultimately, it was in 712 AD when Muhammad bin Qasim conquered Sindh, leading a Syrian Arab army. This conquest converted Sindh (Al-Sindh) into the eastern-most province of the Umayyad Caliphate.

During the three centuries the Arabs ruled this region, the fusion of different cultures went a long way in defining the core values of modern Sindhi society. Furthermore, Turk invasions of Sindh also established the IVC's affiliation with the Ghaznavid Empire. More importantly, it was during the Mughal era that Sindh was a part of the flourishing kingdom, and during the reigns of Sammas (1350-1524) and Kalhoras (1700-1783), that Sindhi Sufis played a crucial role in converting a large segment of the native population to Islam.

Following the British annexation of Sindh, the region was amalgamated with Bombay, a move that generated much resentment amongst the Sindhis. The locals felt that their distinct culture had nothing in common with Bombay. Eventually, Sindh was awarded the status of a separate province under the auspices of the British reforms introduced in 1935.

The demographics of Sindh underwent a conspicuous alteration after the Indo-Pak partition of 1947. At the time of partition, many Hindus – who comprised 25 per cent of the total population of Sindh – left the region. However, Sindh as a province still holds the largest number of Hindus living in Pakistan, as compared to other provinces of the country. According to the census of 1998, almost 22,80,000 Hindus were residing in Sindh at the time.[2]

As an epiphenomenon to the exodus of the Hindus, Sindh received many immigrants from not only other provinces of the country, but also from other regional countries in the following years. The Afghan wars and the secession of East Pakistan accelerated this influx, which has fueled Sindhi grievances founded in expropriation and marginalization.

Worship of the Feminine in the Indus Valley Civilization

Fertility cults were a vital part of the belief systems of the Indus people. Many rituals involved terracotta figurines of the mother goddess. These mother goddesses were in the form of heavily adorned females, mostly in the standing position.

These figurines may have served as votive objects meant to express gratitude on the occasion of the birth of a child, or to pray for their long life and happiness. They may also have been used in ceremonies in which a couple prayed for the birth of a child. Some figurines of nude males have also been found from various sites which have been a part of the rituals where the central theme was procreation. However, the female figurines far outnumber the male ones.

'One piece of the artistic flavour is the figurine of the famous dancing girl from Mohenjo-Daro. The little figurine is shown resting her right hand on the hip, left arm fully covered with bracelets and bangles hanging closely downwards over the bent left leg, a necklace with three pearls hanging on the breasts. She has a braided coiffure and the head is tilted back in a rhythmic pose.'[3] There is also an interesting image of a

dancing girl engraved on a rock at Sado Mazo in Johi tehsil
in the Kirthar mountain range.[4] Apart from this image of the
dancing girl, there are many engravings which show women
dancing before their dwellings. This is testimony to the fact
that dancing has been practiced since ancient times. Tombs of
the Kalhora period also depict scenes of dancing and women
are also shown dancing with men.[5]

Ever since the Vedic period, dancing has been an expression
of the joy of everyday life in Sindh. Dancing supposedly
transposes the overall effect of music on the mind, manifesting
itself in the visible motion of the body. In Sindh, dancing,
like music, was associated with religious rites during pre-
Islamic times when the emotional effect of the movement,
the rhythm and the music heightened religious excitement
and enriched associated rituals. Evidence found in the tombs
of Larkana, Thatta and Mithi districts gives credence to this
theory and reflects the secular attitude of the people of this
region towards the religion. Such attitudes were not limited to
the artists who created the images. The rulers of the area also
made no concrete effort to purge their dominions of this form
of representation from funerary architecture, even though
Islam prohibits the production of figurative images. Except
for a few images in Chandia tombs, these figural paintings
have not been defaced and remain intact to this day, reflecting
the pluralistic ethos of the local people regarding matters of
faith. Such a pluralistic and inclusive approach to heritage was
influenced by the mystic traditions, which have historically
remained pervasive in Sindhi society.[6]

'...The importance of mother-worship in religion,
the abundance of female figurines, rich ornaments, the
comparatively lesser importance given to males, would all

indicate that society in the ancient Indus valley was more favourable to women than to men.'[7]

As Dr Fahmida Hussain conjectures, 'This land of peace, harmony and love had a matriarchal society, where because of her powers of procreation the woman held a high position and status. She not only gave birth but also brought up future generations. She was the cultivator too. She enjoyed a status of a goddess because of these qualities.'[8]

The archaeological evidence uncovered from the Indus Valley also shows how the mythology was deeply influenced by the goddess cults. Goddess figurines dated 6000–2500 BCE have been discovered at the Mehrgarh ruins in Balochistan on the western banks of the Indus.

At Harappa, numerous figures of gods and goddesses have also been found. Many terracotta statues of the mother goddess have been dug up that suggests she was popularly worshipped.

The cult continued to inspire people and gradually found its way into the worship practices associated with the Hindu faith. Scholars have noted that the Sakta sect in Hinduism, focused on worship of female deities only, could have come into being due to the continued devotion to the mother goddess.[9]

The issue with conflating Indus civilization with ancient Hinduism is that the distinct symbols found on artifacts and scriptures are yet to be fully deciphered. Currently, there are three widely held views about the civilization and its relation with Hinduism. The first theorizes that it was an Aryan civilization and its script is an early form of Sanskrit. Others believe in the proto-Dravidian theory, which considers the discovered culture an indigenous part of the subcontinent. There is a third view however, which conjectures that the

Indus civilization had no relation whatsoever with the Aryans or the Dravidians.

In any case, what we know is that in later eras, the widespread cult of Kali and her various manifestations acquired a major position in the popular imagination and spiritual practices of the area occupied by the IVC.

Origin of the Cult – Myths and Legends

Kali is the Hindu goddess of time and change, also known as the lord of death. She is presented as a violent and fearful deity and is often shown wearing a necklace of severed heads and earrings made of children's corpses. Her sharp fangs and long, claw-like nails add to her frightening and violent disposition[10]. According to David Kinsley, Kali was first mentioned in Hinduism as a distinct goddess around 600 CE, and these texts 'usually place her on the periphery of Hindu society or on the battlefield.'[11]

In Hindu scripture, Kali became more popular and powerful with the composition of *Devi Mahatmya* in the fifth to sixth century AD. According to *Devi Mahatmya*, she was born in a battle against the forces of evil, from the brow of Goddess Durga. She immediately went on a rampage destroying all that lay in her sight. It states that eventually, Lord Shiva – also depicted as the consort of Kali – had to throw himself at her feet to make her stop. The image of Kali with Lord Shiva under her feet bears testimony to this legend.

Conceived on the periphery of Hindu society, her recognition grew over time. Kali's most fervent supporters exist in West Bengal and are not hesitant to offer blood sacrifices for her. She has been presented with different names and forms.

Shyama, Adya Ma, Tara Ma, Dakshina Kalika and Chamundi, all refer to the Goddess Kali. Then there is Bhadra Kali, who is considered gentle, and Shyamashana Kali, who lives only in the cremation ground.

Kali Temples in Pakistan

In Sindh province, there are three main temples of Kali. First, at Aror which is popularly known as the temple of Kalka. Second, at Ganjo Takar, a hill in Hyderabad where sits the temple of Kali.

Third is situated in Laki (Sehwan) in a cave where visitors have to crawl in to worship the goddess. A visit to this was considered essential before a pilgrimage to Hinglaj – another major Hindu temple in Pakistan.

In addition, there are other temples associated with the worship of goddess Kali. Nine kilometers from Sukkur town, there is another temple at Aror. This is also the place where Muhammad bin Qasim built the famous mosque in 726 AD. Close to here in Balochistan, we have the Nani Mandir near Hinglaj on the bank of the Hingol River in Lasbela district, where Hindus come for pilgrimage and perform various rituals. Another Kali Mata temple exists in Larkana.

Kali Temple of Thokar Niaz Beg, Lahore

A Kali temple is situated in the southeast of the town of Niaz Beg. Kanhaiya Lal, in his book *Tareekh-E-Lahore*, writes about the Kali temple of Thokar Niaz Beg, Lahore and his exploration visit in the late nineteen century. He discovered that even though there was no icon of a deity, there was a calf placed inside the dome of the temple. The first floor had been dedicated to Kali Mata. There might also have been minor goddesses and other deities on the first and the second floor of the temple at one time or another, as objects of supplication and general rituals of worship.

Empirical evidence suggests that the edifice was built sometime after Ranjit Singh's capture of Lahore in 1799, when one of the rulers of the area – Subha Singh – fled to Niaz Beg. Haroon Khalid however, argues it is quite possible that some construction might have existed at the site even before the rule of the Sikhs.[12] After the partition of the subcontinent, the temple began to dilapidate, as people who had moved here belonged to different cultures and were not sensitive to local history and traditions. Currently, the structure is in shambles.

Kali Temples in Rawalpindi

There were two temples of Kali in Rawalpindi with one located in Kali Bari – which means 'house of Kali' – and the other in Landa Bazaar where many Hindu temples still influence the landscape of the locality.

There was once a huge image of Kali installed in the open in a mohallah of the same name, where the Bengali Hindus lived – the locality that was situated in Saddar. Bengali Hindus were the theatre performers who would also perform various rituals before the image of the Kali. After partition, most of the Bengali Hindus left for India while some embraced Islam. People living in the Kali Bari still narrate the stories of the Bengali Hindus who once lived there and how most left after the Partition.

The other temple of Kali, situated in Landa Bazaar, has been converted into living quarters by the local people. Within a radius of 500 metres of the Kali Mata temple there are six Hindu temples dedicated to Jogi Nath, Shiva, Ram, Krishana (two) and two Gurdwaras, as well as many Hindu havelis.

Lakshmi and Kali Temple in Saidpur, Islamabad

Nestled within the Margalla Hills is the picturesque village of Saidpur that is noted for its temple complex. The complex includes the shrine of Rama, a gurdwara and a temple. According to Ghulam Nabi, an inhabitant of the village, the temple had two statues (murtis) of Lakshmi and Kali.[13]

Other Hindu Temples in Sindh and Balochistan

Hindu Temples in Sindh and Balochistan	Details
Hinglaj Mandir or Nani Mandir, Hingol National Park, Balochistan	Located in Balochistan. Famous in reference to Goddess Sati. It is believed that when Lord Vishnu cut the dead body of Sati, her head fell here.
Kali Devi Temple, Umerkot, Sindh	Located in Sindh
Kalka Cave Temple, Aror, near Rohri, Sindh	Located in Sindh at Aror in a cave
Sri Varun Dev (god of ocean) Temple, Manora Cantt, Karachi, Sindh	Located in Sindh and 160 years old. It was renovated by the Pakistan Hindu Council.

Hindu Temples in Sindh and Balochistan	Details
Sadhu Bela Temple, Sindh, associated with Udasi Panth who follow the teachings of Babs Bankhandi. Udasi Panth is believed to have been founded by Baba Sri Chand, son of Baba Guru Nanak. The main temple of the Udasis is located in Fair Jo Gotham in Thatta district which is dedicated to Baba Sri Chand.	Located in Sindh
Hindu and Jain Temples, Nagar Parkar, Sindh	Located in Sindh
Jhulelal Mandir/Temple at Uderolal	Located near Tando Adam, Sindh
Ganga Devi Temple	Located in Umerkot, Sindh
Jhulelal Temple	Located in Shikarpur, Sindh
Shiv Temple	Located in Umerkot, Sindh

Krishna Temple	Located in Umerkot, Sindh
Temple of Malhan Devi in Hariar Village, Mithi	Located in Sindh
Temple of Deval Devi[14] located in Kharario Charan near Umerkot city	Located in Umerkot, Sindh
Kali Temple, Gunjo Takkar, Hyderabad	Located in Sindh

Krishna Temple	Located in Umerkot, Sindh
Wani (form of Kali and diminutive of Bhawani) Jo Mandir, Kalankot	Located in Thatta, Sindh
Bhawani Temple at Makli, Thatta	Located in Sindh
Ashapuri or Asha (hope) Devi temple at Makli, Thatta	Located in Thatta, Sindh
Shiva Temple in Kotri	Located in Kotri, Sindh
Shiva Temple in Jhimpir	Located in Thatta, Sindh

Allusions in Sufi Poetry

But the cult of the feminine also finds a prominent place in folk tales as well as Sufi poetry of the medieval era, especially in the works of Shah Abdul Latif Bhittai, whose mystical thoughts have influenced generations in Sindh. The female protagonists of Bhittai's poetry portray the quintessential qualities of the region's spirit: love and tolerance, striving in the way of spiritual objectives, love for the land, pluralism, moderation, resistance to tyranny and a delicate sense of nationalism.

Bhittai's *heroines* – Marvi, Moomal, Lila, Baghul, Sasui, Sohni and Mokhi - are brave, compassionate and devoted to their lovers and the land. 'The heroines of his stories present the true and real image of the woman he had visualized in the society of Sindh.'[15]

Moreover, 'searching and struggling is the main idea in the poetry of Shah Latif. Sasui is in search of Punhoon, Moomal desires Rano, Marvi is desperate to get home, Sohni desperately wants to meet Mehar (Mahiwal). For Shah Latif, a woman is the most beautiful symbol of love.

Love is her habit and she is the greatest creative power of the world.'[16] For Bhittai, not unlike other Sufis, love, and the will to struggle are foundational attributes of a spiritually mature individual.

For instance in Bhittai's 'Sur Sasui Aabri', the female voice is enduring:

> I do not know the place, nor have I taken water, Mountains try to scare me, the sun tries to burn Hot winds try to weaken my will
> O beloved; come to me, I am alone to face them.[17]

In this Sur, despite projecting the image of Sasui as a delicate and weak woman with tender, soft hands and feet, Shah Latif attributes to her character the capacity for constant struggle and willpower to achieve her goal. And through her character Bhittai sends a message to the common people that if the will is strong, achieving any goal or target is not as difficult as it may appear at first sight. A tenacious struggle is a prerequisite for achieving one's own as well as collective objectives; success is the fate of the people who strive for it.[18]

Beyond the poems and the prose, one finds that certain Sindhi women were truly famous for their welfare work and generosity. The likes of whom include the royal women of the Kalhora (1700-1783) and Talpur (1783-1843) periods such as Mai Safi, a sister of Mian Shah Muhammad Kalhoro (1625-1657), Bibi Khadeja, sister of Mian Nasir Muhammad Kalhoro (1657-1692), Bibi Jado and Bibi Baiti, wives of Mian Nasir Muhammad Kalhoro, and Mai Chagli. Mai Jaman and Mai Kheri were famous for building mosques, wells and madrassahs. Mai Chagli ruled over Lasbella and was loved for her sense of philanthropy, selflessness and her substantive welfare work. Mai Saffi has her own shrine in Larkana, in a village named after her, also known as Safi.

The three female devotees of saintly Mian Nasir Muhammad Kalhoro, namely Mai Shamal, Mai Garhi Panhwar and Mai Hawa Khoso were also well known in their times. While Mai Garhi had gifted all of her land to her mentor, Mai Shamal – as a sign of devotion – composed memorable poetry which was called 'Samri Mianwal Faqirs' (the followers of Mian Nasir Muhammad still sing this poetry of at his shrine). Mai Hawa was popular for her recitation of *Azi* (invocation), which was the prevalent ritual among the disciples of Mian Nasir Muhammad Kalhoro.

Mokhi and the Mataras[19]

The tale of Mokhi is another popular fable in Sindhi culture that has been quoted over the years by many villagers and Sufi poets[20] alike. Mokhi was a woman in the fourteenth century during the reign of the Soomra dynasty (1058 AD–1349 AD). She sold wine in a public liquor house near Gadap tehsil in Karachi, having learnt the trade from her mother Natar, who was a famous barmaid in the palace of Princess Moomal of Kak near Umerkot.

Soon the reputation of Mokhi's inn spread far and wide. Many travellers took a break in their journey at the inn on their way to Gadap. The legend has it that eight Mataras (drunkards) belonging to upper Sindh were her regular customers. This group of men is said to have been great admirers of the wine served by her. A local versifier describes this in the following words:

Eight Mataras frequented Mokhi's bar
Two each from the Samma, Soomra, Channa and Chauhan
Clans.

Once when the Mataras were visiting her inn, Mokhi ran out of wine. She did not want to disappoint them, so she poured them the only wine left in a pot, which also contained a dead snake. They came to know about the venomous wine only when they had consumed it. Hearing this, they are said to have died out of shock. Mokhi never forgave herself for their deaths, and passed away herself sometime later. The Mataras and Mokhi were buried near the bar that now exists at the foothills of Narathar.

Mokhi finds her mention in the poetry of poets like Shah Abdul Latif Bhittai, Shah Abdul Karim of Bulri, Shah Inayat and Shah Lutfullah Qadri. In the verses of Shah Abdul Latif Bhittai, the character of Mokhi represents sincerity, love and longing. Today, her tomb is located near Shah Mureed's shrine in Gadap and attracts many devotees from distant lands.

Kasu Ma Sati in Sindh's Mithi District

As legend has it, Kasu Ma sacrificed herself and became a sati when her son, Harnath Dohat Rathore, was killed in battle. According to tradition, Harnath's wife was supposed to become a sati upon his death, but refused to do so. It was then that Kasu Ma came forward and presented herself as the wife's refusal was thought to be a bad sign. She subsequently sacrificed her life and became a Maha (great) sati.

Sati worship until recently was practiced by some inhabitants of Tharparkar, a district in Sindh with a large Hindu population. Many men and women from the community pay regular visits to the shrine of Kasu Ma hoping to find escape, solace and alleviation of their worries. The annual fair at the shrine attracts a large crowd of Hindus from every caste who pack the shrine, singing *bhajans* (devotional songs) and reciting *chhands* (folk poetry).

The devotees visiting seek her benediction at every important juncture of their lives. The memorial stone, locally called Lorti and Paryio, depict Kasu Ma holding her deceased son in her lap or arms.[21]

Mai Bakhtwar of Sindh

Mai Bakhtwar is considered to be a true representative of the women's struggle against feudalism in Sindh. She refused to accept the laws dictated by her landlord and, as a result, was murdered when she resisted his attempts to snatching the produce of her family.

The tale of Mai Bakhtwar is treated as a folklore legend of women's resistance in Sindh and is considered an inspiration for several movements for land rights, which came later.[22] For example, her story inspired a massive revolt among the Haris, led by Haider Bux Jatoi, and who protested against feudal laws which were oppressive. The movement was called the Sindh Hari Committee Movement for land rights, popularly known as the Hari movement.

Marvi of Sindh

Marvi, another Sindhi heroine, is revered by many for putting up a sturdy, strong-hearted resistance against the cruel ruler of Umerkot. Marvi belonged to a village named Malir in

Tharparkar. An orphan boy named Phog, who lived and grew up in her family, wanted to marry the beautiful Marvi. However, she fell in love with her cousin Khet, who lived in a neighbouring village. Phog went to the ruler of Umerkot, a man named Umer, who always sought the company of beautiful women. Phog informed him about Marvi and claimed that she was the most beautiful woman in Sindh. Subsequently, Umer sent a proposal of marriage to Marvi but she refused, as she was loyal to Khet and loved her native land.

Umer did not take the refusal well. He abducted Marvi and kept her in his mansion, imprisoned for a whole year, but failed to break her will. Eventually, seeing her unconditional dedication and commitment to her people, Umer permitted her to return to her homeland. Shah Latif expresses Marvi's thoughts in his poetry:

I feel proud of my folks in the desert They have wild vegetation as their food Leaves of trees as their dress and cover Wilderness is all they have to live with My folks have given me nothingness in dowry.[23]

Or,

Only the shameless can forget The beloved and homeland, Condemned are those who forget the motherland.[24]

And again:

The mud of my land is like musk to me.[25]

The character of Marvi was also recreated in modern Pakistan as a television series. Further, Marvi *mela* (fair) is celebrated in many villages of Sindh to pay homage to her resolution and fortitude, and her refusal to bow down to a wicked and cruel ruler.[26]

I raise both my hands
And ask my children
To raise their little hands
Marvi, of Maru and Malir, In the mists of time
She raised her hands While the world slept To God
Full of hope
Praying to see her homeland Marvi, We raise our hands As you raised yours
To God
In hope
For the homeland I was born in Buried my Father Buried my brother Married
Had my children Served a Nation Helped a people
Without telephone or electricity
Computers or emails
Polio drops or iodine

Hear the wind
It carries the sound Of horses that galloped Of caravans that came Of tanks that rumbled Of planes that flew Before the torch of time Was passed
As history's pendulum swung The desert wind calls Marvi calls
A timeless call
A call

The desert wind carries. Children: Hear the desert wind Hear
it whisper
Have faith
We will win.[27]

'Some people think that Marvi's character symbolizes patriotism. In this context some researchers believe that "Marvi" is a symbol of "Sindh" itself, bound in chains and crying for her rights but the people are doing nothing for her deliverance and people watch everything with a feeling of helplessness.'[28]

Using Marvi's legend as a literary device, Bhittai was referring to the collective as well. For Marvi's life story was one of 'removing all obstacles using ones determination.'[29]

These examples illustrate how Bhittai encapsulates the tradition of the feminine transcendence in the face of worldly evils through the creation of female protagonists who, all in their own specific way, establish their affinity with the people of Sindh and attempt to provide them with a panacea for their perceived grievances.

'He wanted to show that a woman has unique qualities; she is more intense than a man in patriotism, height of character, sacrifice and determination; she has been made a victim of different complexes and despite her poverty, has superior human qualities (Marvi). She can defy and rebel against a forced marriage and to get her rights and the beloved, she can stare into the eyes of death and with her sacrifice she can drown the river (Sohni); and if she wants, she can walk on thorns to seek the beloved and fight the mountains on the road to love – she can melt stones with her will power (Sasui). She, after realizing her mistakes can save herself from being abandoned by man, and with her wisdom she can console the angry husband (Leela). Shah Latif desired to show that these various characters with different positive qualities can be presented as examples for womenfolk as well as the nation.'[30]

In presenting a diverse set of such archetypes in the form of his poetic heroines, Shah Latif has also captured the intergenerational veneration of the feminine, and its connection to Sufi thought that has historically remained pervasive in the region. It is valuable to note here that the Sufi tradition of the subcontinent is mainly associated with Sunni Barelvis, but Shias have also been influenced by it to a great extent. Conservative Shias, who mostly identify with the Iranian ones, are different from the Ismailis, another sub-sect of Shia Islam that espouses Sufi doctrines. The founder of Pakistan, Muhammad Ali Jinnah, also belonged to a moderate Ismaili-Shia community.

Historically, Barelvi Sunnis who follow Sufi practices have also been seen to be tolerant of Shia rituals unlike their counterparts, the Deobandi Sunnis. There is a large community of Shias living in Sindh and also in the Gilgit-Baltistan region. The ancient Sufi culture of these areas has borrowed much from Barelvi-Sunnis as well as from Shias.

More recently, the 'martyrdom' and 'sacrifice' of Pakistan's twice-elected prime minister, Benazir Bhutto, is a continuation of the way feminine legends are constructed and worshipped.

The Marvi of the Twenty-First Century – Benazir Bhutto

Benazir Bhutto was elected as the prime minister of Pakistan twice (1988-90 and 1993-96) and was also the leader of the Pakistan Peoples Party (PPP), a centre-left populist political party. She was the first female ruler of Pakistan and therefore, also of any Islamic country in the world. She took over the reign of PPP at a young age when her father, Zulfikar Ali Bhutto, also the founder of PPP, was sentenced to death by the nexus of a military government and the judiciary through what is considered by many to be judicial murder.

Benazir's life was a tale of the struggle against autocratic military rulers and the extreme right-wing parties. Having earlier suffered the pain of losing her father under Zia ul Haq's military regime, her government was dismissed twice, on charges of corruption. She was forced to live in exile twice in her political career. In 2007, when another military autocratic ruler, Pervez Musharraf, was at the helm of political affairs, Benazir vowed to return to the country amidst threats to her life and in a vulnerable security environment. Upon her arrival on 18 October 2007, her welcome caravan was attacked by a suicide bomber. Though she survived, this attack resulted in 130 deaths, the victims being mostly those who had come to welcome Benazir Bhutto.[31]

On 27 December 2007, just two months after the first attempt on her life, she was again targeted after having delivered a speech during a political rally at Liaqat Bagh, Rawalpindi. This time, the terrorists struck successfully and she reportedly died on her way to the hospital.

In December 2008, on Benazir Bhutto's first death anniversary, almost 35,000 people flocked to the mausoleum of Bhutto at Garhi Khuda Bakhsh and since then her death anniversary is a massively attended event.[32]

Much like the divine status of the Pirs of Sindh, the Bhuttos overwhelmed the imagination of the people of the province through their charismatic political appeal, their struggle for the rights of the indigenous people and most importantly, through the sacrifices made by the family. Bhutto's two sons – Murtaza and Shahnawaz were also murdered. It is a common belief in rural Sindh that the Bhuttos, having acquired 'shahadat' for their people and their land, continue to live in essence. '*Kal bhi Bhutto zinda tha, aaj bhi Bhutto zinda hai*' (Bhutto is as alive today as he was yesterday) is a popular slogan amongst the people of the Sindh province, which traditionally refers to Zulfikar Ali Bhutto, but now alludes to Benazir Bhutto too.

The perception of Benazir held by the majority across the Sindh provides a semblance to the image of Bhitai's heroines, that of a woman who is the flag-bearer of her people, the daughter of the land, the mother of the oppressed and one so pure that she borders on divinity. On her return from exile, thousands of men, women and children rushed to Karachi to receive her. Beyond a purely political constituency-based explanation to this mass movement were myriad anecdotes of how the population's down-trodden had put their pennies together, at times mortgaging their scarce land and other belongings, to generate sufficient resources for a visit to Karachi to pay homage to Benazir. In the background of the political ruckus that was unfolding, a transcendental narrative was being written, one within which scores upon scores of the oppressed moved in unison to welcome Benazir Bhutto, as if performing a ritual in reverence of a deity.

Presented at The International Festival of Sacred Arts, Delhi, in February, 2011.

LITERATURE

5

The Enigma of Dual Belonging: Qurratulain Hyder's Enduring Popularity in Pakistan

Writing about Qurratulain Hyder is a daunting task, to say the least. The breadth and range of themes and subjects that her works traverse can overwhelm any reader. More often than not, her writings can remind the reader of the inadequacies of their creative response given the boundless ideas, energy and themes they are confronted with.

It is with much trepidation that I venture to discuss the popularity of Hyder's works in Pakistan. Her magnum opus *Aag Ka Darya* (AKD) was published countless times in Pakistan and remains perhaps the most popular novel in the Urdu language. The paradox is noteworthy here: this novel is strictly not in line with the version of history that Pakistanis are familiar with; yet it is so popular.

There is no definitive hypothesis that I wish to articulate through the succeeding pages; nor would I make any claims of original research here. My standpoint is that of a devoted reader, a handful of secondary sources and limited interviews.[1]

Briefly, this chapter will focus on three major aspects of Hyder's writings which interestingly are also the highlights of her rich, complex and sadly, little-known legacy in the subcontinent. These three elements, in my opinion, also provide some explanation for her enduring popularity among Pakistani readers despite her decision to migrate to India in the 1960s. Notwithstanding the views of the mainstream Pakistani literary establishment, the officialdom and tragic turbulences in Indo-Pakistan relations since the 1960s, Hyder's works have continued to attract a wide readership in Pakistan.

At the outset, it should be reiterated that the sheer quality and innovation of her major and minor works place Urdu fiction at par with global contemporary literary currents. Some, including me, also argue that her work in many instances transcend several typologies of 'great' international literature.[2] Javed Akhtar's impromptu tribute at her demise is instructive:

> *When I say that it is a great loss, it's not only to Urdu literature, not only to Indian literature, but to the word literature. I am not exaggerating at all. In the years to come, Hyder's novels will reach everywhere… The kind of work she has done… it's only because she was born in a third-world country and wrote in a language that is not of the imperialistic powers, her novels have not reached everywhere. I am sure the time will come when they will reach everywhere.[3]*

Therefore, it is apparent that the intrinsic and universal quality of her work has been the primary reason for her appeal among Urdu readers. A leading Pakistani newspaper in its editorial summed it up:

*Perhaps she was to Urdu fiction what Iqbal was to Urdu
poetry; as towering a presence for the second half of the
twentieth century as Iqbal had been for the first half. She was
a great writer who brilliantly captured an entire civilization
in transit.*[4]

But then there are many other celebrated and popular writers
in Pakistan. What differentiates Hyder's work from theirs?

The purpose here is not to draw comparisons, as Hyder
would not have approved of it. Her classic view on this has
always been the same: do people in the West compare Hardy
and James? So why are we, in the world of Urdu, so keen to
harp on *mawazna-i- Anees o Dabir?*[5]

Therefore, I shall identify three major issues or elements of
Hyder's works that point towards her immense legacy as well
as provide some clues to her popularity among the readers of
Urdu language, especially in Pakistan. In short, these elements
are:

(a) Hyder's mastery over the genre of social history and
    its creative use in fiction, thereby laying formidable
    groundwork for future historians and writers. In
    employing this genre, Hyder explores the concept and
    contours of a civilization that is, in great measure, free
    of borders, religions and national identities; narratives
    which suggest that history and eras are concurrent
    and non-exclusive. Therefore, the parochial national
    identities might determine citizenship; the past looms
    large over the lives of individuals and is neither separate
    nor irrelevant to the lives of humans. Therefore, Hyder

presents the histories of people as opposed to rulers
and of individuals, groups and characters that would
otherwise be invisible or at best exist on the margins of
what we know as history.

(b) In her articulation of post-colonial traumas, not
restricted to migration, Hyder takes the literary
approach to the Partition of India to a different
level. This 'level' is beyond the brutality of riots and
the blame-games. Hyder's narratives place the 1947
watershed within the framework of South Asian history
and the continuous process of travel and migrations.
Furthermore, the tragedy of 1947 in Hyder's vision is
also located in the death of the old order and creation
of a new world where new values such as wealth and
consumerism define the civilizational value-system. By
doing so, Hyder, in a foretelling manner, links the role
of literature in the contemporary milieu of market-
obsessed globalization.

(c) In her endeavours as a chronicler of the Indo-Muslim
civilization, Hyder dug deep into the complexities
and contradictions of the history of Muslims in India.
The ethos and construction of Indo-Muslim identity,
therefore has to be composite and not communal for
it would negate history with anarchic results. Thus,
Hyder subverts the communal discourses and thereby
de-legitimizes them while providing alternative
sources of popular historical notions such as the
Bhakti movement in *AKD* and twentieth-century Sufi
practices in *Gardish-i-Rang-i-Chaman*.

Social History Narratives Versus the Official Histories

What is India all about, what is the problem, why are we so full of problems, why are we like no other country? It's because there's too much history, we have too much of everything, and some of it is excellence but too much of excellence in one country, one period over so many centuries creates problem, it's not a simple story, it becomes a very complicated story.[6]

History as compiled, documented and distilled has entailed histories of rulers and the state. This tradition was also appropriated by the new states of India and Pakistan. The Indian nationalist discourse had its counterpoint in the Two-Nation Theory that is supposed to have led to Pakistan's creation. Other narratives, perhaps best typified by H.M. Seervai's frank interpretation[7], were by and large sidelined. In a contested terrain such as this one, Hyder took no sides and came up with what was later to become a major discipline of historical studies: examining the concurrent eras of Indo-Pak history from 'below' and from the point of view of the common people rather than rulers, nobles and court-historians.

Social history, often described as 'history from below', concerns itself with the ordinary people, the 'ruled', and how they define and steer history rather than the rulers.[8] It ventures to view itself as an inclusive form of history, not limited to the statement of so-called historical fact but which can probe historical data from a people's perspective. This perspective also examines whether the masses follow the leaders or whether it is the other way around.[9]

Not that there was no tradition of popular social history versions in the subcontinent. Oral tradition, the folklore and folk literature and several other modes of social history have existed since pre-historic times. But Hyder's modern and creative use of such a technique, often supplemented by original research, in Urdu fiction was novel.

Aag Ka Darya (AKD) was written and published in the highly contested milieu of post-partition Indian subcontinent when the new nation states were re-writing their historical discourses. In Pakistan, AKD was a sensation right from the start when it was published in 1959. The controversy it created became its hallmark too. Hyder was allergic to this topic as it had been beaten to death in the course of innumerable interviews, profiles, essays, et al. It is ironic that such a discussion continues to inform debates on her legacy years after her passing.

AKD, for its canvas, historical consciousness and characterization, surpasses most novels written in any language. This novel dealt with the plight of the human condition in the Indo-Pakistan setting from the fourth century BC to the 1950s. Starting with the Mauryan Empire under Chandragupta, it traced the multiple eras with characters disappearing and re-appearing in different guises pitted against the broad strokes of history and time.

The innovative structure of AKD is truly unprecedented, at least in the languages of the subcontinent. It covered four historical periods: first, the expansion of the Mauryan Empire under Chandragupta in the fourth century BC; second, the end of the Lodi dynasty and the beginning of Mughal rule in the late fifteenth and early sixteenth centuries; third, the late eighteenth-century beginnings of the East India Company rule until its consolidation in the 1870s; and fourth, the two decades leading up to the 1950s that encompassed nationalist struggle, Partition, and Independence. These constitute four sequential, yet discrete, experiential moments that also show a grand, individual attempt to understand a civilization. We take the case of a major character, Kamaal from AKD who would inform the argument below.

A key character, Abdul Mansur Kamaaluddin of Nishapur, son of a Persian mother and an Arab father, arrives in Hindustan in the fifteenth century. Mansur is a fortune hunter and passes through various stages in his Indianization, romancing with Ruqqaiya Bano Begum, a kinswoman of Sultan Husain Shah, falling in love with Champavati with whom he is never united as the war separates them. By the time Sikandar Lodi emerges as a successful power-wielder, he quits the world defined by power. By this time he has imbibed the message of the Chishtiya Sufis, the Buddhist thought and Kabir's *baani*, and ends up in Bengal as a land tiller. His tragic end is caused by the rise of another fortune hunter, Sher Shah, whose soldiers kill him for being a traitor.

However, it is Kamaaluddin's life and the India he describes that sets the contours of modern Indo-Muslim consciousness. Hyder's lyrical prose describes his India in these words:

Leaving the world of Kings, Rajas and commanders, Kamaal saw the other world. This other world was inhabited by labourers, barbers, shoe smiths, peasants and poor artisans. This was the democratic Hindustan ruled by saints who patronized artisans and their guilds. The egalitarianism of Islam was profoundly influencing these Hindu Bhaktas. Islam was being spread by peace-loving Sufis -- here the sword was irrelevant. Tormented over the centuries, the untouchables were chanting Ram with these Sankats without the intercession of upper caste Brahmins. This was a unique world that was beyond

> *the Hindu and Muslim identities. Here Love reigned – and*
> *Kamaal was in search of Insaan.*[10]

Kamaal reappears in the third phase of AKD as well. He is the poor Bengali boatman Abdul Mansur, as well as Kamaal, a landowner in Oudh. In this phase he is again witness to the events of 1857 and the harbinger and embodiment of the civilizational ethos that became the hallmark of Oudh.

In the modern narrative of AKD, Kamaal is now the left-leaning, nationalist Kamaal Reza who is educated at Cambridge, returns to a ruined Lucknow and fails to find a job; the land reforms take away family wealth, his family's ancestral property is confiscated in an unfair manner and labelled as evacuee property. Thus, a dispossessed family migrates to Pakistan whilst Kamaal's alter ego, the Switzerland-returned Amir Raza, has already migrated to Pakistan and entered the elite service of the new state. Amir Raza has already rejected Champa – another recurrent character who represents the more nationalist brand of Muslim consciousness in the novel.

At the time of its publication, the novel represented what the middle classes (obviously the ones who comprised the readership in Pakistan) experienced. The migrants empathized with much that was said. However, Hyder's narratives were not limited to the migrant syndrome alone. It was an anguish that several Pakistanis felt and found a voice in the master chronicler of history and the present that in any case had seamless boundaries:

> *The black marketer is frustrated because he cannot put any more*
> *stuff on the black market. The left-wing intellectual bewails the*
> *fact that there appears to be no possibility any longer of a*

revolution. The Jamaat-e-Islami follower is screaming because he sees Muslim women going about unveiled and dancing in the ballroom. The middle class has a million things to worry about. Employment without a recommendation is not to be had, nor can children find admission in school or college without a word from someone in authority. Then there are those Bengali and Punjabi refugees who are tense because of their conflict with the locals. This struggle is as intense as the one between Hindu and Muslim in undivided India. Some people say that the last hope lies in a military revolution. There is one party, that is, the party of the refugees. This by far is the strangest of creatures in this country. It has come from India and is to be found in every city, town and village of the country, with Karachi serving as its headquarters. The special racket of this class is called culture.[11]

The succeeding novel *Aakhire Shab Ke Hamsafar* (ASKH), equally acclaimed, was about a group of highly charged idealists who struggle in the pre-Independence era. They are the victims of the vagaries of time, get disillusioned with life only to compromise their principles in India, Pakistan and Bangladesh, respectively. However, within the subtext runs a fascinating account of the contemporary historical consciousness, one that was not based on what the major schools of historiography could recount. As Asaduddin[12] writes:

In describing the lives of Deepali, Raihan, Jahan Ara, Rosy and others, Hyder makes implicit comments on social mores and educational attainments of different communities at that point of time. While the girls in Hindu and Christian families have been shown as actively participating in different spheres of life, Muslim girls have been depicted as yet struggling between restrictive social norms and their half-articulated desire to achieve selfhood.

This is where the young Pakistanis in the Western part were introduced to the magic of Bengal, its rivers, culture and poetry in a well-crafted format. ASKH also proved to be hugely popular in Pakistan with many a reader terming it as a more immediate novel as it was less complex than AKD in bringing together the strands of Indo-Pak history.

In *Gardish-e Rang-i-Chaman*, she explores an impressive range of subcultures, dying and flourishing, such as Anglo-Indians, Sufi *khanqahs*, street performers, prostitutes and the nouveau riche classes of the post-1947 subcontinent. Storytelling, therefore, is a statement on the concurrent eras of history and reminds the readers of what, for instance, a Mughal princess would have gone through during the post-1857 tribulations or how the farce of history twice repeated plays out in ordinary, everyday lives.

Agle Janam Mohay Bitya Na Kijo (AJMBNK), a novella, ostensibly a work of fiction, can also be read as a sociological treatise of sorts, as it closely studied class exploitation. AJMBNK also presents an anthropological record of the dialects, music, vanishing crafts and groups of performers. Unlike several accounts of the fall of civilizations, this dealt with the death of a civilization 'from below', to liberally apply this subaltern term. AJMBNK will prove to be a crucial text for historians and students of history in the future decades. The novella has already inspired a range of theatrical performances and feature films.

Hyder's popularity in Pakistan has been termed a 'backhanded compliment'[13] as her books were and perhaps remain bestsellers in Pakistan. It is a separate matter that most of them were pirated editions; and an unregulated publishing industry profiteered from their appeal. However, it is also metaphoric as to how history and a search for personal truths can remain an unstated activity in Pakistan.

By exploring the pain of partition; and reiterating that 'civilization' was a larger domain than a nation, Hyder made a point in Pakistan and, in many ways to the limited Urdu readership in India as well. It was through the English translations and Hindi versions of her novels that this point was also made in India. As stated by Sangari:

> *Civilizations were not divisible into nations, national boundaries came and went; civilizations endured. Civilizational unity was perceived as made up of long-term and contemporary bonds, the textures of lives and memories and friendships.*[14]

In the next section, we explore the emergence of separate identities, howsoever problematic they might be and the inherent dilemmas and conflicts that were faced by the new citizens of Pakistan, especially those who migrated from Punjab and United Provinces of the British India.

Migration, History, the Shifting Sands of Identity

Pakistan's eminent historian K.K. Aziz is said to have remarked that Hyder displayed a firm grasp on history and *Kar-i-Jahan Daraz Hai* (KJDH) is a testament to that. Hyder's most experimental work was this autobiographical novel, which traced her genealogy from Central Asia and recounted her family and personal stories in a complex mosaic of style, technique and ever-changing ambience. Its third volume was published in 2000. As is the case of her novels, KDJH remains the best in its genre and the ability to expand the 'potential of experiencing life.'[15] Navigating through its interconnected stories, social commentary and ambience, the reader, slowly, becomes a part of the narrative, and starts viewing the world in a grand historical perspective and travels with its real characters.

We have to revert to AKD here, yet again. Kamaal Raza, the archetypal Muslim refugee from Lucknow, after his migration to Karachi, wonders:

> *This one has learnt only after Partition. The Hindu says when your culture and your beliefs are different, then you should go to Pakistan. What are you doing here? So these people came to Pakistan as "mohajirs", but once here they learnt that while they had got rid of the Hindu, there was a different problem facing them. The mohajir felt frustrated both at Lahore, where there was the Punjabi, and Dhaka where there was the Bengali. Therefore, the mohajir made a beeline for Karachi. So Karachi is the mohajir centre.*

To date, these words of Hyder are true for what followed decades later, a movement of Mohajir identity and political struggle that is now a part of the mainstream political process of Pakistan with Karachi as its hub.

But the existential question of identity became a recurrent theme of Hyder's works. Her early novels treated these thorny issues in a romantic and idealistic manner. But her later works starting with the magnum opus AKD went deeper. In her later years, with her subsequent return to India, the themes of migration and identity and emergence of a new order echoed in most of the writings. Having been a migrant twice, and having lived on both the sides, she had the unique experiential insight into the process of migration and what it entailed.

Housing Society explored the lives and tribulations of three migrant families and how their world is turned upside down in post-Partition Karachi. In this novel, two affluent families of yore become homeless, while their poor country cousin, through an alliance with the new political and economic classes, becomes a powerful business magnate (this aspect of Hyder's writing is explored in detail in the succeeding section). Another one, *Patjhar ki Awaaz* (*The Sound of Falling Leaves*) has a protagonist who meets an old acquaintance in a Lahore bazaar, bringing back memories of her teenage years in Delhi. The migrant has a new home, a new identity but there is existential angst as well as the bitter turn of history.

In later works such as *Chandni Begum*, Hyder incisively traces the 'love-hate relationship between the emigré Muslims of Pakistan and their relatives left behind in India'[16]; and needless to mention this is another theme that has not been delved into by most writers. For instance, the clichés on the plight of Indian Muslims was also treated in *Chandni Begum* by Hyder among others.

We conclude once again with what Kamaal has to say on Karachi on the shifting sands of historical reality:

'Here's Karachi, the God-given state of Pakistan, the world's largest Islamic country and the capital of the world's fifth largest country, whose slums and refugee shelters can be counted among the world's marvels, especially those horrifying

and filthy makeshift refuges that lie all around the resting place
of the Quaid-i-Azam. In the *Housing Society*, some extremely
beautiful bungalows have been built, which leads one to the
conclusion that the Muslim middle class has never had it so
good in its entire history. Here the new rich rule, with their
new social order and their new principles.'[17]

...And the New States, Classes and Sensibilities

Much like India where the initial reformism gave way to the
politics of caste, elites and bureaucratic stronghold, the new
state of Pakistan underwent quick transformations. A whole
new set of classes emerged and fuelled by the bounties of
evacuee property, a culture of consumerism became the norm.
Our eternal Kamaal therefore cries in AKD:

> *Karachi is an ultra-modern city. Every night its swank hotels
> and clubs bring to life a world of resplendent lights. Sociologists
> ought to investigate the quite fascinating birth, in just nine
> years, of this new class and its culture. The basis of this class is
> money: how to make it, how to get rich. While the river flows,
> leap in and swim because who knows, tomorrow it may run
> dry or it may start flowing in another direction.*[18]

Raihan, the fiery revolutionary in *Aakhir-e-Shab Ke Hamsafar*
ends up as an industrial tycoon and tainted politician in the
new Bangladesh; and the erstwhile idealists of this epic novel
embrace these new realities. How ironic that we are also
witnessing how the Communists in India are now attracting
foreign investment, whilst the ones in Pakistan are allies of
the right-wing parties. For instance, in AKD her statement

rang true: the 'anti-British leftists' who made 'a bee-line for England, deserting the toiling masses for whom their hearts used to bleed.'

More significantly, Hyder commented on what was happening in India as well. In *Gardish-e Rang-i-Chaman*, there is a legendary satire concerning Nigar Khanam, a prolific writer and more of a plagiarist and her sister, Shahwar Khanam. Through the two sisters who are stupidity incarnate, Hyder lambasts the colossal vulgarity of the nouveau riche for whom money is the magic that can buy everything – even culture, decency and grace. In their interaction with other people, the sisters always flaunt money, exult in their malfeasance and unregenerate willfulness.

The archetypal characters of Nigar Khanam and her sister were not unusual, exaggerated though they might appear. In Pakistan, the nouveau riche had established themselves as new role models for many. However, the average middle-class reader in Pakistan considered this to be a pertinent comment. Not that others were not writing about it but the fact that it came as part of the composite panoramic whole of Hyder's novels was the unique feature.

A Chronicler of Our Times

Hyder was a grand chronicler: '*A kind of Tolstoy in Urdu that our critics have ignored. When someone asked her in Bombay to write about the Iran-Iraq war she naturally began with the Arab conquest at Qadissiya.*'[19]

KJDH is a testament to her status as an original chronicler whose style is original and connects with lay readers. We have noted AKD's attempt to explore history and that too in voices of everyday characters, invaders, scholars, lovers and common

men and women of ancient and medieval India. Similarly,
in *Gardish-e Rang-i-Chaman*, labeled as a semi-documentary
novel by Hyder herself, there are chronicles of three kinds. At
the broader level, it traces and records the post-1857 tragic
lives of the Mughal descendants. But that is not what the
novel is about. There are records of the Anglo-Indian contact
and hybridization, something that William Dalrymple has
painstakingly researched in *The White Mughals*.[20] Hyder had
already explored this sub-set of the complex Indian universe,
decades before Dalrymple's book was published. And then
there is documentation of the Khanqahi system, its evolution
and manifestations in the twentieth century.

Not content with fiction, Hyder's creativity in later years
found an outlet in rediscovering the essentials of Indo-
Muslim civilization. She dug out the first subcontinental
novel, entitled *Nashtar*, authored by a late eighteen-century
East India Company official, Hasan Shah. This invaluable
script and its 1890 translation were lying neglected and Hyder
translated and published it under the title *The Nautch Girl*, with
overwhelming excitement that the modern novel was not the
preserve of the English speaking world. This discovery is lesser
known and (like many others) underrated. There were critics
and skeptics, but she held her ground and had no patience for
the self-flagellation which a post-colonial South Asian mind
often indulges in. This is her outstanding contribution to the
corpus of South Asian and world literature. Posterity will treat
it as a major landmark in the evolution of subcontinental
literature.[21]

This is also where Hyder stood shoulder to shoulder
with her contemporaries and successors as she explored the
complexities, contradictions of the history of Muslims in

India. The ethos and construction of Indo–Muslim identity, therefore has to be composite and not communal.

As pointed out, Hyder's vision has been validated by several views on History. For instance, Irfan Habib's view, 'that the "idea" of India as a cultural unity was not a modern secular invention but a much older one, that it was a product of conquest (Mauryan emperor Asoka's inscriptions in 250 BC) and travellers' visions or a view from outside (Alberuni's *Kitab–ul-Hind* in the eleventh century), while the affect-laden idea of India as a distinctive composite culture or a common heritage emerged from immigrants and converts (such as Amir Khusrau's *Nuh Sipihr* in 1318).'[22]

Thus, Hyder's emphasis on the fact that the history of the Indo–Pak subcontinent is a narrative of travellers where eras overlap, merge and are generally concurrent. Hence AKD shows a repeating sequence of characters through over two dozen centuries. And her autobiographical novel, KJDH, she invokes this view as a personal and civilizational account. The ancient and the medieval 'culture', 'whether Arab, European, or Indian was a cross-national traffic, always conflict-riven, yet always familiar with, affected or influenced by, and aware of "other" cultures, and at times almost cosmopolitan.'[23]

In such a context, her vision therefore is multi-religious, directed by an unending process of change with the old influencing the new and the new invoking the old. Therefore, it does not subscribe to 'insider's hegemonic assimilation' or to an 'outsider's imperious hegemony'.[24]

In AKD, the narrative starts with the convergence of Greek, Vedic, Buddhist, Persian, Bhakta and later 'the hybridization both of the British – from innkeeper to nabob – and the Indian – from feudal aristocracy to the colonial middle class. In each period, there is an interplay of different epistemologies, languages, and literatures.'

In this process of recounting history, Hyder demolishes the stereotypes that emerge from the particularism of religious identities. Neither is this a propaganda tool that invokes the 'One India' stereotype. There is immense complexity that confronts the communal versions of history and the Partition saga. The nationalism of Pakistani or the Indian state becomes a secondary issue. The religious or communal narrative also becomes a constructed reality. And the reader can see through it, feel with the author and flow with her grand sweep.

Kamaal, therefore echoes the popular sentiment of educated Pakistanis in the 1950s and perhaps fifty-eight years later too:

> *Islam! Islam has had a rough ride here. If the Pakistani team begins to lose at cricket, Islam falls into danger. Every problem in the world is ultimately reduced to this word, Islam. Other Muslim countries resent the fact that the sole contractors of Islam are these people from Pakistan. Everything is being upholstered with narrow-mindedness. Music, art, civilisation, learning and literature, they are all being viewed from the perspective of the Mullah. Islam, which was like a rising river whose majestic flow had been augmented by so many tributaries to turn it into a cascading force, has been reduced to a muddy stream which is being enclosed from all four sides with high walls.*[25]

In fact, the current dangers of extremism were not missed by Hyder in 1959 when Kamaal articulates this common sentiment:

The joke is that those who raise the slogan of Islam in the loudest voices have nothing to do with the philosophy of this religion. The only thing they know is that the Muslims ruled Spain for 800 years, that they ruled Bharat for a thousand years, while the Ottomans kept East Europe subjugated for centuries. Apart from imperialism, no mention is ever made of Islam's great humanism, nor is it considered necessary to speak about the open-heartedness of Arab seers, Iranian poets and Indian Sufis. There is no interest in the philosophy of Ali and Hussain. Islam is being presented as a violent religion and a violent way of life.[26]

AKD has also been termed as a means of 'reclaiming the subcontinent from the violence that had torn it apart, bulling it into a consoling civilizational lounge duree in which the repeated destructions of the composite culture of Awadh (in 1846, 1857, 1947) could be accommodated to the recurrent rise and fall of kingdoms' (Hasan, ibid). In doing so, Hyder also unwittingly follows Ibn Khaldun's philosophy of history by mourning for the past that is gone and articulating a vision for the future. Therefore, for the Indo-Pakistan readers, AKD brings forth the 'civilizational' consciousness that asks for a 'loyalty that was different from older loyalties of region, religion, or language; a loyalty to the idea of civilization that was wider, deeper, and more compelling than its division into separate nations' (Hasan, ibid).

Even in her last Urdu novel, *Gardish-e Rang-i-Chaman*, the depiction of faith and conversion of a colourful card sharper is a fascinating study. It joins the narrative back to the Bhakti movement descriptions in AKD. The major sub-plot of *Gardish-e Rang-i-Chaman* brings forth a modern Sufi and a twentieth-century Khanqah practices which are not different from the popular face of Islam in Pakistan too. The vast majority of Pakistanis are not adherents to the puritan movements that exist in the annals of corporate media but in the quintessential Sufi vision and reverence for dargahs. But in Hyder's account, this narrative becomes another point of reference for popular history. Such an Islam is beyond the Hindu-Muslim divide and is independent of all political nationalism.

Hyder's nuanced and highly sophisticated vision was not easily apparent to the officialdom or state-sponsored literary critics in Pakistan. She writes in her introduction to the 1988 edition of AKD about one such critic who raised a storm:

> Siraj Rizvi was somebody about whom it is said (I don't know how true it is) that he tried once to gain favours in a personal matter from a Brigadier who was appointed at that time [1959] as a sort of 'Literary Overseer' under the Martial Law. Siraj Rizvi had published a long and very improper essay against my novel, which was published in the daily Jang, Karachi (in which he had also revealed that the author was the real niece of the Indian Communist Dr Rasheed Jahan).[27]

And Hyder was aware of the permanent connection that she made with Pakistan:

> Noon Meem Rashid's view that *Aag ka Dariya* was published in the expired time did not come true because during the last thirty years, the most saleable book in Pakistan after *Iqbal* and *Faiz* is *Aag ka Dariya*. Numerous unauthorized editions of this book have been published

and the irony is that the front pages of these editions invariably bear the statement 'rights of publication are protected in favour of the author'.[28]

The sheer humanity of her vision, therefore struck the Pakistani reader; as this was in sharp contrast to what the state wanted him/her to believe. For Hyder, the divisions of insider and outsider were irrelevant. She was more concerned about identifying the ceaseless cycles of greed and hate that disrupted the world's beauty. Her scrutiny was also the thinking man's vision.

Conclusion

Hyder's remarks in her acceptance speech at the Jnanpith Award function (1991) were telling:

> My concern for civilizational values about which I continue writing may sound naive, wooly-headed and simplistic. But then, perhaps, I am like that little bird which foolishly puts up its claws, hoping that it will stop the sky from falling.[29]

So what is her legacy, after all? Is it just another woolly headed, quaint vision of a secular India? Such a cliché will not do justice to her magnificent writings. It is beyond the labels of 'secular', 'Muslim', 'Indo-Muslim' and so on. Her works are arresting for their complexity and richness, of the inextricability of the Muslim and non-Muslim cultures in terms of literature, poetry and music, and the forces of history like colonization and Independence of the subcontinent. But above all, they leave behind a legacy of humanism and the primordial human quest for love, belonging and search for enlightenment.

Ironically, in her long literary career she proved her early critics wrong, especially high profile ones such as Ismat Chughtai who had accused her of being bourgeoisie and removed from the people of India. Her continuous narrations of the subcontinent's myriad social history remain unmatched. And her characters, victims of the vagaries of Time and rulers' History, bear eloquent testimonies on societal modes of class exploitation. But these characters are not part of an ideological or a deterministic script. They are continuations, manifestations of the history, relating to the present day reader.

The eminent Urdu writer Enver Sajjad held[30] that Hyder challenged the kings' history in Pakistan and warned her compatriots of the dangerous seeds that the new bourgeoisie of Pakistan was planting in the new homeland. Whether this was the case with illegal raids on evacuee property, abuse of Islam, mishandling of the Bengali cultural separateness or denuding history, she unwittingly became an oracle of events to come. Her art was such that she said all this in the context of history – that was grander and larger than the post-Pakistan linear versions. Hyder therefore assumed an important position in the collective consciousness of Urdu readers.

This is why Hyder remained a unique bond between India and Pakistan till her last day. She was a regular visitor to Pakistan, her second home in actual terms. Her family, friends and admirers were in large numbers that never distanced her from the country. Like her characters, she travelled, migrated and re-migrated, becoming a chronicler of our times, not as a historian but as a fiction writer. In the process she defied the label of being anti-Pakistan.

There is nothing in her huge corpus of work that can be remotely termed as 'anti-Pakistan'. Her move to India may have been propelled by the controversies but it remained a personal decision. Hyder's re-migration to India was an afterthought as she originally moved to the United Kingdom.[31] However, she eventually landed in India where luminaries like Nehru and Azad welcomed her with open arms. Pakistani officialdom, and rival authors and critics may have wronged her; but the readers in Pakistan remained loyal to her and gave her the recognition that writers cannot do without.

For years, Hyder will live on as the doyenne of Urdu fiction. Immensely respected and widely read in a country that in her view was not the 'other' but another facet of the rich, complex historical legacy of the subcontinent. In the words of Mustansar Hussain Tarar,[32] she created her own cult, a sort of a literary creed that kept all her readers fascinated and faithful throughout.

Hyder was truly a dual citizen in an age where acrimonies of Partition and officialdom made it impossible to hold concurrent citizenships. But Qurratulain Hyder even defied that; she proved that like her vision, her belonging could be concurrent and beyond the accepted definitions.

Published in *Qurratulain Hyder and The River of Fire, The Meaning, Scope and Significance of Her Legacy*, Edited by Rakshanda Jalil, 2011, OUP.

6

Reclaiming Humanity: Women in Manto's Short Stories

❧

He saw dimly lit humanity even in the characters that appear to us evil. He perceived glimmers of this humanity both in the oppressed and the oppressor, perceiving a distant flame of human frailties flickering both in the pimp who goes out selling in the streets the body of an exploited woman, and in that woman herself. The moral principles in this given everyday universe of ours hide underneath our prejudices and our ideological agendas. Manto created a pure universe on the other side of the horizon; in his universe ambiguities twinkle as virtuous stars.[1]

Perhaps the most well known and also controversial Urdu writer of the twentieth century happens to be Saadat Hasan Manto. He left us with a stupendous literary output, which continues to remain relevant decades after his death. He – like other 'greats' – died young and lived through the greatest upheaval in the Indian subcontinent, i.e., the Partition. As a sensitive writer, he was influenced and traumatized by the political turmoil of 1947 and beyond. His stories reflect his repeated attempts to come to terms with this cataclysmic event for millions in North India. For Manto, Partition remained a mystery but he did not keep himself in a state of denial about it. He, however always used the word 'batwara', never partition.[2] He felt that it was the ripping apart of one nation and would lead to greater divisions among the people of the subcontinent. This coming-to-terms with the 'batwara' is experienced in his works by unusual characters driven by plain ambitions, mixed emotions and above all, sheer humanity. Like Nazeer Akbarabadi, Manto's characters are universal and it is often difficult to condemn them for the writer's humanity remains overarching.

This essay focuses on the female characters in Manto's short stories. The construction and treatment of these characters turns them into complex, and sometimes ambiguous metaphors for humanity. This is why the story of suffering during 1947 is often a tale of women surviving the horrors of crimes against humanity, rescuing and salvaging life when men turn into communal butchers and not giving up even in the face of the greatest adversities.

Other than in the stories of Partition, women characters in Manto's work are strong and unique, given the general trend in Urdu fiction among male writers of sounding as patronizing[3], reflective of the prevailing mores in a conservative, colonial society. Manto's female characters appear defiant and righteous, even though their circumstances are mired in taboo and social marginalization.

Manto's Humanism

Manto was a cosmopolitan humanist who rejected narrow-minded bigotry and refused to let religious or cultural differences override the common notions of humanity. His characters are drawn from real life. They are commoners – many of them from a lower strata of society – who suffer the fate of decisions taken by 'leaders' and those in the upper echelons of power. They are based on the stark reality of situation and his characters seem natural and authentic.

According to a recent biographer Wadhawan[4], the authenticity of Manto's characters emanates from his experiential insights and humane understanding:

> Manto's characters are drawn from the flotsam and jetsam of society – down and outs; rakes and debauches. Manto had spent a large part of his life among them, observed them day and night from close quarters, and had the inner feel of them as if he was one of them... They comprise a portrait gallery such as Sogandhi, the pimp, Khushia, the debauch and a womanizer like Babu Gopi Nath, a procuress like Mummy and a call girl like Mozel. Such are the characters among whom Manto spent his life and that is why they look so convincing in his stories.

Beyond religion, race, caste and creed, Manto was a humanist and had a grand vision of humanity whereby even the dregs of the earth like prostitutes and swindlers had innate humanity, and in many cases proved to be better beings than the pious and the moralists. By narrating stories of evil and horror, he seeks to point out the much-needed absence of good and human dignity. Dr Zehra[5] writes: 'By narrating stories of evil he desires to highlight the good, not the evil. He is not narrating lust for lust, coercion for coercion, oppression for oppression, sin for sin; but to evoke a deeper understanding of the hidden agenda of a hypocritical society.'

Manto's characters exhibit his conviction that happiness does not lie in winning conflicts on religious or nationalist lines, but in fostering human ties based on feminist threads of love, care, respect and tolerance. He raised the slogan of humanism at a time when the subcontinent presented the picture of a boiling cauldron of religious riots and protests, of acts of misogyny committed in the name of communal honour and 'nationalism'.

Manto examines violence without taking sides. He is particularly cautious of the perpetrators of violence who seek to divide humanity on the basis of religions. The instigators in his stories often belong to well-defined groups of Hindus, Muslims or Sikhs. For example, in the story Sahai, he states, 'Don't say that one lakh Hindus and one lakh Muslims have died. Say that two lakh human beings have perished.' As Syed Nomanul Haq[6] has written,

It has often been observed that when telling a story about atrocities that are consciously wrought, exploitation that is deliberate, injustices done by choice, shady businesses carried out by pimps and loafers in dark urban streets, in none of this does Manto take sides. He would not sit in judgment; he would not establish some phony moral balance between two parties – for example, he was never heard saying that though a train arriving from Amritsar to Lahore following the fateful Indian partition in 1947 was drenched in human blood, a train going the other way too had turned into a blood pool ...

Manto uses his characters as metaphors to highlight the prevalent abuse of humanity in those times. Like characters Sharifan and Bimla in his story *Sharifan* and Sakina in *She is alive*, Manto signifies the offering of the female body without resistance as the helpless surrender of humanity to savage cruelty.

Several of Manto's writings are illustrations of communalism, religious intolerance and Hindu-Muslim-Sikh rivalry that befell the subcontinent during the years of Partition. Manto could not fathom why members of different religions could not peacefully coexist. His helplessness and confusion on the subject are apparent in many of his writings. Take this for instance: '... my mind could not resolve the question: What country did we belong to now – India or Pakistan? And whose blood was being so mercilessly shed every day?'[7]

A little prayer Manto once wrote mirrors his search for answers in the darkness of human experience:

Dear God, Compassionate and Merciful, Master of the universe, we who are steeped in sin, kneel in supplication before Your throne and beseech You to recall from this world Saadat Hasan Manto, son of Ghulam Hasan Manto, who was a man of great piety. Take him away, O Lord, for he runs off from fragrance, chasing filth. He hates the bright sun, preferring dark labyrinths. He has nothing but contempt for modesty but is fascinated by the naked and the shameless. He hates what is sweet, but will give his life to sample what is bitter. He does not so much as look at housewives but is entranced by the company of whores. He will not go near running waters, but loves to wade through slush. Where others weep, he laughs;

where they laugh, he weeps. Evil-blackened faces he loves to
wash with tender care to highlight their features. He never
thinks about You, preferring to follow Satan everywhere, the
same fallen angel who once disobeyed You.[8]

Portrayal of Women

Perhaps the most distinctive feature of Manto's stories is
the nuanced portrayal of women characters. Kumar[9] writes
that 'Manto demonstrates an androgynous sensibility and
an extraordinary sensitivity.' The women in Manto's stories
come from diverse backgrounds and form a colourful range
of characters along with a clear conduit for his humanism.
According to noted Urdu poet and writer Fahmida Riaz,
Manto 'saw women the way he saw men.'[10] Women are a
prominent feature in Manto's stories and are categorized in
three main prototypes: the girl, the homemaker (house wife)
and sex worker (prostitute).[11]

In the story *Hattak* (meaning insult), Saugandhi, a sex
worker, is awakened from her slumber late at night to attend
to a client. She gets all dressed up and puts on her makeup
but when her client meets her, he rejects her and leaves. The
rejection proves devastating for Saugandhi. She is enraged and
her wrath frees her of all her illusions. She resolves to put an
end to the recurring exploitation. The next day her lover visits
her, a cunning man who professes love for her but is actually an
extortionist who meets her only for money. Saugandhi kicks
him out of the house and vows not to be victimized anymore.
She returns to her huge empty Sagwan bed and tries to sleep,
hugging her dog, the only living creature from whom she can
expect love and companionship. This is how the story ends:

This roused Saugandhi. She found herself surrounded by
a terrifying silence. Never before had she experienced
this sort of dead stillness in her room. Everything
seemed to be empty, like a train that has been shunted
into a shed after all its passengers have alighted. She
had an uneasy feeling that there was a sort of vacuum
sucking at her from within. She tried her best to fill this
void somehow, but failed. She would crowd a number
of thoughts in her head, but her mind was like a sieve.
It remained empty.

For a long time, Saugandhi sat in the cane chair and
could think of no way of distracting herself. Suddenly,
she picked up her dog and lying down in her spacious
bed, went to sleep, with the mange stricken animal in
her arms.[12]

Saugandhi's character emerges as a self-aware woman who
becomes determined to put an end to exploitation and live
her own life. She prefers the company of a harmless dog
rather than continue to bear subjugation and falsehoods. In
many ways, her character is more powerful than that of many
virtuous wives, a character who has ambition, desire and
intelligence to end her own exploitation.[13] This description of
Saugandhi is memorable for its elevation of humanity:

*Saugandhi's capacity for loving others was large. She could
have fallen in love with any of the men who paid for her
love and she could have sustained that feeling. Even now she
was in love with four men whose pictures adorned her room.
Saugandhi always felt that she was very large hearted, but
wondered why the same quality was not to be found in men.*

She could not understand this and once involuntarily she said to her image in the mirror, 'Saugandhi, the world has not treated you well.'

The events of these last five years, every day and night of them, had left their mark on every aspect of her life. She had not got all the happiness she had wanted in this period, but she still wished to pass the rest of her days in the same manner. Money did not interest her much. She was not very ambitious and had no desire to accumulate great wealth. Her usual rate for the night was ten rupees, of which, one-fourth was kept by Ramlal as his commission. Seven and a half rupees were more than enough for her needs. She even managed to save something for Madho, whenever he came from Poona, as Ramlal put it, to collect tribute from her.

She always gave him ten or fifteen rupees and this, as Ramlal had also observed, because she had a soft corner in her heart for Madho. Ramlal was right. Saugandhi had been drawn towards Madho since their very first meeting. ...

Manto's portrayal of women is explicit, with no use of symbols. Some of Manto's writings put great emphasis on women's anatomy. When he wanted to say 'breasts', he would say so regardless of social norm or taboos.[14] His writings invited criticism from conservative readers, bigots and later the State apparatus who were not used to such a provocative portrayal of women.

'Mozel', a memorable story by Manto, is about a gutsy and beautiful Jewish woman who lives in Bombay. The name of the piece comes from the Jewish woman in the story whose beauty Manto describes in great detail. The story proceeds to an unsettling conclusion to reveal what women's beauty is

used for in society. It is set at a time of communal carnage in
Bombay between the Hindu, Muslim and Sikh community.
A Sikh falls in love with Mozel, but she turns him down on
the pretext of being too religious and conservative. He later
gets engaged to another girl and Mozel is happy for the two's
future.

One day, Mozel finds out that the Sikh's fiancée is in
danger and religious extremists plan to attack her. She forces
him to dress as a Muslim and makes him rush to the building
where the Sikh girl is stationed. Mozel gives up her Jewish
robe and asks her to wear it so that the two can escape the
religious protestors safely. She herself is left stark naked and
as she descends the building's stairs, Mozel is confronted by
the angry crowd. The blood thirsty mob gets distracted and
fascinated with Mozel's beauty. But as she descends, her foot
slips and she comes tumbling to the ground. The beauty that
Manto had praised so heavily is now reduced to shambles. As
one protestor proceeds to cover her body with a sheet, Mozel
shrugs it off saying, 'Off with it, your blasted religion.' Mozel
is a free-spirited woman who has control over her own life.
She overruns her religious leanings to save the lives of two
individuals of a different faith. She is intelligent, independent
and far sighted – unlike the several men who surround her.
Fahmida Riaz's assessment of this story is spot-on:

> Mozel in this story is a free spirit, free like the mountain
> breeze that she enjoys. She is intelligent, far-sighted, [a]
> decision-maker for her own life, strong of heart and mind and
> not at all sentimental – far more sensible and practical than
> most of the men around her. In Indian parlance, she is Shakti
> incarnate, as she rises to save two lives. She can clearly see the

dreadful hoax religion was turned into in those ghastly days of
communal rioting and rejects it in her last breath.

Another of Manto's stories, Khol Do, typifies what the
traumatic partition did to ordinary people. In recounting the
stories of nameless and faceless millions, Manto chooses the
metaphor of a woman to highlight the 'gang rape' of humanity
that was a hallmark of 1947. This is a story of a girl abducted
from East Punjab, who is finally discovered by her father in a
hospital where she lies traumatized, raped by her abductors as
well as rescuers. The ending of the story is chilling and makes
the reader shudder at the violence and barbarity unleashed
during the tumult of 1947.

> *The doctor glanced at the body lying on the stretcher. He felt*
> *the pulse and, pointing at the window, told Sirajuddin, 'Open*
> *it!' Sakina's body stirred ever so faintly on the stretcher. With*
> *lifeless hands, she slowly undid the knot of her waistband and*
> *lowered her shalwar. 'She's alive! My daughter is alive! Old*
> *Sirajuddin screamed with unbounded joy. The doctor broke*
> *into a cold sweat.'*[15]

The important point to be noted here, as writer Zahida Hina
has suggested, is that Sakina has suffered 'within the boundaries
of Pakistan at the hands of Muslim volunteers.' Hina adds,
'We turn our backs to this point.' According to Khalid Hasan,
Manto is said to have cited 'Khol Do' as his greatest story.[16]

In Dus Rupay (Ten Rupees), Manto describes the story of
an innocent young girl named Sarita who works as a part-
time sex worker. Grinding poverty has forced her widowed
mother to send her daughter, barely in her teens, for 'outings'

with men in exchange for money. Personally, Sarita loves these adventures as they mostly involve visits to the beach and she enjoys the car rides too. One day, two young boys visiting Bombay pick her up and take her to the beach. The trio enjoys as they laugh, play and sing together. Sarita has never seen such happiness before. When she is dropped home, she returns the 'dus rupay', or ten rupees, that she is given at the beginning of the meeting. She was used to taking money from clients in the past, but this time she had only enjoyed herself.

In describing Sarita's character, Manto emphasizes her innocence and delicacy. She is playful, fun-loving and cheery, like all young, teenage girls. The character description tends to break away from stereotypical imagery of sex-workers and the reader shares Sarita's joy.

The story 'Sharifan' comments on how violence begets violence. A Muslim father avenges the rape and murder of his daughter by committing the same atrocity to a Hindu girl whose father then stumbles out to his house just like the Muslim father and goes on to rape a girl from another religion. Manto often ends his stories on a running note as if to suggest that violence and revenge cannot have an end and continue in a vicious cycle. In this story, he begins with the Muslim father shouting his daughter's name 'Sharifan, Sharifan', and ends with the Hindu father's shouts of 'Bimla, Bimla'.

The epic story, *Thanda Gosht*, (Cold Meat), illustrates the episode of a Sikh named Isher Singh who abducts a Muslim girl during the riots and rapes her, only to realize that she had been dead the whole time. His jealous partner Kulwant Kaur rebukes him after she finds he is unable to give her sexual pleasure. She suspects he has been sleeping with another woman. Isher Singh pants, breathless as he narrates the chilling

encounter that rendered him impotent. The following lines
present his narrative of one particularly shocking experience:
'There was a house I broke into ... there were seven people in
there, six of them men ... whom I killed with my kirpan one
by one ... and there was one girl ... she was so beautiful ... I
didn't kill her ... I took her away...'

Manto blends the Partition so meticulously into the
lives of his characters that it creates a living memory of the
bloody event. More importantly, the dead Muslim girl is more
symbolic than either Singh's impotence or Kaur's desire. It is
the most powerful metaphor for what humans did to each
other during the 1947 bloodshed. Yet, it is the libidinal urges
of Kaur that represent the force of life amid the harrowing
darkness of this story.

This passage from a collection of essays by Pakistan's
feminist writers is worth citing here:

*In Manto's stories, there is nothing definite ... these (stories)
came about in a particular historical moment and due to special
circumstances ... in these stories what is eternal happens to be
lies, hypocrisy and cruelty with a societal group ... and hatred
towards those who defile humanity. Manto's artistry is such that
he never preaches but continues to enlighten your mind and
stir your conscience. Women have been subjected to humiliation
and Manto through his stories has empathised with their
plight and shown solidarity with their cause ... this is why
we women consider him to be a mature feminist. He raised the
character of a prostitute ... and familiarises the reader with the
humanity of women. His portrayals of domesticated women
and prostitutes are unique for he associates unconventional
attributes — for example, determination, will, not being content*

*in every situation and above all the ability to laugh. But
Manto also showed 'real' men who were unconventional and
sensitive ...*[17]

Realist-Feminist?

*Manto just could not accept pigeon-holed and straight-jacketed
ideas and systems. That, in a manner of speaking, was the
tragedy of his life, and, ironically, a point of salvation for his
art ...*[18]

The literary critique of work that exhibits female exploitation
often sees a lack of attention to the suppressed female under
patriarchal protection, for it would seem more likely that the
emancipated housewife would ring a bell with the majorly
bourgeois readership in Pakistan than the 'fallen' prostitute.
And that such work sexualizes the inhumane nature of acts of
violence. For Manto, sex is a serious subject and anyone who
takes it lightly is an enemy of beauty.[19] One of his primary
grudges towards married women is their keenness to cover
up their sexuality due to superficial norms of society. He
appears partially frustrated about his own personal liberties
being restricted by married life and goes to great lengths
in critiquing the homemaker. Manto's criticism is directed
towards pretentious saints who preserve chastity in order to
boast about it. Additionally, the shock value of his work needs
to be seen in light of all his work that has a major theme of
a revaluation of the status quo of selfish and power-obsessed
human nature.

His explorations are of a specific nature where he focuses
on the 'worst' of humanity, and this 'worst' part of humanity

for him is clearly of a physical nature. He writes as someone confessing on the part of the silent degenerate and inhumane majority. Manto's work screams that true morality is not silent, nor hidden under tradition, rules or a white veil of religiosity. He explores the degenerate as a mirror. As Kumar[20] writes,

> They live in an infernal underworld, invisible to the respectable society which pretends ignorance of its existence. Ironically, not only has it produced this world, it also provides it full sustenance. Its hypocritical indifference to such a world is not just a quiet consent to its existence. In fact, it is due to the vested interests of patriarchal society that prostitution survives because it does not seem to threaten any of its fundamental principles. Let it be so then!

While discussing sex workers, Manto regards them as legitimate workers in a free economy.[21] He rejects the idea that they lead to a rise in immorality and sees them as providing an outlet to society as well as an essential service to the people. He, however, accepts that these workers are often underpaid and are not meted with equal respect as compared to non-workers. Intizar Hussain, the great Urdu writer has correctly stated: 'Prostitutes, who figure prominently in his stories, are not of the Umrao Jan Ada[22] type. They are downtrodden prostitutes.' But Manto asserts that they are his favourite characters: 'I accept them with all their vices, their disease, their abusiveness, their peevishness'. But why? Why has he chosen them as characters for his stories?[23]

Much has been written about the question of feminism in Manto's works. It is important to remember that the notion of a feminist in the 1940s was different from that of today.

Additionally, since he portrays the abuse his female characters endure, his work redefines long-held patriarchal notions of vulgarity and taboo through teaming up humanism with taboo. Here it is just a man-made convention that cannot stain the humanity of the character. At the outset the notion that Manto used the female as a 'sex exhibit' needs to be discarded. The feminist worldview emerges out of an awareness of institutional exploitation and inequality, and willingness to do something to improve the entire system.

Khurram Ali Shafique[24] writes that Manto is half-way between eugenic or utilitarian feminism (that tries to improve the female condition without systemic change), and left-wing socialist feminism.

> *As a student of socialism he recognises the exploitative institutions of the society and raises fundamental questions about the moral and ethical values regulating the lives of women. But just when we expect him to come out as an advocate of unconditional freedom he takes an about turn and betrays his own utilitarian longings for women as men's favourite sex toys.*

Manto does expect the readers to consider the patronizing attitude of male lovers to their mistresses in love, but as Shafique says, 'we must not forget that the traditional nuances of heterosexual love had not been seen as exploitative by those times'. Manto was primarily concerned with his own literary agenda, which was to emphasize the creative aspect of human nature. This agenda in itself wasn't misogynic, thus we can argue that his portrayals were realist and feminist.

As one begins to analyse Manto's female characters, the first facet that strikes you is the immense diversity and colourful range of characters. In Manto's literary oeuvre, no two women are alike. The notion of the 'prostitute' as the feminist works because in the sub-continental society, it was these women who could claim to be free. While the homemaker may be a paragon of conservative security, she has never been free. The sex worker is free, even though the choices she has to exercise her liberty are constrained, and that too by the same rules that keep the homemaker's freedom in check.

There is one element of Manto's writing that completes the argument for him being a feminist. Not only did his female characters fight against the constraints of society, some of his male protagonists were also feminists. Hence, one can state that he looked at women the same way he looked at men – as unique individuals, living their own lives and dealing with it as best as they could. Yet, here was a species more despised, exploited and trampled upon than any man. So by nature a friend of the underdog, he took special care in exploring their situation and their mettle while facing the situation.

In Manto's story 'Mahmuda', we witness the protagonist Mustaqim in anguish, unable to actively save Mahmuda from slipping into the gruesome circumstance of becoming a sex worker for her sheer survival. In this story, the male is as constrained by patriarchal rules as is the 'fallen' Mahmuda. Mustaqim is drawn towards her beauty on his wedding day and she remains in his heart forever as he follows her life through the news from his wife. A simple girl of a humble background, Mahmuda is married to an eccentric maulvi who within two years of his marriage leaves her to fend for herself. The greater Mustaqim's sympathy, the greater his wife's alertness, in echo of the fact that in modern society there is no 'pure' emotion, because all empathy is perceived to be covertly sexual in patriarchy. When Mahmuda is driven to 'bad ways', Mustaqim wishes to save her and bring her home. Kulsum, his wife, will not hear of it, whether due to jealousy or concern for impropriety. As Kumar notes, Mustaqim is incapable of action, and like hundreds of other men and women of respectable society, he becomes an accomplice in contributing to the degeneration of humanity.

'Sharda', another memorable story, recounts the physical lust of its protagonist Nazeer and the excitement he finds in infidelity. Sharda, a prostitute however, is more than a sex object. She turns out to be a sensitive woman capable of loving and also taking decisions. Nazeer cannot marvel at the devotion shown by Sharda but also cannot bring himself to appreciate her given his patriarchal and stereotypical attitudes. Though even in this state, he cannot help admire the physical attributes of women. One such passage in the story relates to Nazeer's reflection on how women were endowed with the capacity to nurture and give life to children through breastfeeding. This thought comes to him in a state of semi-arousal. Sharda leaves Nazeer sensing his guilt (of cheating on his wife) and burden (of responding to Sharda's love). However, Sharda repays him by providing him with his favourite brand of cigarettes when he has no money. There is a deeply ironical tone which clearly vindicates Sharda and shows Nazeer in poor light.

Conclusion

Manto's stories are testaments of fallen humans who somehow end up uplifting themselves and others out of darkness. Women and their stories become literary devices for Manto to reaffirm and reiterate his humanistic vision. This vision, it should be noted, is more expressly stated in the wide corpus of Manto's non-fiction work which is yet to be fully appreciated. This essay has cited some of the better-known stories with powerful women characters who reclaim humanity as well as represent its trampling by political events, greed and simple misogyny perpetrated in the name of communal or nationalistic honour.

Manto's outstanding characters betray the author's sensitivity and impartial scrutiny of human behaviour. As Kumar notes, Manto's treatment of human experience 'results in a positive salvaging of the dignity of human existence'.[25] Despite the turbulent, disturbing stories he narrates, there is a redeeming aesthetic: a 'gesture of reclamation and solidarity in identifying intense moments of cognition of human anguish, which in turn arouses compassion for the oppressed.'[26]

If Manto were writing today, he would have written about the lives of those who are looked down upon and are victim to religious extremism in the subcontinent. Manto's stories have special relevance as they celebrate diversity and foster belief in humanism. The multi-religious, multi-lingual and multi-cultural societies of India and Pakistan can only salvage themselves by adhering to the principles of humanism as laid forth by Manto in his stories.

It would be pertinent to conclude with these lines from a recent essay authored by Pakistan's feminist poet and political activist Fahmida Riaz:

It is strange that other writers, specially in Urdu, are so blind to the reality of women. They would not even notice bravery or intelligence in their female subjects. On the contrary, they are capable of giving the most perverse 'psychological' twist to the most remarkable traits in a woman. Even today, Manto stands more or less alone in the position that he takes on women. After Manto, there is none like Manto.

Published in *Social Scientist* Vol. 40, No. 11/12 (November–December 2012), pp. 75–86.

7

Remembering Intizar Husain

I remember the languid afternoon in Lahore where, surrounded by his friends and admirers, I met Intizar Husain. This formal introduction happened as poet-writer Fahmida Riaz was visiting Lahore and wanted to see Intizar Sahib – as we all called him. This was nearly a decade ago and my memory of that meeting is a bit hazy now. All I remember is that Intizar Sahib showed extraordinary enthusiasm when he heard my name.

'*Arrey!* I have been reading you in *The Friday Times*', he said. Bewildered, I thought he was trying to humour a young novice with literary pretensions. Noticing my maladroit attempt to hide my expression, he added in chaste, homely Urdu, 'I had thought that this guy Rumi was some old man writing about the shared cultures of the subcontinent ... *Aap tau naujawan nikle* (you turned out to be a youth).'

In those days, I was regular feature writer at (TFT) and had penned many a rant on the civilizational ethos of the Indian Subcontinent that has fast eroded in the past few decades. Little did I know that it would be noted by – of all readers – Urdu's master fiction writer and columnist, essayist and a critic!

This was a moment of reckoning for me. I was but a pygmy in front of this literary giant and man of all proverbial seasons. Hearing his acknowledgment was almost a homecoming – a process that continues, distracted by the necessities of garnering jobs and nurturing pretenses of a 'career'. Among other reasons to change direction in my life, perhaps Intizar Sahib was a major one. His encouragement – to an utterly unimaginative person like me – acted as an elixir.

This meeting was the first in which I managed to speak to him. One had seen him for years at various events in Lahore. Unlike other senior writers, Intizar Sahib had resisted the temptations of turning into a cult figure, a pop star or a *pir*. We have had many a celebrated writer turning into feudal patriarchs and patrons. This is not an exaggeration. Former bureaucrat-turned-writer – and also the architect of censorship under the Ayub regime (1958–1968) – Qudratullah Shahab was declared a mystic *pir* by his groupies, and for some time his formal *urs* (commemoration) celebrations were also held. Perhaps these still continue but I have lost track.

For the next few years, I met him as regularly as possible. Every Sunday, Intizar Sahib was found with Eruj Mubarak, Khaled Ahmed, Zahid Dar, Gulnaz and Zaman Khan among others. I would join them occasionally as I shuttled between Lahore and Islamabad for work. These were soirees that shall never be equaled. Intizar Sahib listened quietly, interjecting here and there. Seldom did he attempt to assert his seniority or wealth of knowledge.

On many occasions, I witnessed a most rare, civilized discourse on language between Khaled Ahmed and Intizar Sahib. Khaled Ahmed's thesis – that Urdu had been appropriated by the extremists and therefore become a vehicle of retrogressive ideas – was politely challenged by Intizar Sahib, who always maintained that Urdu was in fact a vibrant language in both Pakistan and India. Such discussions in the age of talk shows on TV and abusive social media interactions appeared as a leaf from a fading world of ideational exchange.

When I was working on my book *Delhi by Heart*, it was Intizar Sahib's world that had inspired me. In his travelogue *Zamin Aur Falak Aur* (*A Different Land, A Different Sky*), he writes:

'Dear traveller, do not waste your journey because of your mental reservations. Keep your heart open when you go travelling and leave unfastened the windows of your mind. Every habitation has its own atmosphere and its special fragrance. No town is devoid of evil men, nor empty of good ones. And every journey has its own sufferings and its own delights. For all this, it is meant that the traveller keeps himself open. Out of this very "all this" comes the special fragrance of his journey.' (Translation by Safdar Mir.)

I did not consciously follow this advice but having read it while I was still in high school, these lines stayed with me. It was only in recent years when I picked up the book after two decades, I realized that Intizar Sahib's fascination for the peacock near Nizamuddin Dargah and its voice representing the 'spirit of Delhi that had lost its way in the bushes around' was calling out to the lost ones. For Intizar Sahib this had to do with physical separation from the soil but for my generation it was the delinking – and a conclusive one at that – from a civilization. It was about a thousand years of history rubbed into the dust of jingoism.

When I told him about my book and its obsessions, Intizar Sahib was delighted. He was also the first one to read and review it for *Dawn*. He sensed that I had unwittingly treaded his path: 'Rumi feels that he is moving in a vast world which carries a touch of the divine, where the past and the present merge into each other and the Hindu–Muslim divide loses its edge.' For a beginner, this was nothing less than a windfall, a memory I cannot cherish enough.

From 2010 to 2014, I attended the Karachi Literature Festival (KLF) and in the initial years, I had the privilege of interviewing him as well as participating in several panels where Intizar Sahib held forth. I travelled with him to India for a Manto conference and another event during these years as well. In a session with him, he spoke of his early memories and the writing process. He also made the famous statement that he had seen two paradoxical forces rise in Pakistan: the power of the mullah and that of women.

Averse to being didactic or patronizing, Intizar Sahib was always eager to listen. Curious about what I did other than my work for TFT, he had a list of questions. It was a little difficult to speak to him on the telephone as he had become hard of hearing, so our conversations almost always took place in person. When I took translator and noted author Rakhshanda Jalil to his house, Intizar Sahib was more than hospitable. Our meeting was extended by hours and as we sat in his bedroom, one had books everywhere, I realized how his writing was his life. So whenever I would ask Intizar Sahib about his writing schedule and techniques, he would laugh and say it was a perennial part of his existence.

He was different from most of the luminaries of Lahore's literati for a host of reasons, foremost being his status as an outsider. He moved from the United Provinces (UP) of undivided India to Pakistan and landed in Lahore. The city,

its physical and cultural environs became his new 'home.' As
the certainty of Partition became clear and an iron curtain
between India and Pakistan was erected after the 1965 war,
the new 'home' could only be imagined with the memory of
what was left behind. This is why *hijrat* or migration became a
perennial theme of his fiction.

As time flew by in the new Muslim homeland, the theme
became sharper and more pronounced. It was not only that
Husain left a world behind but a civilizational ethos that was
multi-religious, multicultural and composite. It was ironic that
Intizar Sahib invoked Hindu, Buddhist and other mythologies
in a country that he – like thousands of others – had seen as
the new haven for a migratory populace.

In the initial years, Intizar Sahib was part of the intellectuals'
club that viewed art as being separate from politics. On the
other hand, the Anjuman-e-Taraqqi Pasand Musannifeen
(Progressive Writers' Movement) viewed literature as a vehicle
of social change and engaged with the politics of the time.
Intizar Husain and his mentor-friend Mohammad Hasan
Askari, a towering literary critic and commentator, challenged
the progressives' worldview and held that the craft of fiction
must not be subordinated to the political concerns of the day.
This division continued for decades and became even more
intense as the state cracked down on the Communist Party,
setting a new ideological framework for Pakistani 'identity'
using Islam and everything that was not Indian in nature.

But Intizar Sahib was no rabble-rouser, nor was he an
ideologue. He straddled this world and by the time he wrote
Basti in the late 1970s, he had seen the dismemberment of
Pakistan in 1971 and the decline of Pakistan's imagined ethos
(one still has to figure out what exactly that was – given the

contested imaginations of Pakistan that bedevil the national narratives). The novel refers to the 1971 crisis but the characters refuse to take overt sides in the political conflict. The protagonist Zakir remains a participant in the larger flow of history but is trapped in the memory of a lost abode.

I remember reading an interview by Intizar Husain in which he had admitted he had been writing one story all his life. To be precise, this was the story of a lost identity, roots and the dilemma of finding new anchorage on different soil. In an earlier story, *Sheher-i-Afsos*, there is a line which sums up this anxiety: 'Have you seen that those people who get estranged from their own land are not accepted by any other land?' (Translation by Safdar Mir)

In 1983, a special number of the *Journal of South Asian Literature* was devoted to the works of Intizar Sahib. Herein, a key interview reveals the writer whose earlier engagement with Pakistani and Islamic identity is clearly under transformation: '…The Muslims came to India and formed ties with its soil … This attempt to understand the Islamic revelation in terms of our land, this endeavor to merge that revelation with our soil which yielded a unity that later was shaped into what we know as Indian–Muslim culture … But we did not permit this unity to continue for long, as its progress has been constantly obstructed and halted.'

This rupture of a unity – and its later manifestations in Hindu–Muslim discord, the colonial experience and the Partition – is what influenced the exploration of the *hijrat* mystique by Intizar Sahib through much of his large corpus of fiction.

Intizar Sahib's contemporary Enver Sajjad, who was one of the pioneers of the Nai Kahani Movement (or the postmodernist style in Urdu) questioned in one of his essays (published in a volume entitled *Talash-e-Wajood*): 'What would have happened had there been no Partition and if "Intizar had never to migrate, what sort of fiction would he then have written? Would he have become a *patwari* of his soil due to the immense love for it?"' Indeed this was a tongue-in-cheek remark by a contemporary and a 'progressive' author but it does raise an important question.

It is therefore appropriate to say that Partition and the experience of exploring a new identity made Intizar Sahib a unique and creative voice. And his layered craft – of using mythologies, colloquial references, folk expression and time-travelling – added to the richness of his storytelling.

Basti was published in 1978 and Intizar Sahib's other major novel *Agay Samandar Hay* (*The Sea Lies Ahead*) was written in 1990s. I received the news of his illness and death while reading Rakhshanda Jalil's excellent translation of the novel. The novel continues the stylistic features of Intizar Sahib's fiction but there is even greater disillusionment with the Pakistan project here. Once again, the 1947 *hijrat* is compared to Prophet Mohammad's shift from Mecca to Medina in the seventh century. Even in the Middle Ages, legends of migration took place when Muslims were evicted from parts of Spain. The protagonist Jawad Hassan faces forces larger than his agency. He is continuously haunted by memories of his birthplace, his childhood love and all that he left behind.

The dilemma of Jawad has autobiographical shades as the Pakistan dream has turned sour. Living in the backdrop of Karachi's anarchic violence, Jawad is bitter about the corruption, the distorted society and the increasing religious–supremacist discourses.

Jawad's existentialist crisis is deepened as he sees the new elites of Karachi, amidst intense violence and curfews, indulging in '*kabab-paratha*' parties, and '*mushairas*'. Intizar Sahib also weaves a jihadist character in the form of Ghazi Sahib in the novel – a figure whose later real-life manifestations have greatly harmed Pakistan in recent decades.

This was the transition of Intizar Sahib who had distanced himself from literatures of a political variety. His column, translated by Basharat Peer for the *Granta* magazine's 2010 issue, remains a fine critique of Zia's Pakistan that we know all too well: 'What an era General Zia had brought to Pakistan! The echoes of prayer and the roar of public hangings…'

Perhaps the most incisive line in this historic writing is: 'Along with religion, an unthinking nationalism had become the other god of Pakistan.' Describing the culture initiated by Zia, Intizar Sahib writes:

'General Zia aggressively nourished the Islamism that Bhutto had midwifed. Overnight, bureaucrats began showing up in mosques and rows of the faithful became a feature of the offices. At my newspaper, *Mashriq* (the East), there were a few devout men. The moment the call for afternoon prayer sounded, their pens would stop and they would leave for the nearby mosque. And now, the moment the editor appointed by the General stepped out of his cubicle, every reporter and editor would rise from his seat and head for the mosque. The madman stood with a razor on our necks. Rumour had it that two lists were being made: those who prayed regularly would be considered for promotion; those who didn't …'

There cannot be a wittier, sadder testament to this era. In his thousands of columns and essays, as he wrote consistently, the tone was never abrasive or self-promotional. This defies the Urdu column format which is largely ideological or political propaganda laced with self-praise and VIP attention-seeking. In Intizar Sahib's columns was a pronounced focus on the environment, particularly the trees, birds and references to nature. In fact, when India carried out the nuclear tests in 1998, a key concern for Intizar Sahib was the fate of peacocks in Rajasthan. Such was the heart that remained pure, and a vision unalloyed despite all the disillusionments he faced and lived with.

I have been away from Lahore for more than twenty months. It is difficult to imagine a place without Intizar Sahib. I waited for him to return from the hospital. There was much that I wanted to tell him especially about my own *hijrat* experience and the way it impacted me. Leaving Pakistan, even for some time, was not an easy decision. And not having visited the *watan* (homeland) for so long is even more traumatic. All of Intizar Sahib's literary preoccupations make so much more sense to me. But I have also learnt from him that the sum total of human experience entails movements, explorations and the ultimate search to make sense of a chaotic world.

It would be a cliché to say that an era has ended with the passing away of such a colossal figure. For me, an old *jamun* tree was suddenly removed from the landscape of my life. I think Intizar Sahib would approve of my sentiment as the ancient Buddhist and Hindu cosmologies place a gigantic jamun tree at the centre of the universe. Of the seven continents of cosmos, the central happens to be *Jambudvipa* (the Isle of Jamun).

Losing that is tantamount to a sorrow untold.

Published in *The Friday Times*, Pakistan, 19 February 2016.

8

Fahmida Riaz

❧

If there is one word that describes Fahmida Riaz, it has to be a 'rebel'. A woman who has always been true to herself, fearless and outspoken without cavil. Her poetry is what has made her rightly famous. Yet the irony of her literary persona cannot be ignored: she is also under-published, for pirated editions of her earlier works sell and a major anthology of her poetry was published after a gap of twenty years. Her prose was not available in bookshops for years until the Oxford University Press started publishing it in recent years. Yet she has been translated widely across the globe. A voice that mixes the East and the West, the sacred and the profane leaving at least two generations enchanted. Perhaps a milestone of my life has been knowing her and in no conventional manner. I am young enough to be her son, devoted to be her *shaagird* (sans literary spark) and mesmerized to be her follower. Well, almost.

Writing about her life and works in not easy either. There are layers of her persona which require a lifetime of research. Not unlike the dialectic of the Arabian nights, her mind and emotion work at various levels; and so has her rather eventful life traversed: odd and straight, rough and mellow, moody and banal. From the ordinariness of a middle-class household to working with haris (landless peasants) in rural Sindh, from the spotlights of literary events to the ignominy of an unfortunate exile in India. She has imbibed the electricity of life like nobody I know and drunk the poison of existence to the fullest. A single evening with Fahmida is akin to living a tale through and through where a poet – admittedly self-absorbed – takes over and sets the rhythm of time.

Fahmida Riaz was born on 28 July 1946 in an educated and cultured family in the city of Meerut, Uttar Pradesh, considered as ground zero for the Indian Revolt of 1857. Her family later moved and settled down in Hyderabad, Sindh following her father's employment in tone of the first educational institutions for Muslims in Sindh. Her father – Riaz-ud-Din Ahmed – was an eminent educationist, loved by his colleagues as well as students. Her mother was well-versed in Persian and Urdu classics. However, Fahmida's father passed away when she was only four years old, leaving the burden of managing the household on her mother, Husna Begum.

Once in college, Fahmida Riaz took over a share in these responsibilities and started to work as a newscaster at Radio Pakistan, also using this time to graduate from Sindh University. During this period, her poems began to be published in literary journals. This was also the decade of the students' uprising in Pakistan, with Fahmida became deeply involved in it. Later, in early 1967, through an arranged marriage, she moved to the United Kingdom. The publication of the first volume of her poems coincided with her marriage and a new phase began in her life.

In London, Fahmida worked with the BBC Urdu Service. At the same time, she studied in the famous London School of Film Technique (the only other Pakistani who had studied there before her was Mushtaq Gazdar). In this cosmopolitan institute, she made many friends. During her stay in London, the counter-revolution in Chile and the massacre of Bengalis in East Pakistan had a deep impact on her. Unfortunately, her marriage did not work and a divorce led her back to Pakistan, where Riaz found work at an advertising agency in Karachi. By this time, Fahmida had started to mature as a poet, potential for which she had begun to exude from a very early age. She had written her first poem at the age of fifteen and had a collection to her name by the age of twenty-two.

She became a sensation in the early 1970s when her bold, feminist poetry created a stir in the convention-ridden world of Urdu poetry. Riaz was expressive, sometimes explicit, and politically charged. She created a completely new genre in Urdu poetry with a curiously modern sensibility. Her work, despite its inventiveness and challenging of conventions, did not compromise pure literary merit. Her collection 'Badan Dareeda' became a new marker of a self-assured woman's angst as well as confidence. Here was a passion unfettered by taboos.

Her famous poem 'Bosa' (Deep Kiss) celebrates the beauty of love:

> *Deep myrrh-scented kiss, Deep with the tongue, suffused With the musky perfume Of the wine of love: I'm reeling With intoxication, languid To the point of numbness....*

One can easily imagine how the guardians of middle-class morality among the literati reacted to lines such as:

> *After love the first time, Our naked bodies and minds A hall of mirrors, Wholly unarmed, utterly fragile, We lie in one another's arms, Breathing with care Afraid to break These crystal figurines.*

But this was not a passionate lover that her voice represented. It also dealt with the process of procreation and its complexities. In 'Come Give Me Your Hand', the modern woman addresses the man whose child she is nurturing:

> ...*touch my body and listen to the beating of your child's heart....*
> *Let your fingers know its body.... How you have transformed*
> *me! Within me was a haunting darkness, A limitless, endless*
> *space I wandered around aimlessly. Yearning for a taste of*
> *life....*
> *You filled my womb in such a way That light pours forth from*
> *my body.*

TRANSLATED BY PATRICIA SHARPE

She had returned to Karachi with the determination marry a man of her own choice and devoting her life to bringing about social change in Pakistan. She was isolated amongst the mainstream Urdu writers because of her insistence on the rights of sub-nationalities, but found friends among Sindhi and Balochi writers and even young political workers. In Karachi, she initiated 'Awaz', a politically charged Urdu publication. During this time, she met Zafar Ali Ujan, a Sindhi left activist and married him. Soon they had a daughter Veerta and a son, Kabeer.

Her unconventional and robustly progressive publications put her at loggerheads with the Zia regime, which attempted to implicate Fahmida Riaz and her husband on multiple charges, including those of sedition. One of her fans however, came to her rescue and provided her with bail. Using this window of opportunity, she, together with her sister and children, fled to India for a self-imposed exile that lasted seven years. Her husband joined her after his release from prison.

Across the border, Fahmida was appointed poet-in-residence at Jamia Millia Islamia in Delhi. During her exile, her poetry flourished and found a new South Asian dimension and imbibed influences from her complex interaction with India. Exile did not bedraggle the fighting spirit of the indomitable Fahmida, who discovered a newfound cause to raise her voice against the rise of Hindu nationalism in India. As was the case back in Pakistan, this put her at poles with her hosts, many of whom were quick at jumping to ludicrous conclusions. Claims that she was a 'Pakistani agent', stirring up factionalism in India was typical of the demagoguery she had witnessed back home.

Her poem 'Naya Bharat' remains a testament to how religious fundamentalism is plaguing the Indian spirit. Comparing the polity with her home country, she addresses the Indians and complains how they turned out be 'just like us'.

Your demon [of] religion dances like a clown,
Whatever you do will be upside down.
You too will sit deep in thought,
Who is Hindu, who is not.
Keep repeating the mantra like a parrot,
Bharat was like the land of the brave.

TRANSLATED BY KHUSHWANT SINGH

My favourite poem from this phase of her expression remains 'Purva Anchal' which was written during a journey through Eastern UP (India) as she looks through the train window while passing through the lands where Buddha, Kabir and other sages once walked. Fahmida laments:

Brick and stone
Reduced to rubble.
Mosque and temple
Still locked
In the same old squabble.
Every brow
Disfigured by a frown...

Listen to Kabir,
Who pleads with you:
Wars of hatred
Do no honour to God.
Both Ram and Rahim
Will shun a loveless land.

TRANSLATED BY PATRICIA SHARPE

Her muse had matured and like Buddha's true disciple, enlightenment was descending on her — an enlightenment fashioned by a holistic understanding of civilizations, nations and communities. The lines of these poems should be popularized across South Asia and wherever there is conflict, hatred and competing gods.

When two are locked in conflict
And ready to lose their lives,
Neither can win in the end,
Unless both do — and equally...
Such are the paradigms of war,
Such the insight of the Buddha.
Why are we, his heirs, so blind?

TRANSLATED BY PATRICIA SHARPE

The rise of Benazir Bhutto in 1986 saw the return of Fahmida Riaz to Pakistan. During Benazir's first tenure, Riaz was appointed Managing Director of the National Book Foundation, and then given a post at Quaid-e-Azam Academy during her second tenure. In between, she was constantly on the state radar, termed as an 'Indian agent' and denied government employment. Her turbulent relationship with the state invokes memories of poets such as Daman, Jalib and Faiz.

Pakistan had, by the 1990s, turned into a polity infested with conflict, sectarianism and deeply penetrated conservatism promoted during the rule of military dictator General Zia ul Haq.

Fahmida's poem 'Mantra' deals with the Indus River (Calm- breathing, mighty River/Deeper than the secrets of the heart), and shuns sectarianism:

> *...only with a vicious dogma*
> *That calls the land my enemy, The river my foe...*
> *Far beyond the farthest sky*
> *Lives God, an alien, not of this earth.*
> *How can I love and hate*
> *At his command?*
> *How can I, born of the soil,*
> *Renounce it?*

TRANSLATED BY PATRICIA SHARPE

Fahmida Riaz has served as a vanguard in the feminist struggle in Pakistan. Challenging male dominance in the subcontinent, she has published several stories, translations and the deconstruction of criticism of feminist work. One famed poem, 'Chadur and Char-diwari' is notable for its startling imagery and boldness. Addressing the patriarch, Fahmida opens the poem with questions as to why a chadur is being imposed on her and other women.

> *I am not a sinner nor a criminal*
> *That I should stamp my forehead with its darkness.*

The poem uses stark images of women's travails in our society and makes forceful points in a truly original diction and rare sensibility. Perhaps a resonant voice of every Pakistani (or even South Asian) woman is what the poem ends with:

> *Bring this show to an end now*
> *'Sire, cover it up now*
> *Not I, but you need this chadur now.*

> *For my person is not merely a symbol of your lust:*
> *Across the highways of life, sparkles my intelligence*
> *If a bead of sweat sparkles on the earth's brow it is my diligence.*

> *These four walls, this chadur I*
> *wish upon the rotting carcass.*
> *In the open air, her sails flapping, races ahead my ship.*
> *I am the companion of the New Adam*
> *Who has earned my self-assured love.*

TRANSLATED BY RUKHSANA AHMED

Today, Fahmida Riaz is Pakistan's leading poetic voice and perhaps the most undeterred. The freshness of her diction combined with her intellectual courage has set new standards in Urdu literary expression.

For instance the poem, 'Aqleema' looks at the predicament of Cain and Abel's sister:

But she is different.
Different in her gut
And inside her womb...
Aqleema has a head, too.
Let God speak to Aqleema sometimes
And ask her something.

TRANSLATION BY PATRICIA SHARPE

It is a pity that Fahmida is better known as a poet and her unique prose is lesser known. Her short stories and novels (*Godavari, Zinda Bahar* among others) are extraordinary pieces of literary work. Often it is difficult to determine the genre of her 'prose' as the lines between watertight compartments blur and fade away, only to reappear as a gentle reminder to the reader that our author is experimenting in her inimitable style. She wrote *Godavari* when she was in exile in India during the 1980s. This was the time she had a relatively safe environment. However, this was also a time when she was uprooted; and was disappointed with the promised secular land because of its deep-seated biases, its roving communal demons and above all, its typecasting of Pakistanis. Therefore, *Godavari* emerges as a tale of exile as much as it is about the marginalization of women and India's lower castes. In the recent years her short stories have turned semi-autobiographical and indicate a new trend in her style.

In the late 1990s, Fahmida Riaz discovered Jalaluddin Rumi, the twelfth-century Turkish poet and jurist, and now an international celebrity. One of her recent collections, *Yeh Khana-e aab-o-gil*, is an outstanding translation of Rumi's ghazals in the same rhyme and meter. From citing the *Nahj al Balagha* to countering rigid feminist/political stereotypes defining Pakistani state-led narratives, she has maintained an eclectic approach towards not just the style of her writing, but also towards the intellectual and philosophical content therein. These lines from her poem, 'Condolence Resolution' are self-evident:

> *Don't be distressed if I am left unburied*
> *If the priest denies me the final rites.*
> *Carry the remains to the woods and leave it there.*
> *It comforts me to think that the beasts would feast.*
> *Their bellies filled, they'll clean their paws*
> *And their sinless eyes will gleam with a truth*
> *That you, my friends, dare never express:*
> *'She always said what she had to say,*
> *And for all her life had no regrets.'*

TRANSLATED BY PATRICIA SHARPE

As a provider in her household, Riaz had to find work. The last government of Pakistan People's Party (2008–2013) after much hesitation found employment for her at a dictionary board in Karachi. This vocation was short lived as the hyperactive Chief Justice placed a ban on government contracts to people over the age of sixty. The Oxford University Press rescued her and since then she has been working for the publishing house. This has been a fruitful engagement as Riaz has published more fiction, translations and books for children.

Pakistan has to treasure her writings for she is not just a poet or a writer. She represents much more; perhaps the withering soul of Pakistan endangered by bigots and warriors. What a fortunate country we are to have icons like her: celebrated not for their family, dynasty or power. But for the sheer force of creativity, beauty and tenacity to resist.

First published in *Monthly Herald* (2010).

9

'Who Will Listen to the Tale of My Woeful Heart?' The Portrait of 'Nautch Girls' in Early Urdu Literature

❧

The opening of the Suez Canal ushered in a change in the social life of India. The 'nautch', a highly sought-after art form slowly took on explicit immoral connotations under the judging eyes of Christian missionaries as well as a colonial obsession with the exotic Orient. Essentially, a colonial construct, a nautch girl referred to the popular entertainer, a *belle beau* would sing, dance and when required also provide the services of a sex worker.

It is not a coincidence that the earliest novels of the subcontinent dealt with the intense and memorable characters of the nautch girls. The subaltern accounts of the women from the 'dishonourable' profession are nuanced for they concurrently represent the duality of exploitation and empowerment. Perhaps only the genre of novel could do full justice to all such nuances.

Long before the feminist discourse explored and located
the intricacies of the lives and work of sex workers, male
novelists in the eighteenth and nineteenth centuries were
busy portraying the strong characters of women in the 'oldest
profession', who were rarely found indulging in self pity. In fact,
stereotypes of the hapless and suffering prostitute find a rare
mention in two texts. Through these we find out that contrary
to the perceptions about the inherent moral inferiority of
women associated with this profession today, early Urdu
novelists of the subcontinent portrayed them to be defiant of
conventional morality, sophisticated and, paradoxically, socially
empowered.

The Unrepentant Umrao Jaan of Lucknow

Mirza Hadi Ruswa's *Umrao Jan Ada* is an early novel written in
Urdu.[1] The novel's origins itself are of note as the Lucknow-
based poet Ruswa persuaded Umrao to reveal her life history
in several parts. Many critics have inferred that the narrative
was perhaps authored by Umrao herself and the forthrightness
of the story suggests that she had a huge part in drafting this
classic, semi-documentary. Although to treat it as an historical
account – or even a semi-historical account – will have to
be done with a pinch of salt; it still remains relevant to the
authentic portrayal of the nautch girls' circumstances in that
period.

Umrao's woes originate in a typical patriarchal mold.
As a young girl, she is kidnapped by a hooligan in an act of
vengeance against Umrao's father for giving testimony against
him. The villain sells her to a Lucknow *kothi* (a high culture
space also operating as a brothel) managed by Khanam Jan.

There, Umrao receives an education and induction into arts and culture by an elderly Mawlvi who recreates Umrao as a civilized poet–cum–entertainer. Her quest for knowledge and attainment of self-confidence to handle a predominantly male world takes place within this space. Thus, the tale of exploitation turns into a narrative of self-discovery.

Umrao Jan Ada, an archetypal courtesan steeped in *Avadhi* high culture and manners, emerges as a voice far ahead of her times. Her views on sex work are startling:

> … *though it may well be one's desire to be loved, a desire that swells as she grows older, it is not given to a whore to live out this desire … A tart's only friend is her money; she is no one's wife, and if she is foolish enough to give her love to some man, she does so at the considerable risk of jeopardizing her livelihood.*[2]

The empowerment of Umrao is in many ways linked to her profession. For instance, when asked about 'love' by the narrator, she is quick to clarify that the need to preserve her livelihood is paramount: 'Whenever we want to ensnare anyone we pretend to fall in love with him.'[3]

The novel by Ruswi is a complex and sophisticated portrayal of human character. Through the vicissitudes of her life, Umrao acquires a deep knowledge of human nature, and this brings her wisdom and peace:

> *Personally, I think that no one is wholly bad, and there is some good to be found in everyone. You have probably heard it said about the thieves of the past that if you make a friend of*

them, then you will always get along very well. Without some
element of goodness, life would be impossible.[4]

Her more complex understanding of moral issues comes out
in several places through her defence of her own way of life.
When the narrator asks her what punishment she anticipates
for her sinful existence, which has required hurting many
hearts, she says:

> *There should not be any. In the way that I harmed hearts*
> *there was also much pleasure, and the pleasure makes up for*
> *the pain.*[5]

At a time when women were more or less completely
dependent on men for financial and social sustenance, sex
work emerged as one kind of a safety net. Also in line with the
inner culture of courtesans, prostitutes who decided to leave
the profession were looked down on as those who had gone
astray. And, Umrao remains contemptuous of such women
who leave their position of power and independence and
subject themselves to the whims of respectable men who may
or may not reciprocate in terms of social respect.

The novel also chronicles the disruptions caused by the
deepening of colonial rule; and Umrao is quick to recognize
that her survival is linked to the British rule. She witnesses the
destruction of Lucknow, which was at the centre of the 1857
war, and the subsequent crackdown by the British and also
records how her *kotha* is destroyed. There is resignation as well
as proactive adjustment to political and social changes. Towards
the end of this book, Umrao is not only a thoughtful woman
but also stronger woman. She is neither fatalistic nor depressed

about her life even though she employs a chaste *Lakhnawi* Urdu style that romanticizes the vicissitudes (and tragedies) of history. For its robust yet ambiguous portrayal of characters and vivid glimpses of mid-nineteenth century UP courtesan culture, detailing the elaborate conventions and rituals, it remains a modern novel unsurpassed for its truthfulness. For instance Umrao tells the narrator that 'no man ever loved her, nor did she ever love any man'.

The female characters in particular come alive on the pages (Khanam Jan, the *kotha* Madame), Bua Husaini (a housekeeper in her old age) and Umrao's contemporaries Bismillah Jan and Khurshid. As a great novel straddling between the quest for self-realization as well as being a victim of larger, systemic exploitation, it remains matchless.

In Pakistan, *Umrao Jan Ada* was adapted into a film in 1972, but it transformed the narrative into a moral framework and Umrao into a suffering beauty exploited by destiny and men.

Towards the end of an otherwise well-made film by eminent Pakistani film director, Tariq Hasan, Umrao is presented through the middle-class lens: a repentant, sinful, hurt woman who ultimately dies for the respectable (middle class) world that may not have the space for her. The Indian version of 1979, directed by the legendary Muzaffar Ali, gave a better treatment in terms of the ambience and the *Avadhi* culture, but only partially captured the layers of Umrao's worldview on her profession and the social commentary on it. Its ending was also melodramatic as Umrao is rejected by her mother and brother. The last frame of the film, however, redeemed it as Umrao clears a mirror and perhaps hints at a new phase of self-discovery.

Khanam Jan and the East India Company

Prior to *Umrao Jan Ada*, another Persian text *Fasana-e Rangin* translated into English as *The Nautch Girl* in 1992[6] by Qurratulain Hyder (1928-2006) is arguably the first subcontinental novel. Or at least Hyder passionately held this view until her last days.[7] This autobiographical novel by Hasan Shah (1790) narrates the story of an East India Company *munshi* (a clerk) and his doomed love for a dancing girl Khanam Jan. The novel, originally written in Persian, translated into Urdu in 1893 as *Nishtar*.

The young Shah in the service of the Englishman Ming Saheb, in Cawnpore (Kanpur), spots a beautiful dancing girl in a visiting troupe camping in the town through the patronage of the English saheb. Ming Saheb also lusts after Khanam Jan but she rejects his advances. Ming moves to another member of the troupe but the confident Khanam Jan falls in love with a lowly clerk, Hasan Shah.

The starry-eyed lovers enter into a secret marriage as both the protagonists' professional compulsions inhibit their public declaration of love. However, Jan in due course leaves Cawnpore with the employer. The troupe has to move to another city when the English officer is transferred and the patronage ends. The two fantasize about escaping but their plans cannot materialize.

The hallmark of this novel is the portrayal of Khanam Jan who appears to be a confident, learned and strong-willed character. Her ability to say no to a *gora saheb* and her subsequent subversion of her place in the troupe are remarkable for eighteenth century India. Even though Khanam has vowed not to be a courtesan, she does not leave the troupe. Though not as empowered as her successor-to-be – Umrao Jan – Khanam Jan is cognizant of her social position. After the Englishmen leave, Shah has planned to meet Jan by the river but he is fatally delayed by his official commitments. Crossing the river is also a metaphor that runs across the folklore of the subcontinent and Shah employs this device in a subtle fashion. While it remains a simple story of love in times of a changing India, the characters and nuances of human behaviour announce the arrival of the Indian novel.

My Candle Burns at Both Ends

Avadh (Oudh, in later-day United Province) state, annexed by the British formally in mid-nineteenth century, therefore becomes a parable of the political and social transformation of India. Amid these changes, the voice of the dancing girls is distinct and individualistic. It is neither pathetic nor morally flawed. In fact, it is reasoned and powerful. As recounted by Hyder[8], the case of Oudh reminds us of the verse:

My candle burns at both ends
It will not last the night
But, Ah my friends and Oh my foes
It gives a lovely light.

As Hyder puts it, the Oudh state was India's Camelot, where Khanam Jan becomes the torchbearer of an emerging high culture, and Umrao Jan – like a burnt candle – narrates its dénouement. These two women represent, and are also shaped by, their sociological environments. Umrao in the twilight of Oudh culture relates the realization of empowerment within the patriarchal fold. It should be remembered that Malika Jan, the wife of the last ruler of Oudh, was also a dancing girl and she issued a *farman* (edict) defying the Ordinance of Empress Victoria and declared that the state have nothing to do with religion. This extraordinary document is a unique instance in modern subcontinental history. Thus, fiction and fact were producing what one may roughly call a proto–feminist stance on the issue of sex-work as we knew it in Victorian India.

Towards Gauhar Jan

> *Gaisberg eagerly waited for the morning of 11 November, when the woman he was besotted with would arrive at the makeshift studio. Gauhar's entry into the studio on that Tuesday morning in Calcutta was to place her forever in the annals of world musical history. Her imposing persona and her flair in dress and manner had captivated Gaisberg completely...*[9]

Urdu's legendary writer Qurratulain Hyder who translated Hasan Shah's novel in English remained, through her literary career, fascinated by the various permutations of the Indian nautch girl. In her later novel *Gardish-e-Rang-e-Chaman*, a semi-documentary novel, through literary devices she blurs the boundaries between the respectable and the non–respectable. Mughal princesses orphaned after the anti–Mughal killings by the British led to a major upheaval in the comfortable zones of Muslim rule in India. The central character of the novel – Nawab Begum – is a descendent of one such Mughal progeny who later becomes a courtesan; after a long career and several tribulations revels in her status as a powerful woman. In the true tradition of courtesan lineage, Nawab Begum launches her daughter as a theatre performer in early twentieth-century Calcutta. The textual tenor moves between the context set by Ruswa – between the pathos of exploitation and the energy of empowerment.

In her novel, published in 1987, Hyder fictionalized the character of the early twentieth-century singer from Calcutta, Gauhar Jan for the first time. This is decades before the excellent book on Jan by Vikram Sampath hit the bookstands. From Avadh, the deposed ruler Wajid 'Ali Shah had moved to Calcutta and this is where new converts to Islam, Malika Jan and her daughter Gauhar Jan, found their performative abode. The mother-daughter duo became the best-known *ba'i*s (singing women, singular: *ba'i*) of Calcutta. Based on this formidable reputation, Frederick William Gaisberg, the Gramophone Company's first India agent, in 1902 selected Gauhar as the first Indian artiste whom he wanted to record. Thus popular culture's interface with modernity in India came about through these empowered and public singing women.

As Sampath records faithfully, Gauhar recorded close to 600 records in over ten languages during her stint as a playback singer. The vast repertoire, husky and flirtatious voice encapsulated myriad musical forms: *khayal*, *dhrupad* and light genres such as *thumri*, *dadra*, *kajri*, and *bhajan*. With her cosmopolitan vision and command over several languages, Gauhar was a trendsetting flamboyant star long before Bollywood adopted glitz as a policy. Jan's extravagant party that cost ₹20,000 was infamously publicized. The purpose of the party was to celebrate the birth of several kittens by her favourite cat. Gauhar Jan gained much attention for flouting government regulations for gallivanting in a four-horse-driven buggy. She had to pay a fine of ₹1,000 per day to the viceroy.

This was the colourful character that made Hyder's novel inimitable for its mixing of fact and fiction; and also for redefining the status of courtesan – moving it away from the well-defined zones of morality. The universe of South Asian literature, especially in the regional languages, has been ignored as a tool to understand the evolution of our sociological attitudes towards dancing girls, courtesans and sex workers.

A Century of Confusion

ibtida' awargi ki josh-e wahshat ka sabab hum to samjhe hain magar nasih ko samjhayen ge kya

(I know fully well about the wild times when I started going astray But Oh! Advisor! How do I make you give up finding faults and understanding my plight?)[10]

Urdu's celebrated short story writer Sa'adat Hasan Manto has explored the societal attitudes towards sex workers with a surgeon's precision. Prior to 1947, he was writing about the hypocrisies, but the mayhem of 1947 gave him an additional perspective when he saw ordinary sex workers as finer human beings than the religious *shurafa'* (the honourable people – usually from the upper middle classes). One such memorable character is that of a Jewish sex worker in Bombay named Mozail. In the backdrop of the 1947 riots, Manto portrays vacuous religiosity of a Sikh character in sharp contrast to the innate humanity of Mozail as she parades naked and gets killed to distract a rioting mob to rescue people. Mozail emerges as a towering character in this story. Manto chronicles the socially fallen – the pimps, prostitutes and the brothel-keepers – and by removing them from the rigid moral framework, elevates their humanity. Thus, Manto refuses to judge his characters, otherwise viewed as the subaltern dross.

The new nation-states since 1947 (Pakistan and India) and 1971 (Bangladesh) have been unable to set a clear approach towards sex-related professions. The whole gamut of male sex-workers, not a recent phenomenon either, remains relegated to relative ignominy. If anything, the inherited Victorian colonial state has defined public morality and 'righteous' conduct. Offences concerning public display of affection and obscenity remain on the statutes across South Asia. The sad part is that the voice of a sex-worker is lost in the regulatory framework imposed from above.

In postcolonial, morally charged societies, courtesans of yore have found other avenues. For instance, due to the late President Zia-ul-Haq's 'Islamization' policies in Pakistan – during much of the 1980s – and brothel-focused cleaning up in South Asia, sex workers have moved and integrated into the mainstream social fabric. In Pakistan specifically, Lollywood has absorbed a large number of these individuals and after the decline of the film industry in recent decades, commercial theatre is the new playground for the exploited-empowered courtesan. One such theatre company in Pakistan's cultural centre, Lahore, pays two million rupees per month to a theatre actor whose identity as a sex worker is now blurred with other labels. The rise of massage parlours and private services via the Internet and the advertisement chain has further complicated matters.

The Blame Game

Ghulam Abbas' Urdu short story *Anandi* (also translated into a classic film *Mandi* by the film-maker Shayam Benegal) remains a parable for all times to come. The moralist municipality of an imagined city expels sex workers and brothels to improve public morality. The wilderness of sex workers' new abode soon turns into a new city – *Anandi* – and the land mafia, the trader-merchant class, *dargah*s and temples spring up in a short span of time. The story ends with another irony!

The meeting of *Anandi*'s Municipal Council is at full boil, the hall is packed nearly to bursting, and contrary to normal, not a single member is absent. The issue under debate in the Council is the expulsion from the city of the women of the marketplace, for their very presence has become an unsightly and intolerable stain on the skirt of humanity, nobility, and culture.[11] One eloquent scion of society is holding forth: 'It is simply not known what the policy might have been on the basis of which this polluting class of people was given permission to live in the precise center of this ancient and historical city of ours...' This time, the area selected for the women to live in was twelve kos from the city.[12]

Anandi was written in the mid-twentieth century. Little seems to have changed; at least in terms of social and cultural attitudes.

Published in *Bunyad, A Journal of Urdu Studies*, Volume 2, Number 2, 2012, Lahore University of Management Sciences.

10

Mustafa Zaidi: A Poet Remembered

Thirty-five years ago, Mustafa Zaidi, a poet of notable standing and a dismissed CSP officer, was found dead in Karachi's Hotel Sumar. The mystery of his death remains officially unresolved to date. He was only forty years old and had produced several outstanding, original collections of poetry. He had also tasted and fallen victim to intimacy with the state. He was married to a woman of German descent and had two children; yet his final companion was not a member of his family but Shehnaz, the last love of his life. That October day, in 1970, Shehnaz was found unconscious along with Mustafa Zaidi's dead body. His last five poems were a series titled 'Shehnaz', and it is through these powerful poems that we know of the woman who was immortalized by Zaidi.

As is often the case, Zaidi started off writing in Allahabad under the pseudonym Tegh Allahabadi. His first volume was published when he was a teenager. He was a disciple of another maestro, Josh Malihabadi, and was well-known by the time he migrated to Pakistan after Partition. The later trajectory is also familiar: advanced studies in English literature, a brief period spent teaching and entering the Pakistani civil service through competitive examination. However, his poetic side thrived through various phases and he was published regularly to mixed acclaim.

As inappropriate as it may sound, I have always been fascinated by Zaidi's death. Perhaps a subconscious death wish in me finds this such an alluring case. In real terms, Pakistan lost a fine civil servant and an unsung poet whose stature could be belittled only by a society as dysfunctional as ours. I have followed his path: in Dera Ghazi Khan, where he served as the subdivisional magistrate, in the medieval resort of Fort Munroe, where he spent his summer working away and composing verses; and all the places in the inimitable Murree hills. I have had a chance to stay in proximity of where he lived in Murree. For years, I have studied him in order to appreciate the intricacies of his inner universe. Would I be melodramatic in proclaiming that during this Zaidi trail, I have heard the echoes of his anguish, observed flashes of his infinite genius and traces of his apparent hedonism?

Wherever I have been, culturally endowed locals ascribe the following couplet to the houses in which he lived:

Traverse these stones, if you can, to reach me
The path to my house is not studded by a galaxy.

His last collection, Koh-e-Nida (The Beckoning Mountain) contains a chilling chronicle of a death foretold. Koh-i-Nida is a splendid image borrowed from the Arabian tale of Hatim Tai, concerning a mountain that calls people in and consumes them. How very pertinent for a life such as Zaidi's that was annihilated by its very intensity. Published in 1970, the book's

foreword is titled: 'The Last Word' and declares that this is the
last collection of his verse. For a sensitive poet of Zaidi's ability,
giving up poetry was tantamount to giving up life. If I were to
paraphrase the critical stream of consciousness from this piece,
it would read as follows:

*I shall not write anymore: I have lost the spirit of enquiry over
the last few years and my surroundings and circumstances have
killed my desire to augment knowledge. In a country where I
am considered educated, most people I have come across are
devoid even of my ignorance. The kind of poetry that will be
appreciated here, I am unfit to write.*

Recognition: *Is essential for a poet's soul and I have not
achieved even a modicum of what I deserved. If for decades I
have not been able to achieve that, why should I write more?
I have often composed better verse than many poets whom the
critics notice. I was shocked to see an anthology compiled by
Wazir Agha that contained the names of lesser poets, but did
not find a place for my name. I was heartbroken.*

On being a misfit: *In all circles, I am out of place. The
civil servants consider me an object of entertainment in their
drawing rooms and I suspect the poets find me useful. In my
society where no ideology is accepted other than in its stultified
vision, who am I to complain? Here, great minds such as Josh
Malihabadi have been trampled by the state and society. What
is the value of my anguish? Therefore, when society does not
accept an individual and the individual refuses to conform to
society, then composing verse is the most useless of activities. A*

poet has to be an organic part of the society, not a disconnected irrelevance.

And: *In particular where the religious ideology of a country can easily kill you, what is the solution other than suicide, escape? If neither of these, keep yourself prepared to be slaughtered by knives of the butchers.*

Limited appreciation: *Throughout the world, I have been taking photographs and the state has not even bothered to provide me with even a little physical space to continue my interests. I have a passion for flying and obtained my private pilot's license after much ado. In a crash landing, I could not prevent a small aircraft that I was fond of like my children from being damaged. I am so traumatised by this event that even the flying club management cannot appreciate the depth of this sorrow.*

Harassment: *On April 24, 1969, when I was living in a bachelor's hostel with my family, a subordinate brought thousands of rupees to me as a bribe. The following day, when I complained in writing to the chief secretary of the province, I was harassed for months and tortured to the extent that it was beyond the endurance of any normal human being. What was my fault? I had refused a bribe but my subordinate was enmeshed in the corridors of power and he ensured that my life was a living tale of misery.*

Zaidi's dramatic soliloquy is self-explanatory and a microcosm of the larger existential woe of Pakistani society. It encompasses the dying values of inquiry, creativity and integrity, and bemoans the limited space for individual passions and interests. Notably, it also mentions religious bigotry and the lack of space for individual liberties, even in the pre-Islamized Pakistan of the late sixties. Small wonder, then, that Zaidi uttered forebodingly:

> On whose hands shall I find stains of my blood
> The whole city is gloved in anonymity.

Yahya Khan's famous list of 303 summarily dismissed civil servants included the name of Mustafa Zaidi who, above all, suffered the biggest stigma of non-conformity. Zaidi was a wanderer, a bit of a philanderer and outspoken in his poetic expression. He never refrained from a candid assertion of sexual desire and experience, or from expressing his artistic contempt of all that surrounded him. As a classic misfit, he also had something in him reminiscent of Lord Byron, albeit in a different context.

'Aesthetics is a fire not aware of its inflammability', said Zaidi, and continued to ignite the flames of his creativity until they consumed him. His poetry is diverse: from troubled relationships with women to a poetic critique on the unjust functioning of the United Nations; a dialogue with Polonius (from Shakespeare's *Hamlet*) and on the country of his choice, Pakistan. In 'Musafir' (Traveller), written before his death, he addresses his homeland after a long sojourn abroad:

> There is nothing that I carry from my homeland
> Merely a dream and the fortifications of a dream
> Accept the gift of my soiled shirt
> For its dirt carries the dust from the mosques

This apparel cannot be washed for it enfolds
The splashes of Biafra's sacred blood
This is the soil from Vietnam and its grains contain
The radiant brows of the prophets.

TRANSLATED BY THE AUTHOR

His troubled soul had predicted the pattern of emigration:

I hope you may not end up desolate
Anarchy may not replace the law
Oh my country, so many of your citizens
Are left with no choice but migrate.

By late 1970, Shehnaz, for whom he had declared his true love, was moving away from him. The five Shehnaz poems document in effect the evolution and climax of his passion, the decline and fall of their relationship and his underlying disappointment with life. The early Shehnaz poems profess:

She was not an artist herself, but shared my art
She shared the body in the journey of the spirit
Whose modesty had been revealed page by page
She accompanied me in every crease of the bed
In one way, I was a fire-worshipper
She experienced every angle of the garden.

And the last poem in the Shehnaz quintet complains:

The way you insist on separation now
Even my vows of love did not have such intensity
This new found comfort in our shared unfaithfulness

Eludes the heart's life-blood and the blossoming colour of henna.

TRANSLATED BY THE AUTHOR

Is it not a sorry tale of forgetfulness that no authoritative work has been produced on Zaidi? And perhaps the first PhD on his works was undertaken abroad. He complained bitterly about Pakistan not acknowledging his worth. Have things changed in all these years? He has surely been printed and read much more after his death but has not gained the attention that his original and diverse poetry deserves. Zaidi had an almost romantic craving for recognition and never concealed it. It is tragic that his competence as a civil servant has been forgotten by ruthless power-mongers and his poetry has not been given its due by aficionados of Urdu literature. Even today, he remains on the wrong side of the literary establishment and his poetry has been reduced to the sexual explicitness of some of the poems. Zaidi was never a sentimental poet and he knew it. This is why he complained that he could not write poetry defined as 'right' by critics. However, as Josh said at Zaidi's memorial, he was the greatest poet of the future and aficionados can do little to undermine his creative genius.

Zaidi's death was shrouded in mystery while most believed he committed suicide. As I have learnt — through my interactions with his friends and family — the actual circumstances of his death suggest otherwise. News reports and eyewitness accounts point to the absurdity of the claim that he died in a hotel, as family members claim that he was found dead in his own home. Thanks to Zaidi's ardent fan Abeer Zaidi, I have come to know of more precise facts.

Following are the circumstances of his demise and the lack of evidence to support the commonly held view that he committed suicide:

> On March 20, 1971, under the headline 'Evidence of Zaidi's nephew recorded', the newspaper Dawn reported: 'Mr Shahid Raza, nephew of the former CPS officer and well-known poet Mr S.M. Zaidi yesterday said that there were signs of a struggle having taken place in the room in which his uncle's body was discovered last October 12. He was testifying in the Court of the District Magistrate, Mr Kunwar Idris, in the committal trial of Mrs Shehnaz Saleem, Wife of Mr Saleem Khan, who is charged with the murder of Mustafa Zaidi.'

The report goes on to say that Raza entered his uncle's house with a police official and a maternal uncle the morning after the death and found the body lying on the bed. The receiver of the phone was dangling off the hook and the cord stretched across his body. There were stains of blood on his back as well as on the bed sheet and the furniture. Writer Laurel Steel has mentioned this report in her book, *Relocating the Post-Colonial Self* and has also published some letters written by Zaidi to his wife in Germany to help him get a visa to join his family in Germany. Additionally, Steel also mentions that on the day of his death he rose at 8 a.m. and washed his car. Later in the day, he received visitors including Shehnaz Gul and afterwards told his servant to go home and return the next morning. The question that must be asked is: can this demeanour be that of a man bent on committing suicide in a hotel room?

Zaidi yearned for artistic freedom, the actualization of self-worth and esteem, and he felt stifled. His fears of growing bigotry were not unfounded, as was witnessed in the decade after his death. Unlike many medieval and modern masters of Urdu poetry, Zaidi was politically active and international in his perspective. He felt there was no place for him in Pakistani society; perhaps we never do have any room for deviants!

Zaidi was punished for his dreams but they existed beyond him, continuing to haunt us, often eluding our contemporary consciousness. We owe his tortured soul a lot; not the least of which is remembering why he decided to die.

Zaidi was starved of love and artistic freedom, punished for his dreams. His dreams still fill our contemporary consciousness, reminding us each day of all that we have lost as a nation.

Decades later, this case is still an enigma and has left many of those who appreciated his life and work in both denial and doubt.

11

Silhouetted Silences: Contemporary Pakistani Literature in the 'Age of Terror'[1]

❧

Since the invasion of Afghanistan by the United States and the global hysteria about 'terror' and 'terrorism', Pakistan is facing the greatest existential challenge since its dismemberment in 1971. As a frontline ally of the US in the war on terror, the Pakistani society and polity have been engulfed by growing militancy and acts of violence commonly branded as terrorism. Whilst there is no single definition of 'terrorism', the mainstream media and policymakers – in the service of imperial rhetoric aimed to justify and perpetuate the occupations of Afghanistan and Iraq – have established *terrorism* as the major threat to domestic and regional peace in South Asia. Acts of premeditated and organized violence in India, Pakistan and Bangladesh have thus assumed a central place in discourse on regional cooperation or its converse: the rivalries between the constructed nation states and their irresponsible power-elites.

In this milieu, the South Asian citizens have been the victims of violence, uncertainty and acrimonies that have only led to exacerbation of poverty, inequality, ascendancy of militarism and war-mantra. All of this is taking place when globalization is relentlessly seeping into domestic economies, cultures and social systems. Where does this leave the writers and poets of the region, those who grapple with the complex, confusing and fast-changing social and political realities? Whilst the community of South Asian writers -- traditionally the forbearers of intellectual and political movements -- is beleaguered by the corporate media industry, it has struggled to respond to challenges that events have created.

Explored here is the response of the Pakistani literature in Urdu, English and some regional languages and how these streams are reacting and interacting with the new reality of 'terror', violence and suicide bombing. The kaleidoscope of Pakistani literature is varied and presents a mixed view. The writers' creativity is strangulated by 'ideology' and anti-Americanism. At the same time, the sheer scale of violence and its *direct* impact on human lives and social structures is a key issue faced by the writers, poets and intellectuals of Pakistan.

❧

Considerable attention has been devoted towards literature that has risen out of or focused on life during the age of terrorism, starting with Joseph Conrad's work on Victorian anarchism, leading up to the more recent modern-age literature that reflects the current state of affairs after the 9/11 attacks. Literature as a medium of expression has been representative of the impact that terrorism has had on society in general, and it comes as no surprise that terrorism is now being studied through the many ways various writers capture certain moments in time in their work. As a public phenomenon that concerns society at large, it is very difficult to restrict the study of terrorism to a purely political occurrence concerning the government, terrorists and the media. This reductionist view fails to encapsulate the cultural realm of the ongoing discussion, and tends to view terrorism as an autonomous phenomenon. Hence, by observing literary discourses during troubled times, we obtain a far more nuanced and detailed view of how terrorism impacts the life of the everyday individual – particularly in the social realm, as captured and reflected by the pens of numerous writers[2] (Alex Houen, *Terrorism and Modern Literature from Joseph Conrad to Ciaran Carson*).

Terrorism has often been used as the subject matter in works of fiction, ranging from the thriller genre to books that deal with more detailed questions about politics and philosophy. Some novelists have focused on the social conditions that give rise to terrorists' groups, whilst others concentrate on the cultural and political systems which terrorists claim to oppose. Some try to get inside an individual terrorist's head, either to explain or criticize, whereas others focus solely on the experience of being a victim of terrorism. Perpetrators and victims, causes and effects, social conditions and psychological roots: clearly, the variations are endless. Nevertheless, what all these literary treatments have in common is a deeper curiosity about what terrorists might *represent*, both culturally and artistically. They are constructed and construed as more than a 'mysterious menace lying in wait' to terrify us. Instead, terrorists tell us something about ourselves – for better or worse.

Indeed, since 9/11 it has become much harder to argumentatively sustain, on one hand confident dismissal of terrorism as a threat, and on the other hand, the ironic acceptance of it as a political or artistic act. Certainly, anarchists were a legitimate threat in the nineteenth century as well. Queen Victoria survived multiple attempts on her life, and Scotland Yard itself was bombed once. But nineteenth-century novelists responding to these acts seem to have had more resources to depend upon; they had greater confidence in the ability of Western culture to endure. By contrast, the literary depictions of terrorism that have emerged in the past few years have been much more sombre. Though they give reason for hope, and even transcendence, they do so with a sense of vulnerability rather than contempt or cynicism. And they do this by focusing less on the terrorists and more on their victims (John Utz, *Terrorism in Literature*).

In recent years, the political and social milieu has created deep contradictions for the writers and poets of contemporary Pakistan. Writers have felt bruised by the widespread violence and desecration of humanity. Yet, they are equally aware of the public mood that holds the great powers responsible for destruction in the neighbourhood. First Pakistan was embroiled in the anti-Soviet battle of the 'free world' and since 9/11 it is again a participant in the war on terror. This is what makes the task of the poets and writers extremely difficult.

During the 2001-2008 period, domestic military rule — coupled with a growing incidence of militant extremism — placed the Pakistani writer, like his fellow citizens, in a tight corner.

Since 9/11, Pakistani writers in English have also made their presence felt at the global level. Three novels — *The Reluctant Fundamentalist* by Mohsin Hamid; *No Space for*

Further Burials by Feryal Ali Gauhar; and *A Case of Exploding Mangoes* by Mohammed Hanif – serve as the epitome of the new emerging voices of Pakistani literature in English. More importantly, these novels bring forth the critical issues of war, violence, identity and the workings of the Pakistani security establishment that are central to global debates on South[west] Asian peace.

The Reluctant Fundamentalist[3] is about the inner turmoil of a well-meaning educated Pakistani and his interaction with the post-9/11 world; the book examines the nature of quasi-subaltern rootlessness and its impact on the Pakistani diaspora. The book's examination of this particular phenomenon complements academic work on the structuring of communities, especially for people who reside in isolation and experience anonymity in their day-to-day interactions. Encountering racism and discrimination breeds mistrust, and eventually leads to an invocation of tradition, and a quest to seek identity in various forms such as ethnicity and, as shown in this case, religion. Although a work of fiction, the book has insightful commentary on issues that have received a great deal of attention in the Western academy. The identity crisis and the subsequent breeding of the perception of *us* vs *them* has been an important factor in the trajectory of terrorism and fundamentalism, especially in the post-9/11 context. This aspect perhaps gives Huntington's *Clash of Civilizations* some functional direction as well.

Feryal Ali Gauhar's novel[4] is located in Afghanistan, and recounts the horrors of war and occupation that have brutalized humanity. The characters of the novel testify to this, and the setting of the novel is an Afghan mental asylum. The literary device of using an asylum, as a reproduction of Afghanistan at a micro level is meaningful as it sheds light on years of political turmoil that have beset the country. It also turns into a parable of a society undergoing continued upheavals and in need of healing. The novel presents a narrative from the standpoint of an American army technician, hence casting a move away from the case of Hamid's book that discussed issues of existentialist nature for the Muslim populace.

Hanif's work[5] on the assassination of General Zia, whilst not reflecting the exact theme discussed in the earlier two examples, belongs to the category of literature that also takes into account the role of the numerous agencies and clandestine actors present within the political structure in Pakistan. The agenda — and the ambiguities — associated with these actors are reflective of the present situation of fundamentalism, and their historical roots and linkages with the Pakistani state and its 'strategic' goals. Moreover, this work incorporates the role of foreign actors in a scenario of violence and political turmoil that is, again, relevant to the current situation in the troubled region of Pakistan and Afghanistan.

This literary renaissance comes as Pakistan struggles to contain the militant Taliban, and the political instability. What we find in common with the literary pieces mentioned above is that their medium of expression finds a larger audience abroad and provides an international perspective to a problem that is perhaps transnational in nature itself.

As mentioned earlier, the taboos which had inhibited the writers in national languages to express themselves have started to break. Of late, more and more writers, especially the younger ones, are writing on issues of violence and terrorism. Scores of short stories and a few novellas are talking of the impact of terrorism, and the futility of war and violence in a direct manner. In a short story entitled *Tales Scripted in Blood*, Asim Butt writes from the perspective of a misled jihadi:

He had prayed that he gets an opportunity to crush the enemies;
and he had done quite a bit of that. However, this experience
(of violence) had left indelible marks on the inner layers of his
mind — the sounds of bullets, the bomb explosions and human
cries — this noise kept on blaring cruelly inside him. But it
became even more intense when for some reason blood gushed
in his veins — that is when his mind would get rattled.[6]

In poetry too, this trend is evident. Many poems reiterate
humanism and its threatened status in this age of militancy and
war. For instance, the powerful *A Mourning poem for Bajaur*[7] by
Pakistan's eminent poet Kishwar Naheed[8]:

Coffins have become so numerous
That the city is shrinking

The eye is oozing
And not even a word of association
Like an open wound
On the lips.

The sky looks over everything
And remains silent.
Why does it go on believing
That mankind will awake once again
From its deep slumber
And laughter will ring again
On the threshold of houses.

No, it was not yesterday
But many years ago,
We held hope with our hands

We sat in the shadow of wide-awake walls
And used to think:
Yellow-gold wheat smiles and laughs
In our courtyards

We have the same courtyards, the same threshers
But bullets jump through them,
Riddle holes in my fields
and in the bodies of my children

With my tear-soaked pillow
I sit in the courtyard, watching

Coffins have become so numerous
That the city is shrinking.

Increasingly, regional writings are local voices of resistance to
war and the culture of violence. A Pashto poem *How could I
be silent* by Iqbal Hussain Afkar represents the end of silence.

The fire of destruction, Is setting me ablaze,
And I'm turning into dust and ashes, How could I be silent!
Friends! How could I be silent!

Once my fellow.is now my killer,
As he's convinced to take my life,
Ignoring my agony while I'm floored,
I'm turning into dust and ashes,
How could I be silent! Friends!
How could I be silent!

That my land; A paradise, My lovely heavenly garden,
Is struck by strife and wiping me out,
I'm turning into dust and ashes, Fellows!
How could I be silent! Tell me!
How could I be silent!

Beware! O' Pashtuns! If you could, You are burning and the
fire's yourselves!
How easily I'm being sold!
I'm turning into dust and ashes,
So, how could I be silent!
*Fellows! How could I be silent!*⁹

Pashto literature has undergone several changes since the
advent of violence and fundamentalism to the region, and
especially after the Afghan War and the ensuing crisis of
nationhood in Afghanistan. Moreover, the recent American
invasion in Afghanistan and the rise of fundamentalist forces
in the tribal areas have created distinctions between the forms
of literature that are now being produced.

As literature cannot be viewed in abstraction from the
larger societal structure and its intricate happenings, the case
of Pashto literature is no different as it incorporates some of
the major themes of violence and war in its core expression.
The distinction is between those who propagate the message
of peace and harmony through their cultural invocations of
tradition, whilst remaining in tandem with another branch
that is equally keen on perpetuating the cause of jihad through
their writings. Traditional Pashto literature has been nationalist
and based on glorification of the past by invoking traditions
and folklore. This new dimension within Pashto literature is

reflective of the changing nature of Pashtun society especially in the context of the Khyber Pakhtunkhwa (formerly known as the Frontier province) and its surrounding regions.[10]

❧

For a closer analysis of terrorism and its impact on literature, it is relevant to study the case of Sri Lanka, a country bruised by decades of ethnic conflict and large scale violence. Literature in the Sri Lankan context assumed a prominent role after the political events of the 1980s i.e., the ethnic riots that erupted between the Sinhalese and the Tamils. Literature, as a medium of expression, as is the case with war-struck regions, remained marginalized and repressed.

Poetry, understandably, was the first to undergo new experiments and experiences. An anthology of poems edited by Nuhman, Cheran and Jesurajah was titled *Maranathul Valvom* (We Live Amidst Death), 1984, and it summed up the emotional turmoil of this era. Nuhman's translation of Palestinian poetry opened up a new literary panorama to young Sri Lankan readers. It was Cheran, the son of Mahakavi – a new arrival of the 1980s – who recorded with authenticity the changed feelings and emotions. His anthologies, *Erandavathu Sooriya Uthayam* (The Second Sunrise) and Yaman, though slender in size, left a deep impression. On the burning of a public library, he wrote:

> *What took place? My city was set on fire*
> *My people became faceless.*
> *On my land, my breeze on all the estampage of the Alien.*
> *With your arms inter-locked behind your back for whom were*
> *you waiting?*
> *Fire has writ large its message indelibly on the clouds.*

Conversely, fiction took some time to emerge as a genre that echoed the senselessness of violence. Living in a war ravaged environment, and the sense of loss, uprooting and chaos found expression in the short stories of Ranjakumar, Uma Varadarasan and Tirukkovilur Kaviyuvan. The scale and extent of suffering, and literary interpretation as well as resistance to such a milieu is immensely haunting. For instance, Ranjakumar's Kosalai (the mother of Rama in Ramayana) narrates the woes of mothers whose sons run away from home. Kaviyuvan's stories lament how the societal groups and institutions like family have been affected due to violence.

In the words of Karthigesu Sivathamby, much of these writings are not freely available and even if available, cannot be discussed openly. Even a brief review will reveal how life has changed and suffering has become all-pervasive[11]. However, it should be remembered that by being truthful and empathetic the writer also shows the mirror to the society that is otherwise locked in the narratives of power and war. The humane voices are the strongest condemners of violence and war as they remind the futility of terror driving home the point that militant or militarized ideologies can only disrupt and destroy human lives.

Pakistani literature, after shying away from direct references to the human suffering and terrorism, has followed, with some variations, the Sri Lankan trajectory. Notwithstanding the growing body of literature, Pakistani writers face a herculean challenge today[12]. The larger questions on the marginalization of folklore, the decreasing accessibility of literature and writing in the age of mass electronic media, and corporate hegemony on ideas and expression, are shared threats.

Like other art forms and mediums of social expression, literature is a dynamic, evolving reflection of human and societal experiences. The very fact that there are Pakistani poets and writers challenging the rising tide of extremism and violence – regardless of who the originator of such crises may be – is a welcome shift, and a testament to the rich heritage of Pakistan's literary history and its dynamic present.

These are indeed interesting, confusing times. But each time the groups of various shades gather in protest, they recite that litany of Faiz's hopes, as translated by Maniza Naqvi:

We shall see

Certainly we, too, will see
That day that has been promised to us

......`

When these high mountains
Of tyranny and oppression

Turn to fluff
And evaporate

And we that oppressed
Beneath our feet will have
This earth shiver, shake and beat

.....

Hum dekhein ge

Lazim hai ke hum bhi dekhein ge

*Woh din ke jis ka wada hai jo loh-e-azl pe likha hai hum
dekhein ge*
Jab zulm-o-sitam ke koh-e-garaan

Rui ki tarah udd jain gay

Hum mehkumoon ke paun talay
Yeh dharti dhard dhard dhardkay gi

*Aur ehl-e-hukum ke sar uper jab bijli kard kard kardke gi
hum dekhain gay.*

❧

The importance of literature, and its inherent potential, in
helping confront militancy and building bridges among
divergent communities within the SAARC countries and
between the 'nation-states' clamouring for identity, peace and
progress cannot be underestimated. Terrorism, or whatever
form and shape violence takes, is also a shared curse and a
cause for collective praxis that the regional countries have to
undertake to protect humanistic values.

There can be no other way to improve our present and
reclaim our common bonds and heritage. The culture of
violence and acrimony has to give way to a new dawn.

12

Pakistan's Rich Dissident
Literary Tradition

❧

The long spells of authoritarian rule in Pakistan have nurtured a rich dissident literary tradition. This tradition has its roots in the Progressive Writers' Movement, which originated in colonial India with major Urdu poets and writers as its vanguards. Faiz Ahmad Faiz was, of course, the best-known torchbearer of this tradition, while other luminaries included Sajjad Zaheer, M.D. Taseer, Rashid Jahan, Kaifi Azmi, Ismat Chughtai, Sahir Ludhianvi and Ahmed Nadeem Qasmi, to name only a few.

With the post-Independence Pakistani state continuing the old-style approach to ruling over the masses, the progressive movement too carried on its dissent long after 1947. Those who had migrated to Pakistan faced a new reality, which, in the words of Faiz, was far from the dawn for which they had hoped. "*This blemished light, this dawn by night half-devoured,*" Faiz wrote ruefully, "*surely not the dawn for which we were waiting.*"

The progressive literary movement eventually began to be considered something of a threat to the postcolonial state, and several Pakistani writers faced severe restrictions. Among the several pioneers of the movement, it was the direct yet lyrical poetry of Habib Jalib that stirred the street, echoing the vision of the world from below. While Faiz used the classical Persian idiom, Jalib's expression was more popular and immediate, and related easily to the common language of the streets. During the rule of General Ayub Khan, from 1958 until 1969, Jalib particularly represented the public conscience when he chanted his poem 'Dastoor' (the Constitution), which was about Ayub Khan's tailor-made "constitution". Later, this work was utilised in support of Fatima Jinnah's (the Quaid-e-Azam's younger sister) campaign against the general:

Aisay dastoor ko
Subh-e-baynoor ko
Mein naheen manta
Mein naheen janta
 I do not accept I do not recognise
A constitution that resembles
A morning with no light.

Rejecting Compromise

Jalib did not spare the administration of Zulfikar Ali Bhutto either, particularly when it began to compromise the people's politics on the altar of expedient alliances with Pakistan's notorious feudal barons. However, a second wave of resistance poetry blossomed in Urdu and other local languages when Prime Minister Bhutto was executed after what many saw as an illegitimate trial. Ahmad Faraz, another progressive poet, penned verses that lamented the shock and paralytic effect that Bhutto's hanging had on the body politic.

The eleven years of General Zia-ul-Haq's rule were particularly harsh and repressive for those members of the opposition intelligentsia. As such, writers and poets increasingly chose to express themselves using symbolism and allegories, thus adding new dimensions to Pakistani literature. Enver Sajjad's postmodern novel *Khushion ka Baagh* (The Garden of Happiness) was a notable result of this experimentation. The novel recounted the oppressive Zia regime and, using the allegory of a garden, narrated the tales of political resistance through abstract characters and surrealism.

Jalib was again one of the most outspoken poets of the Zia period. He wrote a popular anthem for the struggle against Gen. Zia:

> *Sar sar ko saba, zulmat ko zia*
> *Banday ko khuda, kya likhnaa'* (How can I call the toxic
> fumes as morning breeze?
> *How can I call the dark night the dawn?*
> *How can I refer to man as god?*)

Pakistan did not enter its quasi-democratic phase until Gen. Zia died in a mysterious air crash in 1988, at which point Benazir Bhutto came to power, after filtering her father's legacy and the anti-Zia struggle through a package that was acceptable to the Pakistani establishment. Jalib, witnessing this compromised democratic rule, could not resist:

> *Haal ab tak wahi hain ghareeboan kay*
> *Din phiray hain faqat waziroan ka*
> *Maqrooz hai daise ka her bilawal*
> *Paoon nangay hain benazeeroan kay*

The plight of the poor remains unchanged
Only the days of the ministers have changed
Each Bilawal [Benazir's son] of the country is indebted
And the Benazirs of the country walk without shoes

When Jalib died in 1993, his widow refused to accept a plot offered by Prime Minister Bhutto, despite the fact that the impoverished Jalib had managed to leave little for his family. He left a rich legacy within Pakistan, however, and during the hectic events of 2007, his name became increasingly prominent. This was particularly due to a recurrent feeling of compromise and pessimism on the part of Pakistani writers regarding how the forces of change had actually become collaborators of the status quo.

There were good reasons for this cynicism. A large portion of the Pakistani civil society had supported General Pervez Musharraf's 1999 takeover and the initial years of his rule. The anti-establishment theatre groups had made peace with him, for instance, while an alarming number of secular poets and intellectuals held him up as a bulwark against the country's growing Talibanisation. The doyens of civil society deemed him a liberator of the media and the state-run arts councils, and General Musharraf was even the chief guest at the International Kara Film Festival in 2006.

Over the course of 2007, Gen. Musharraf's increasingly brazen moves to stay in power led to the widespread withdrawal of support for him among the Pakistani intelligentsia. The March 2007 dismissal of Chief Justice Iftikhar Chaudhry was probably the most important turning point, as the images of an evidently beleaguered Chaudhry saying 'no' to the all-powerful army chief evolved into an improbable but indisputably dynamic symbol of resistance. Much was forgotten: the compromises that the chief justice had previously made; the allegations that Gen. Musharraf had levelled against him; the fact that the Pakistani judiciary, for various reasons, cannot contribute to the realization of broader social justice in the country.

It was during the subsequent campaign for the restoration of the chief justice that Mansoora Ahmed, an eminent Urdu poet and protege of the late Nadeem Qasimi, received a call from Aitzaz Ahsan, one of the country's leading lawyers and one of the leaders of the public protests. Ahsan was calling to ask Ahmed for the text of a poem that she had written that mocked officialdom, particularly the authoritarian images that were emanating from Pakistan's infamous state-run television news programme, Khabarnama. This poem, of the same name, was recited at one of the first public meetings held by the country's lawyers, where the power of Urdu verse quickly, once again, became evident.

Uncle's Uniform

From March to July 2007, as Pakistan was witnessing significant political upheaval, Jalib's legacy of awami, or populist, poetry was re-invoked as a rallying voice for the increasingly vocal crowds. This time, a poem by an unknown poet, composed in the folk Punjabi tradition, proved to be a popular charm. *'Chacha wardi laanda kyon naee'* (*Uncle, why don't you doff off your uniform?*) gave voice to the Pakistani weariness of having to put up with military rulers. One of the most amusing of the poem's lines urged Gen. Musharraf to draw pension, and take a good rest at home. This notwithstanding, the poem was hardly offensive, and perhaps gained popularity because it was much more playful than solemn:

> *Nas ke tu washington jaaven*
> *Bush noon jaa jaa masske laven*
> *Pairi dig dig tarle pavain*
> *Mazlooman noon tarryian lavain*
> *Zaliman naal takranda kiyon naee*
> *You rush to Washington all the time,*
> *And please Bush again and again*
> *Beg at his feet all the time*
> *And threaten the oppressed of your country*
> *Why don't you confront the oppressors?*

That this poem was composed in Punjab province and recited in its hinterland was particularly symbolic. Traditionally, Punjab is considered the primary support base for the military, and the poem's sensibility seemed to allude to a poignant shifting of sands in Pakistani politics. When Gen. Musharraf refused to budge from power, the exasperated sequel to this poem was '*Chacha wardi paee rakh / Qaum nu thallay layee rakh*' *(Uncle, retain the uniform / and keep the nation subjugated).* There were again overt references to Pakistan's acquiescence to the US and its 'war on terror', which was killing more innocent Pakistanis than the militants it was purporting to control.

By the time the Supreme Court restored Chief Justice Chaudhry to his office on 20 July, Gen. Musharraf had made a tenuous peace with Benazir Bhutto. This quickly became another issue of disquiet for many, and a Jalib-esque cry in colourful Punjabi followed by Baba Najmi:

Adhee wardi pa layee sadi bibi ne
Jarnail naal bana layee sadi bibi ne
Bhutto jayree soch ujaagar keeti si
Hathee oe dafna layee sadi bibi ne

Our Bibi [Benazir Bhutto] has worn half a uniform
And has compromised with the general
The ideals that Bhutto had enlivened
With her own hands, she has buried them

This disenchantment was largely undone, however, when Bhutto landed in Karachi on 18 October to a crowd that far exceeded her own expectations. This was the moment when another old verse reincarnated itself within the turmoil of Pakistani politics: *'Har ghar se bhutto niklay ga tum kitnay bhutto maro ge? (A Bhutto will emerge from every household / How many Bhuttos will you kill?)* The ominous foretelling by this verse could hardly be missed when bomb blasts suddenly disrupted Bhutto's homecoming rally, killing nearly 150 people. Reacting to this incident in a poem entitled 'Useless, of no value', Irfan Sattar ends with these chilling lines:

Armano aur khawabon ka yeh dher uthao
Be-masraf aur be-qeemat ye anbaar hatao'
(Remove the debris of aspirations and dreams
Clear these useless piles [of human limbs] that are of no value)..

Following the early-November imposition of the state of emergency, protests were small, though all the while consistent and intense. Demonstrations against media curbs adopted the famous Faiz poem 'Bol' (Speak) as their logo. The lines: *'Bol ki*

lab azad hain tere / Bol zaban ab tak teri hai' (Speak, for your lips
are yet free / Speak, for your tongue is still your own) subsequently
reverberated at nearly every demonstration. Students,
academics and lawyers were charged and mobilized 'perhaps
in part atoning for their earlier blunder in accepting the
proverbial camel into the tent.' Representing the conscience
of the contemporary literati, the senior poet Ahmad Faraz was
also back in business, and his brutally direct (some would say
seditious) poem 'Mohasara' (The Siege) re-surfaced:

> *Peshavar qatilo, tum sipahi nahin Mein ne ab tak tumharay*
> *qaseeday likhay Aur aaj apnay naghmon se sharminda hun*

> *Mercenaries, you are not soldiers*
> *I had praised you all along*
> *Today, I am ashamed of all my [patriotic] songs*

Faraz was unceremoniously fired from his government job as
the chairman of the National Book Foundation in 2003, four
years after Gen. Musharraf's first took over. Since then, he has
been particularly critical of the General's administration, and
returned the civil decorations he had received.

Citizen groups also remembered the great Sindhi poet
Shaikh Ayaz. In particular, his poem 'Echo the call' resonates
those days:

> *So much time has gone by*
> *The woes of this land*
> *Remain still the same*
> *That I have seen.*
> *Rise, O Revolutionaries!*

And echo the call of this land
How long shall I
Echo the call alone?

All was not lost. 'Uncle' removed his uniform, and also lifted the emergency. Elections were announced, and mainstream parties decided to contest and move towards a transition of sorts. The country's lawyers remained defiant, promising to continue to protest the removal of popular judges. Other members of civil society also vowed to join the lawyers, with some strange pairings having arisen in the push for democracy the truncated left parties and the rightwing Jamaat-e-Islami, for instance.

Those were indeed interesting, confusing times. But each time these groups of various shade gathered in protest, they recited that litany of Faiz's hopes:

Hum Dekhaingey
Hum Dekhaingey

Lazim hai ke hum bhi dekhaingey
Woh din ke jis ka wada hai Jo loh-e-azl pe likha hai
Hum dekhaingey
Jab zulm-o-sitam ke koh-e-garaan
Ruii ki tarah ud jaingey
Hum mehkumoon ke paun talay
Yeh dharti dhad dhad dhadkeygi
Aur ehl-e-hukum ke sar upar
Jab bijli kard kard kardkeygi

Hum dekhaingey
Jab arz-e-khuda ke kabay se
Sab but uthwaaiy Jain gay
Hum ehl-e-safa mardood-e-haram
Masnad pe bithaaiy jaingey
Sab taaj uchalay jaingey
Sab takht giraaiy jaingey

Bas naam rahay ga Allah ka
Jo gayab bhi hai hazir bhi
Jo nazir bhi hai manzar bhi
Uthay ga analhaq ka naara
Jo main bhi hun aur tumbhi ho
Aur raj karaygi khalq-e-Khuda
Jo main bhi hun aur tum bhi ho
Hum Dekhaingey
Lazim hai ke hum bhi dekhaingey
Hum dekhaingey.

Published in *Himal Southasian*, January, 2008.

13

The Verse of Freedom

❧

Much has been said about the literary and artistic revolution of Pakistan. Undoubtedly, Pakistani writers, artists and musicians are now recognized globally for their work which engages with the world and brings forth perspectives which alter the unidimensional image of the country. At home, the new wave of literary and creative output is celebrated each year at the Karachi and Lahore Literature Festivals which have emerged as major venues for conversation and the showcasing of what is being produced in the mainstream.

Away from the spotlight of the international media and TV channels, Pakistan's regional poets and writers are waging a far more perilous battle by engaging with their subaltern, marginalized audiences in the local idiom, thereby putting themselves at risk. The days of Faiz and Jalib are not over as we often moan. Instead they have deepened and regionalized. Our region has had a rich, ongoing folk tradition that continues in myriad forms and expressions now. In India, Bangladesh and Pakistan, poets and artists continue to challenge power and injustice; more so in Pakistan where instability, extremism and uncertainty have impacted people in a profound manner for the past few decades.

With the growth of social media, Facebook has emerged as an arena for dissent and regional expression. Despite the censorship of several pages and websites by the state, the outpour of anger and frustration continues. Concurrently, the extremist opinion also uses the Internet to its advantage. Having been pushed out of the mainstream electronic media, I have spent a bit more time on Facebook learning about what Pakistanis are saying and discussing. Admittedly, the conservatives and the mainstream politics such as the narratives pushed by Pakistan Tehreek-e-Insaf (PTI) override everything else, but there is also a far greater space for progressive voices. I do not wish to go into further detail here as the purpose of this essay is to discuss a powerful and moving Saraiki poem that I came across on Facebook.

This poem is by Zafar Jatoi, a Saraiki poet that echoes the emotion of any sensitive Pakistani. The poem is about the loss and distortion of dreams and identity; of losing all colours of existence except one, and that being the hue of radicalization. While some in Pakistan, and now its powerful Army, have come to realize the depth and extent of radicalization, it is only a recent development. For the last decade, phrases such as 'extremism' and 'radicalization' were considered Western ploys to defame Pakistan and it was thought that the entire problem of extremist ideology was a reaction to the US presence in Afghanistan. Jatoi is a voice from the depths of the Saraiki hinterland, echoing what many feel about their land now gifted to a complex web of seminaries and militant outfits that have destroyed the region once known for its Sufi tradition and pluralism. My translation is imperfect but I would like to acknowledge Saleem Malik and Munawar Rind, my friends, for making me wade through the depths of the Saraiki idiom.

My dream ruined
My identity ruined
What kind of a place is this?
Where friends are not friends
Where beloveds are devoid of love
Relationships have no feeling
Where associations are empty
Where fathers and sons fight
What kind of place is this?

What kind of a place is this?
Where I hardly can breathe
Where I barely live
Where beasts inhabit
Where few humans are left
Where trust has evaporated
Where love has disappeared
Where strangers surround me
Where affection has gone

After moaning the loss of the world he knew, Zafar does plain talk in the folk tradition and that of resistance poetry:

What sort of a place is this?
Where a murderer is a messiah
Where the teacher has become a trader
Where a dacoit is a leader
Where a bigot is a teacher

Where you can buy fatwas
Where the mosque is not safe
Where a bomber is sacred
What kind of a place is this?

After the specific protest, Jatoi turns metaphysical and existential. Narrating how diversity has been robbed of the land he belongs to, he uses powerful images to deride the imposition of a singular ideology:

It seems that this land
Has been consumed by greed
In the world of seven colours
Six colours are dead
And only one colour survives
Here black is also white
Here blue is also white
Here red is white too
Here animals are white too
Even I have turned ash-white
Zafar, here I am colourless too
If someone like me [adherent of diversity] exists
He, too, is overpowered
And turned colourless.

Jatoi's protest is not different from the powerful modern Pashtun poetry that has been challenging Talibanization. Shaheen Buneri, a journalist associated with Radio Free Europe/Radio Liberty (RFE/RL) Mashaal Radio, wrote in 2012 that over a hundred poetry collections were published in 2011. Buneri in his essay 'Poetry Fights Back' (January

2012, Boston Review) cited these powerful lines by Zarin Pareshan:

> I could not care less if it's a mosque or a temple filled with idols
> Where my beloved lives, that is my Ka'aba
> You religious fundamentalists stop this bloodshed
> Humanity is the best religion; love, the best worship
> Because of this war I despise the 'dear mullah'
> Love is my religion; unity is my faith.

The tone of this reminded me of a celebrated Baloch poet Ata Shad and his poem *SahKandin*:

> Efforts to put a curb
> On the peoples' consciousness
> Is an exercise in futility.
> Consciousness cannot be snatched away by death;
> It is everlasting, ever vigorous,
> Like overwhelming love and affection.
> This is why the nationalists use poetry of Baloch poets
> to locate their current struggle for rights:
> A people's spirit cannot be destroyed by killings;
> They remain restless, ever resentful.
> This restlessness and resentment lead the people to their
> ultimate goal, Freedom.'

TRANSLATED BY JAN MUHAMMAD DASHTI

Ata Shad is one of the three major modern poets, the other two being Sayyid Zahoor Shah Hashimi (1926–1978) and the iconic Gul Khan Nasir whose lines are used by Baloch youth today. In fact, the poetic expression informs us of the extent of disquiet and it is sad that the Pakistani state has yet to appreciate that and deal with it in a democratic manner.

These lines from Sayyid Zahoor Shah Hashimi's *Sistageñdastunk* haunt me:

My heart bleeds
To wet the barren land of my miserable people
In the hope that one day these lands will turn green
And there will grow red flowers
I will gather the seeds of those flowers
Because these are from
My blood

Islamabad might help itself to read these lines from the same poem and accordingly decide if it needs to change its approach:

We do not want your buildings
Do not set our huts on fire;
We do not require your forts,
Do not surround our hills;
We do not need your stores,
Do not ravage our fields;
We do not demand your ships,
Do not destroy our boats...

Themes of resistance, nationalism and identity are also replete in modern Sindhi poetry. For decades, Shaikh Ayaz's poetry has been an anthem for nationalists. And there continues to be resistance to the Islamist ideology in contemporary poetry despite the fact that Sindh is also being turned into a militant zone. The 1 February 2015 attack in Shikarpur where sixty-one people were bombed in an Imambargah comes as culmination of that unfortunate trend.

After the 16 December 2014 massacre at Army Public School, grief-struck as most, I turned to Rahmat Shah Sail's poem on Peshawar, 'City of Flowers':

When your pretty flesh is plucked like the petals of a flower
I watch in silence, for I have no power
When your precious blood is turned to drizzling rain
I perform your funeral rites with tears, for I have no power
O Peshawar! Our love is ancestral
I would never let you turn to smoke while I watch
O Peshawar! We share the blood of life, you and I
I'd never let you disappear while I watch
We are witnessing the force of history
O Peshawar! Bombs don't suit you.

Not all Pashtun poets have had the freedom to openly express themselves. In the tribal areas of North and South Waziristan, many have faced Taliban-imposed censorship. After the launch of military operations and with the mass exodus of people from the agency, dozens of poets also arrived in Bannu and soon they were back to composing poetry. One of the poets, Saleem Khan, once free of the adverse circumstances wrote about his life as a refugee:

My dignity, don't allow me to beg. Oh my poverty, you made me fight with my soul. Tell me, time, what kind of Pashtun I am that I have become so ugly.

My dignity, don't allow me to beg before anybody. Oh my poverty, you made me fight with my soul.' (Translated by Aamir Iqbal and Tim Craig.)

Across tribal areas, literary organizations have been active in voicing their ideas. In Parachinar, Speenghar Adabi Jirga advocates a secular society with participation of all sects. They bring out a monthly publication called *Speen Ghar*. In Mohmand agency, Mohmand Adabi Ghuncha has been holding peace *mushairas* (poetry recitals). In Bajaur, Pukhto Adabi Tolana has been active and poets continue answering the call of their muse despite the conflict in the Khyber Agency. Mureeb Mohmand quoted poet Saleem Zaheer saying: 'Us Waziristanisare suppressed from all sides ... Not only are we victims of militancy but of Pakistani society as well.' (*Express Tribune*, July 2014)

Akbar Sial, a Pashtun poet titled his collection 'No to War' and in one of his poems 'Rulers of the World', says:

'Don't snatch the pen from our hand
With which we make the picture of our dreams
Don't create violence in our village
Don't bring mayhem to our village
Don't turn this ancient playground
Into a blood-red ammo dump'

In Urdu a much larger corpus of resistance poetry exists. Kishwar Naheed has immortalized the cowardice of terrorists who are afraid of young girls:

Strong men
Afraid of little girls

Found everywhere
Identify them
They are capable of mischief
In this declining city
Be brave and have faith
Those afraid of little girls
Are worthless in their existence.

Fahmida Riaz continues to challenge orthodoxy and injustice. In her recent short poem she laments the society and the ruling classes in a classical style:

The long night has denuded the eyes of any light
The image of dawn turned out to be a mirage
So many fears lurk in the darkness
Every Khizar is suspicious, perhaps a looter
Every sleeve suspect of holding a dagger
Lost the belief, sincerity
Being robbed time and again
We have lost faith too.

Whatever one predicts about the future of Pakistan and its discontents, its poetry is likely to flourish as it attempts to calm its wounded residents. More importantly, it is not giving up on the ideal of a secular, tolerant Pakistan.

Published in *The Friday Times*, Pakistan, 6 February 2015.

ARTS

14

Public Spaces, Architecture and National Identity

❦

Pakistan's traumatic birth in 1947 and its iterative, fluid identity have defined much of its history. A country, ostensibly created for the rights of the Muslim minority in India, promised different things to the Muslim communities of an undivided India. For the modern, westernized and British-influenced Muslim intelligentsia, it was a haven for economic and political opportunity. For many clerics, it was the land where the Shariah would rule; for droves of subalterns, it was an idea to be explored and countenanced in pursuit of a better life.

The country's founder, Muhammad Ali Jinnah, was a secularist who mobilized Muslims invoking both religious and non-religious symbolism and agenda to create support for a separate country. However, Pakistan was not a given; its creation was only legitimized and actualized when the talks between political parties within India broke down. The British who were a weakened colonial power after the end of the Second World War were now moving out of the region.

Independence and the Partition of India took place in the fast-changing context of a post-war world. A 'moth-eaten' and 'truncated' Pakistan, to use the words of Jinnah, came into being on 15 August 1947.

From the very start, the civil bureaucracy – largely composed of the Muslim elites from the United Provinces – attempted to create a distinct identity for the country. The cultural conundrum was how Pakistan could be separated from its 'Indian', 'non-Muslim' past. Even the periods of Muslim rule between the twelfth and nineteenth centuries were not driven by Islamic edicts. Instead, the secular process of governance entailed principles of inclusivism, especially in terms of religious freedom. Conversely, with the adoption of an Islamic identity, the official Pakistan started to reimagine its history, inventing and recreating a mythological, glorious past and began to shun its non-Muslim heritage. This process was at variance with the population's everyday pluralist reality and this remains the case even after seven decades.

Perhaps the greatest of challenges in early Pakistan was the peculiar nature of its physical and cultural geography. Its more populous eastern wing consisted of a Bengali population with a rich cultural identity, pride in the Bangla language, and the relative acceptance of common cultural symbols with non-Muslims. West Pakistan (in 1971 this region became today's Pakistan after the eastern wing seceded) comprised multiple ethnic and linguistic groups, but its elites were wedded to the idea of one-nation-one-religion. As a political gimmick, it was later picked up by the military and to date remains the cornerstone of Pakistan's identity.

Overtime, the use of religion turned from a national unifier to a ploy of legitimizing military (and civilian) rule and authoritarianism. From 1948 to the 1980s, the Pakistani state passed a series of laws and enacted amendments to constitutions turning the country into a hybrid theocracy, or at least popularizing the Islamic nationalist goal that helped shape an anti-India strategic worldview and which then influenced three generations of Pakistanis.

❧

Public architecture reflects the political and religious identities and the creative capacity of a nation. Every society has its own collective, splintered character(s), and cross cutting historical narratives. The diversity of architecture also reflects various historical eras, aesthetic evolution and state-citizen relationships. In Pakistan, monuments and structures built during different eras of history overlap. The territory that is modern-day Pakistan is not a linear manifestation of history as imagined by post-1947. The oldest structures found in Pakistan date back to the Indus Valley Civilization -- around the third millennium BC. The succeeding empires which ruled the subcontinent left their imprint in the form of buildings, gardens and monuments. Even the design of cities such as Lahore, Multan, Bhera (in central Punjab), and Thattha, among others, testify to the unbreakable threads of a complex past.

It is important to ask how the new state asserted its worldview on public spaces.

The new and 'imagined' nation, Pakistan, inherited two dominant architectural styles: those that belonged to the so-called 'medieval' period and those that were constructed by the British Raj during the colonial era. Since 1947, however, a third type of public architectural design emerged. This 'Pakistani' sensibility is a cross between Pakistan's Mughal heritage, its avowedly 'Islamic' identity and 'modernity' that defined twentieth-century ideological and aesthetic movements.

As the new nation struggled to define and pursue its (often unclear) destiny, it constructed monuments, gardens and spaces which were reflective of complex and contradictory political dynamics. The question of identity – at the heart of Pakistan's political and social life – manifests itself in the national 'symbols' designed since 1947. The most significant cultural and design statement can be found in a national monument, the Minar-e-Pakistan (the tower of Pakistan), in Lahore. The monuments intersects with the real and imagined memory of the country.

The Minar-e-Pakistan Prototype

In 1940, the All India Muslim League passed a resolution in the city of Lahore demanding autonomy within the Indian polity for Muslim minority communities. The resolution did not ask for one single separate state. Post-1947 folk history has turned that event into a demand-for-Pakistan movement. It is now called the 'Pakistan resolution', taught to Pakistani children at schools and celebrated by states across the country as the political call for forming a separate state for Muslims.

It was at this time that the country's founder, Jinnah, articulated the famous 'two-nation theory': 'Hindus and Muslims belong to two different religious philosophies, social customs, and literatures. They neither inter-marry nor inter-dine together and, indeed, they belong to two different civilizations which are based mainly on conflicting ideas and conceptions ... It is quite clear that Hindus and Musalmans derive their inspiration from different sources of history.'

The ideo-political separation of Indian Muslims from their Hindu compatriots also entailed the assumption of distinct historical memory. For the Indian Muslims, the centuries-old Muslim rule 'defined and distinguished them from the other cultures and religions of the subcontinent.'[1]

To commemorate the anniversary of the Lahore Resolution, the military government of General Ayub Khan in the 1950s decided to build a national emblem in Lahore. Nasreddin Murat-Khan, a Pakistani of Russian origin, was entrusted to design and oversee the development of the project. Government officials asked that the tower be topped with a dome.[2] Though some consider Minar-e-Pakistan a replica of Paris's Eiffel Tower, the dome distinguishes Minar-e-Pakistan. It represents a commonly used symbol in Muslim architecture. The base of the Minar is illustrated with floral inscriptions, which include the text of the Lahore resolution in multiple languages. Qur'anic verses and the ninety-nine attributes of Allah are also inscribed in Arabic calligraphy on various plaques, as are excerpts from speeches of Jinnah and selected couplets from the national poet Allama Iqbal.

These inscriptions reflect a construction of Pakistan's identity that later became formally known as the 'ideology of Pakistan'. This so called 'ideology' was officially declared by another military government in late 1960s and made into orthodoxy by the third military government of General Zia ul Haq in the 1980s.

Minar-e-Pakistan, as a physical manifestation of Pakistani nationalism, adequately engages with Islamic references. The Minar also evokes the memory of Muslim invasions of the Indian Subcontinent. One of the earliest Muslim monuments in India happens to be the Qutab Minar[3] in Delhi built in the thirteenth century and which celebrates the conquest and rule of Turkic Sultans.

Remembering the Founder Jinnah

After the death of the country's founder, Quaid-i-Azam (the great leader) Muhammad Ali Jinnah, the state initiated the construction of a memorial as a tribute to him and invited international architects to submit their designs. The mandarins decided[4] that the memorial would be a blend of traditional Islamic and modern architecture. Yahya C. Merchant, an Indian architect, was assigned the task of designing and overseeing the work.[5] In 1960, the construction began. The main building of the mausoleum is distinguishable by its modern structure. A graceful, gold leaf-covered chandelier, with forty-eights haded lights in four tiers, was gifted by a Muslim association of China and hangs from the ceiling of the dome. Another distinguishing feature of Jinnah's mausoleum is the use of white marble, not unlike that of the glorious Mughal buildings such as the Taj Mahal.

In line with the Islamic architectural traditions, it was decided in the 1980s that a garden be developed on the premises of Jinnah's Mausoleum. In Islamic architecture, gardens are representations of the Qur'anic vision of paradise, an ideal garden reflecting symmetry, rhythm and order. This task was completed in the year 2000 under the rule of General Musharraf. It is ironic that the memory of the 'democrat' who created Pakistan was imagined, developed, extended and refined under three different military regimes.

New capital – Islam[abad]

Under the supervision of General Ayub Khan, the first military regime (1958–1968) embarked on an ambitious project of creating a new capital for the nation. Since Pakistan lacked a real capital, it was decided that a new city would be built. It was named Islamabad, with 'abad' as a traditional suffix relating to city. It was, on the whole, a religious and political symbol for a nation that revered Islam as its core identity.

The chosen site was close to the dominant province of Punjab in the western wing. The site selection, the cost and 'neglect' created much political resentment in the eastern wing. In the 1970 election that led to a civil war, the building of Islamabad by West Pakistani military elites was cited as one of the key grievances by the East Pakistan's politicians.

A Greek architect and urban planner, Constantinos Doxiadis, was hired to design the city. He based the design on a grid system with the north of the city facing Margalla hills.[6] It was the first planned city of Pakistan, which was divided into eight sectors and zones: the diplomatic enclave, the business district, the educational sector, the industrial area, and the housing sectors for the government's officers and employees, each with its own marketplace and a park.[7] Islamabad has grown beyond its original design and its contemporary reality reflects the distribution of political power, land and building conglomerates and an inept development authority that negotiates the interests of these power groups instead of an accountable, independent public service institution.

Since it was the seat of the government, a presidential complex housing the Office of the President, Parliament's building and a centre for Islamic ideology was constructed.

These three buildings were considered the core government machinery. The design of the buildings mix Islamic architecture influences with modern textures and lines.[8] The Prime Minister's Secretariat entails many opulent design features from Mughal architecture.

[Re]creating Public Spaces

The Charing Cross landmark in Lahore has remained the centre point of the city since the British era and continues to be the better-known venue for political mobilization. In 1904, a grand statue of Queen Victoria was placed under a canopy and the monument stood at the crossing until 1951. The statue was moved to the Lahore Museum thereafter. In the 1980s, during the 'Islamist' regime of General Zia, a wooden model of the Holy Quran was placed where the statue once stood. Earlier, under the civilian Prime Minister Zulfikar Ali Bhutto, another modernist tower was erected to mark the 1974-summit conference of the Organisation of Islamic Countries (OIC). The summit monument – as a cultural space – commemorates the ideal of Unity of all Muslims and that of the *Ummah* – the Muslim Brotherhood – and denotes a new acquired role by post-1971 Pakistan. These design innovations and reworking of the colonial landscape also indicate Pakistan's official aspirations to be a pure, unifying Muslim nation that follows religious commandments in both its public and international life.

It is not an isolated event that Pakistan's nuclear bomb has been officially termed the Islamic bomb. Its architects, Bhutto and General Zia, considered it a means to enhance Pakistan's place in the world and make it into a leader of the Ummah.

Despite its nuclear capability, it is unclear whether Pakistan has ever acquired that mythical position. Internally, the Muslims of Pakistan have been a victim of sectarian militias and since 1979, Pakistan is anything but a symbol of Muslim 'unity'.

Pakistani leaders relied on Islam to forge national cohesion and concurrently used pan-Islamism as a slogan. Prime Minister Bhutto, a firm believer in folk Islam, promoted symbols and adopted policies to secure the support of Islamist political parties. The 1973 Constitution advanced the Islamist cause, declaring Pakistan an Islamic Republic and Islam as the state religion. To promote pan-Islamism, Bhutto hosted a Summit of Organisation of Islamic Countries, and proposed the idea of establishing a 'Muslim Commonwealth'.[9]

General Zia-ul-Haq, who deposed Bhutto in a coup, joined hands with fundamentalist Jamaat-i-Islami (JI), and the traditional Sunni interpretation of Islam became the state policy. Though political and military elites practiced a modernist version of Islam, pronouncing a traditionalist version allowed Zia to legitimize his rule and establish control over the state and society.[10]

In the 1990s, short spells of civilian rule were unable to change the legacy of Bhutto and Zia. Also, the weak democratic governments were unsuccessful in balancing the demands to impose similar interpretations of Islamic Sharia with the aspirations of a reform-seeking multi-ethnic society, asking for progressive legislation. Islamist parties never gained enough electoral strength but their role as an ally of the military and intelligence agencies and street power is enough to keep a government under pressure. Owing to popular pressure, Nawaz Sharif introduced a Shariah Bill in 1991 that would have transformed the nation into an Islamic state and society, though this wasn't approved by the parliament. In 1999, he again attempted, in vain, to amend the constitution and make Sharia the supreme law of Pakistan but the Senate opposed the bill.

General Pervez Musharraf, who took over in a coup in 1999, promoted 'enlightened moderation' as an attempt to push back against militancy and extremism within Pakistan. This was also a response to post-9/11 alliance that Pakistan's military forged with the United States. Despite the public pronouncements, Musharraf only took half-hearted measures to control the Islamists. He ordered military operations in Pakistan's tribal regions, which bred popular resentment. Facing pressure, he withdrew several progressive changes announced by his government to the draconian blasphemy laws. He also co-opted Islamist parties by giving them power in two provinces for five years, and relied on the support of these parties to maintain his legitimacy.[11]

Militarization

Pakistan's army is not unique in its self-assumed role as a national unifier. Many countries in Asia and Latin America have also accorded such a role to their militaries. Pakistan's military has acquired influence over most facets of the country's political and social life, and now runs educational institutions, business groups and construction companies to build its own housing colonies. Such wide-ranging activities and a sizeable budgetary allocation provide it with the necessary resources to control the state and its policy. Furthermore, non-transparent military policies are designed and implemented in the name of 'national security' and 'national interest', granting the military the legitimacy to maintain its hegemony over the Pakistani state and society.[12]

Pakistan's militaristic identity is manifested through a public display of military weapons and religious war symbols. In Islamabad, a model of the Ghauri missile is centrally displayed. Ghauri is also the founder of the Sultanate dynasty in India during the twelfth century. At the entrance of Islamabad, a model of Chaghi Mountain, where Pakistan conducted its nuclear tests,[13] has been built. Such symbols of nuclear nationalism can now be found in public spaces across the country. Air bases across the country display the models and retired aircrafts flown by the Pakistan Air Force (PAF). In military cantonments, various military equipment items such as tanks adorn public squares.

In its early years, Pakistan turned into a national security state and with repeated martial laws, its original ethos now stands defined by its military muscle. *Pakistan Today,* a national newspaper recently lamented that militaristic pride and its inculcation through visual symbols 'underscore one of the major reasons behind the promotion of the culture of militancy which continues to fray the social fabric of the Pakistani society.'[14]

It is not uncommon to see children dressed as military personnel carrying toy weapons on national days such as 23 March -- which has turned into a day when Pakistan's military might, rather than its republican or democratic credentials, are presented to the nation. *Pakistan Today* rather forthrightly stated that the 'unending promotion of a militant mindset indicates why terrorist organizations continue to get fresh volunteers for suicide bombing. It is in the vital interest of the state to promote a culture of tolerance and inculcate the desire to turn Pakistan into a modern welfare state rather than a national security state.'[15]

The building of Pakistan's parliament, which houses both the National Assembly and the Senate, also reinforced the Islamic identity of Pakistan. The first Kalima of Islam, the line a person pronounces to join the Muslim religion, has been engraved on the edifice of the parliament of an Islamic country. The forehead of the parliament of Pakistan tells a clear story.

The Arabization

The Bhutto and Zia regimes also marked Pakistan's espousal of the increased role of the Gulf States in its political and economic life. Since the 1970s, the oil-rich Gulf States have been a major provider of employment to Pakistan's working class. As of early 2016, 8.7 million workers[16] were employed in Middle-Eastern countries, which in turn send nearly $20 billion as remittances to their families.[17] Saudi Arabia happens to be the largest source of remittances for Pakistan.[18]

In 1979, the Iranian revolution and the Soviet invasion of Afghanistan were opportunities for Pakistan's military to build formidable ties with the Saudis and the western powers. Within a short period of time a Sunni–jihadist coalition with Pakistan at its centre emerged both to contain Iran's Shiite influence and to expel the Soviets through jihad. The political and social consequences of such policy choices have been drastic to say the least and merit a separate discussion. However, the power of the Middle East started to manifest itself as the state espoused a more rigid Islamic identity partly inspired by the Gulf countries in particular the tenets of the Wahabbi strand of Islam practiced in Saudi Arabia.

The Faisal Mosque in Islamabad – a global symbol of Pakistan and its capital – is named after King Faisal of Saudi Arabia, who provided generous funding for its construction. It also happens to be Pakistan's largest mosque. The design of Faisal Mosque fuses contemporary structural lines with a traditional Bedouin Arab's tent and the conventional minarets. Unlike other symbols of Islamic architecture, especially in South Asia, it lacks a dome and pillars. In a way, Faisal Mosque also shows a break from the Indo-Persian legacy of Pakistan as its state through a public statement announcing its allegiance with the [Islamic] Middle East (as opposed to India, the 'non-Muslim' neighbour and Iran, the minority Shia Muslim state).

Faisal Mosque accommodates more than 300,000 worshippers at a time. During religious occasions like Eid, national leaders of Pakistan offer their prayers at this mosque. It is no coincidence that the champion of Sunni (sectarian) Islamization, the architect of a full-throttled jihadist policy, General Zia, is buried within the premises[19] of the mosque. In recent years, seminaries have also grown in and around the mosque. The capital of Islamabad itself is home to more than 401 seminaries[20] representing a high density of seminary growth experienced by an otherwise small city by Pakistani standards.

Islamabad's design as a deliberate spatial order and linearity with symbols of Islamic grandeur and military prowess is encircled[21] by religious seminaries today. The 2007-Red Mosque conflict also testifies to the power of religious lobbies as the military operation against this law-breaking mosque and seminary could not result in a vacation of the premises. Ironically, President Musharraf who ordered the operation faces a trial for it and the chief cleric who wants to bring down Pakistan's constitution and governance structures has been acquitted of all charges by the courts. Nothing could be a more disturbing metaphor for the direction of the state.

Concluding Thoughts

The purpose of this essay was not to present a comprehensive political history or a review of how public design has been imagined. But the key aim here was to highlight the moments in the nation's history where ideas about imagination of an Islamic homeland, a unifier of world Ummah, the military might, have intersected, overlooking the folk traditions and diversity of Pakistan. Half of the country was lost in 1971 in pursuit of a centralized, linear imagination of a nation. Because the state's ideology remains religious and centralized, battles between traditionalists and modernists, between regional identities and central diktat, continue today. The people of Pakistan have chosen many a form of artistic, political expression to defy the centralized identity of Pakistani culture. This is a separate topic for inquiry. For now, it is important to remember that the Pakistani state's efforts to forge a one-religion, one-culture 'identity' remain both unaccomplished and bitterly contested. Efforts to cement national identities through public design require material progress, and people's participation in the political processes for long-term, substantive traction.

Submitted for Encyclopedia of Asian Design, Volume 2.

15

Global Icon, Unsung at Home

❧

'Not to be boxed in, to be able to transcend boundaries: for an artist, it's essential.'

It is a pity that I got to discover Shahzia Sikander's work only after I left Pakistan. After her initial successes in the 1990s, with her migration to the United States, she slowly disappeared from the local art scene and the narratives within her country of birth, almost rendered invisible, like the mythical characters one reads in folklore. In a different country, she would be celebrated for being a global icon, intensely original and gifted. Though not in her country of birth where talent is subjugated to the cliques that define 'excellence' and where history has to be doctored to make the present legible and comfortable.

Sikander graduated from the National College of Arts in 1991. Her innovative work struck everyone since she had done something remarkable with the miniature form. Reinterpreting the format of a traditional Indo-Persian miniature, she crafted a personal relationship and in a way liberated it from the clutches of 'tradition'. Prior to her work, the late Zahoor ul Akhlaq inducted postmodern ideas during

211

the 1970s and 1980s and suggested how miniature remained
a relevant form for 'contemporary' artists. In his own work
he borrowed elements of the miniature form and merged
them with the abstract style he practiced. Sikander went
beyond and, using miniature as the foundation for her work,
created something new. Her teacher Ustad Bashir Ahmed
encouraged her and thus began the great revival. Later, Imran
Qureshi, Aisha Khalid, Ambreen Butt, Saira Wasim and many
others took this movement forward and they are all globally
celebrated artists in their own right.

Soon after a short stint at NCA, Sikander left for the
US and joined the Rhode Island School of Design where
she earned a Masters degree in 1995. The global audience,
particularly in the American art academe and practice, was
stunned by the sheer creative force exhibited by the young
Pakistani artist. Much of her work in the 1990s is about
pushing the boundaries; and she continues to strive to create 'a
new language', as she calls it. The Scroll (1988–91), a five feet
long miniature visualized her own relationship and intimacy
with the medium, where she mapped her home and its details,
architectural limits and imagination with a woman protagonist
dressed in white. That woman, the artist, was almost a ghost
as Sikander explained to me roaming around centuries of
'tradition' and finding her own space in a busy environment. It
would not be an exaggeration to say that Sikander is a pioneer
of a new form and during the last twenty years or so countless
young artists have been inspired by her exploration.

Sikander's departure from Pakistan was beneficial for her
artistic journey, like her departure from the traditional form
of miniature. At Rhode Island she dabbled in new media
and conversed with the feeling of being uprooted that she

must have experienced at some level. Inspired by Eva Hesse and Ana Mendieta's works, Sikander too created many versions of a female heroine traversing between cultures, borders and religions. Another Residency at the Glassell School of Art in Houston enabled her to experiment with scale. So the miniature form – the basis of her creative muse – turned into massive murals that continued her own conversation and intimacy with the form. By creating wall and floor drawing, Sikander was setting a new frontier to be followed by others a decade later. Where she was once an apparition turned into an abode – both a refuge and a means of protest. This subversion required the kind of confidence and skill that only Sikander possessed. Perhaps this is what makes her work incredibly original and path breaking.

In 1997, Sikander moved to New York and there was one success after the other. Her works were displayed in the Whitney Biennial that year, and she was the first Pakistani artist to be featured in the landmark exhibition that occurs every two years. Thus began her dazzling and bolder experimentation with form and content. At Yerba Buena Center for the Arts in San Francisco, she studied and incorporated street-art by creating drawings directly on the wall. At the Cleveland Center for Contemporary Art (2001) her wall installations turned three-dimensional as she became interested in the dimensional capacity of tissue paper. By 2001, Sikander was working on animation and in all the forms she worked, drawing and engagement with the miniature art form evidently stayed with her. Except that it found new meaning through her own explorations of identity, migration and understanding of the 'other'. A variety of media including animation, video, mural, and collaboration with other artists since the 2000s has turned her art work into an intricate process of navigating and challenging 'contested cultural and political histories'.

As she told me, it was vital to respect and acknowledge the autonomy of the 'other' and this is why multiculturalism does not appeal to her as a reference to her works. Sikander's hallmark is that she stands out everywhere even when engaging with elements of American, South American and other cultures and never loses sight of their sovereignty.

Sikander's video animation *The Last Post*, which takes the opium trade and the British East India Company as a point of departure was installed in Norman Foster's Kogod Hall, a space between the Smithsonian American Art Museum and the National Portrait Gallery in Washington, D.C. Sikander says that her 'process' focuses on rediscovering cultural and political frontiers, to 'create new frameworks for dialogue and visual narrative'. Contemporaneity is about remaining relevant by challenging the status quo, not by clinging to past successes. She challenged the traditional and contemporary divide and holds that deconstruction in her narratives is a means to re-imagine 'historical content and entrenched symbols…open the discourse' and 'to challenge and re-examine our histories'.

An earlier digital animation *SpiNN* (2003) satirized cable channel CNN as it highlighted the mass of spiralling, abstracted forms, almost like a swarm of angry black crows or bats that land at a Mughal durbar hall. In turn the hall is full of gopis whose black hairdos turn into the central motif underlying women's agency. In *Unseen Series* (2011), large-scale HD projections deal with landscape in the night, where drawings are juxtaposed with architecture and foliage. A multi-armed female form refers to Doris Duke looming over Shangri La;

and her majestic home overlooking the Pacific (where her ashes were sprinkled).

Later in 2011, Sikander travelled to Sharjah to participate in a local biennale. Inspired by the desert and observing the coastline at Hormuz resulted in *Parallax* – a 15 metres long, cinema-sized video installation. The *Parallax* employed hundreds of miniature drawings and gouaches and turned them into living animations. They replicate and separate and resemble images of soil, sand, water and blood providing an overview of Hormuz only to transform into flocks of innumerable birds, black oil and then hordes of people. It delineates the narrative of power, control and its complicated relationship with nature.

It is a sign of her success in evolving a unique global language that Sikander's work is included in the permanent collections across the globe. In the US, the Museum of Modern Art, New York, The Hirshhorn Museum and Sculpture Park, the Whitney Museum of American Art, the Solomon R. Guggenheim Museum, the San Francisco Museum of Modern Art, Museum of Fine Arts, Boston, Philadelphia Museum of Fine Arts, Museum of Contemporary Art, Los Angeles, and many more exhibit her paintings and installations. Outside the US, The Museum of Contemporary Art Tokyo, Royal Ontario Museum, Centro Nazionale per le Arti Contemporanea Rome, Bradford City Museum, Art Gallery of New South Wales, the Birmingham Museum, the Burger Collection, Hong Kong, MAXXI Museum, Rome among others showcase her work. In 2015, Asia Society has honoured her for having made a 'significant contributions' to contemporary art.

The honours started with her achieving the Shakir Ali and the Haji Sharif Awards at NCA in 1992. During the last two decades she earned the Art Prize in Time-Based Art from Grand Rapids Museum (2014), the Inaugural Medal of Art by Hilary Rodham Clinton (2012), John D. and Catherine T. MacArthur Foundation Achievement 'Genius' award, (2006-2011); SCMP Art Futures Award, Hong Kong International Art Fair (2010), The DAAD, (Berliner Künstlerprogramm, Deutscher Akademischer Austauschdienst) Berlin (2007-08), Tamgha-e-Imtiaz, the National Pride of Honour by the Pakistani Government (2005). *The Newsweek* in 2004 listed her as one of the most important South Asians transforming the American cultural landscape. In 2006, the World Economic Forum, appointed her as a Young Global Leader and in 2010, Sikander was elected a National Academician by the National Academy in New York City.

Sikander's two decades of practice has seen three distinct phases: first, pushing the boundaries of miniature and subverting the tradition; second, the early 2000s where she distanced from the form but not its essence and delved into larger questions of global relevance. Her third and more recent phase is turning her art practice into a three dimensional endeavour where the form holds a dialogue with the content, the artist engages in a discourse with her medium; and the viewer is pulled into that conversation. This is reflected in her recent works such as *Parallax* and 'The cypress despite its freedom is held captive by the garden' based on a dilapidated cinema Khorfakkan and a Pakistani labourer.

This amazing repertoire, unmatched by any artist of her generation, is nearly invisible in her own country. As Faisal Devji wrote last year in a hard-hitting piece entitled 'Little Dictators': 'Sikander's pioneering work is under threat, being routinely censored...' Devji cited two books – *Modernism and*

the Art of Muslim South Asia and *Art and Polemic in Pakistan*
(by Iftikhar Dadi), *Cultural Politics and Tradition in Contemporary
Miniature Painting* (by Virginia Whiles) that ignored the
'foundational character' of Sikander's work. These are two
major art histories of Pakistan and both omit Sikander's vital
contribution to contemporary Pakistani art at home and
abroad. Devji added, 'If anyone can break this stranglehold on
the narrative of Pakistan's cultural history, it is Sikander, who
achieved global fame in the pre-9/11 world and whose work
is not over-determined by the 'war on terror,' itself now an
aesthetic commodity.' (*Newsweek Pakistan*, February, 2014).

The two authors however denied the deliberate omission
and cited research frames for not mentioning Sikander. Devji
responded with another long piece on the factionalized art
world of Pakistan. Sikander has also been accused of not
engaging with Pakistan even though much of her work abroad
has referred to the country where she was born and trained;
and throughout the world she is known as a 'Pakistani' artist.

This is not surprising. Skipping Sikander's story is a
figment of the larger Pakistani malaise to deny its own history.
Reinventing histories and concealing information is a larger
trend at work. Take the example of 1971: the memory of the
Bengalis, their struggle and independence is something we
have erased. Sikander's central role in redefining the scope of
miniature and globalizing its form, acknowledged by the world,
is ironically not mentioned in art histories being compiled
within the country. Pakistan generally has a problem with its
citizens recognized abroad: be it Dr Salam or Malala, there is
a strange, complex reaction at work. It has something to do
with a country not at peace with its identity and position in
the world.

When I arrived at her New York studio on a freezing December afternoon, I felt as if I had entered into an ocean of possibilities – exhibited, un-exhibited, familiar and unfamiliar. Almost like the magical *zanbeel* (bag) of the mythical Amar Ayyar. There were grand works in progress, nothing similar to what I have seen. And hundreds of works that inform her installations, projections, etc., were scattered. On the wall on the right, I saw the original 'Scroll' that was unbelievably mesmerizing. It took a few minutes for me to travel within this extraordinary work. We had been exchanging emails over the past decade and this very first meeting was therefore quite special. I remember sending her an email exactly a decade ago to which she responded promptly. I had seen some of her work and could not believe that powerful ideas could be treated in such a delicate manner.

Sikander's brush with global academe has also turned her into a unique artist with a formidable verbal expression. I had hundreds of questions and she responded with stories – personal, technical and political. It turned out to be one of those conversations where one simply wants to hear and travel with the narrator: into the words, into the syllables, into the subtext. Sikander told me how her own hybrid identity was constantly shifting with the conceptual boundaries she recognized and challenged. Her art therefore was an open-ended conversation with herself and the craft she had innovated over the years.

Slender, tough and brimming with energy, she is an enchanting persona. From the paintings and installations, we moved to her computer where she showed me her animations. I have to confess that I have not seen something so original before. Sikander's craft as a post-miniaturist is so central to her range that one cannot miss the haunting intensity of her lines and strokes. Projecting them on larger scales and in different media transforms the tradition into an entirely new artistic style.

Sikander was perturbed about the fact that she was being put through a loss of her own history which she 'owned'. The year 2014 was tough for her with all the commentary by her peers and art critics in Pakistan. She had been accused of catering to the West. 'I respond to my own quest and medium with which I work,' she added. In fact, Sikander's poignant work entitled 'The Resurgence of Islam' was painted in 1999 (two years before 9/11) and it remains one of the more nuanced renderings on the subject. My advice was to completely ignore what is said since her work was the best answer to all the jibes and criticism. Sikander agreed but only partially.

'Success is not what it is perceived to be. It's a lot of hard work and almost a hermit-like existence' she remarked, when I asked her about her meteoric rise on the global art scene. 'It's all push, push, learn to invent...all the time', she added. Referring to the process of painting she called it 'meditative' and this is why being a hermit has become her second nature. Looking at her oeuvre, I cannot help but agree. How could anyone produce so much if he or she were not a hermit!

I also saw her recent work that was featured in The New York Times. Aptly titled, 'The World Is Yours, the World Is Mine', it reflects on the news about the Ebola outbreak from Africa to the US and how isolation was being conducted in a globalized world through screenings and quarantines. Playing with the idea of active and dormant microbes, Sikander transports it onto the broader story of how 'narratives lie dormant until someone culls them from history's rubble.'

Sikander wants to work more on 1971 as a means to familiarize herself with the history that she was not taught. In that process she would perhaps reclaim some of her own histories that have been taken away by the art establishment of Pakistan. The best way to view Shahzia Sikander's work is to look at the themes of displacement and the universal need for 'fictive transport' (to borrow the term from artist David Hunt) from the 'more personalized sense of alienation that clings to each of us.'

I am still struggling to grapple with her work and by no means have I engaged with even a fraction of an incredibly vast and rich corpus. The good part is that Sikander has promised to continue the conversation: both with viewers (such as myself) and with that delicate, layered craft of hers.

Published in The *Friday Times*, Pakistan, 20 February 2015.

16

Neo Miniature: The New Face of Pakistani Art

❧

Steeped in the past, and yet, modernist in its application, neo-miniature is the new face of Pakistani art. Having evolved as a genre that is entirely indigenous in its expressions, it has also globalized Pakistani cultural idiom and has inspired a generation of artists within and outside the country. The neo-miniature movement is located within the resilience of Pakistani society as well as its struggle to reinvent aesthetic and cultural parameters of identity.

Nearly two generations of Pakistani artists have experimented with the traditional genre of miniature art; some have even gone on to expand its scope and vocabulary. It is on the shoulders of such artistic endeavour and innovation that Pakistan's neo-miniature movement has now turned global.

Neo-miniatures retain traditional techniques while incorporating contemporary themes, and some have even deconstructed the format and articulated sensibilities that would otherwise be identified with postmodernism.

Its entry into the Western markets – galleries and private collections – is a recognition of the rigorous technique and innovative thematic inferences employed by Pakistani artists. Undoubtedly, Pakistani art has found a discernible niche in the global art market.

'In the postmodern framework, where skill has been put on the back burner in preference to conceptual art, miniature is viewed with much awe and fetches high prices,' says Nafisa Rizvi, an eminent art critic and curator. 'Gallery owners and curators tend to emphasize the painstaking and meticulous effort needed to undertake a painting of this nature.'

The neo-miniature movement is not a continuation of tradition or a completely new event. It is located within the resilience of Pakistani society and its struggle to reinvent aesthetic and cultural parameters of identity and social change. This is one of the key reasons why the world takes it so seriously and provides patronage to it.

Rizvi notes that of the two Pakistani artists invited by documenta (an exhibition of contemporary art which takes place every five years in Kassel, Germany) for the first time in our history, one was the miniaturist Khadim Ali.

'Khadim Ali, an Afghan Hazara, has found the freedom to express the persecution of Hazara community, something that may not have been possible without global patronage,' explains Iftikhar Dadi, an art historian at Cornell University.

'Pakistani artists who fetch the highest prices and are represented by galleries abroad include key miniaturists,' adds Rizvi.

After 9/11, the miniature movement found renewed and greater resonance in the West. The earlier themes that the iconoclasts had chosen – the burqa motif, clerics, nihilism – had become both relevant and exploratory.

As Dadi puts it, 'The playfully subversive miniature was well-suited to participate in a globalized and postmodern cultural sphere in which Pakistani art is inextricably linked to diasporic practices, international mega-exhibitions and promotion by Western galleries.'

The interest in Pakistan and the quest to understand it better also contributed to wider interest. Aisha Khalid's work, for example, which questions the concept of veiling, gender hierarchies and the repetition of Arabesque pattern, found great traction.

Saira Wasim's explorations of the US foreign policy and the 'war on terror' narratives under the Bush administration were visual allegories that highlighted manipulation and exercise of imperial power not unlike the Mughal court. Her works have also been used as book covers.

But the movement has had its naysayers too: art critic Virginia Whiles in her recent book *Art and Polemic in Pakistan* explains that the neo-miniature movement is split between the traditionalists who prefer to work within conventional boundaries, and the iconoclasts who have broken the shackles of convention and given the form a new dimension.

It is the power of the latter group that has turned the courtly miniature into a radical form of artistic expression. The movement therefore found resonance in the West where Pakistani artists have negotiated global trends using the intimate, demanding techniques of miniature painting.

Many trailblazers in this group emerged from the National College of Arts (NCA), Lahore, originally known as the Mayo

School of Art. The institution had been set up by the British in an attempt to preserve and mainstream traditional South Asian art forms.

With the decline of the Mughal Empire, the advent of British colonists and photography, tradition witnessed a rupture. Patronage, not unlike music, was relegated to regional kingdoms and principalities. Patronage had enabled the miniature form to flourish for nearly a millennium; and the colonial period saw its decline.

But it was only in the 1990s when younger artists such as Shahzia Sikander, Imran Qureshi, Aisha Khalid and others, under the tutelage of the legendary instructor Bashir Ahmed at the NCA, spearheaded the new miniature movement. Almost all the influential contemporary miniature artists have been trained at this art institution.

Iftikhar Dadi credits Abdur Rahman Chughtai (1897–1975) as the first major Pakistani artist to revive Mughal miniature style after the independence. From 1980s onwards, artist Zahoor ul Akhlaq (1941–1999) employed the stylistic features of the tradition to create a new, modern sensibility.

In fact, Akhlaq also oversaw the setting up of a miniature painting department at the NCA along with Bashir Ahmed. Akhlaq's own work explored conceptual and formal scale of miniature painting. His vision became the basis for a major movement a decade later.

Critics such as the late Akber Naqvi were initially sceptical about miniature's 'revival'. But ardent defenders such as artists-educators Salima Hashmi and Naazish Ataullah, among others, carried forward the legacy of Zahoor ul Akhlaq and some of their gifted students such as Shahzia Sikander and Imran Qureshi. Their involvement as academics is an important element of the revival and new avatar of the miniature movement.

But greater success abroad has also brought about greater critique and introspection at home. Despite the wide corpus of outstanding artistic output and its global acceptance, there have been critical voices questioning the authenticity of tradition and practice.

Commodification, for instance, has been cited as a pitfall of this movement where, according to critics, some younger artists have indulged in copycat formulas for commercial success.

The rise of the miniature painting at the end of the twentieth century, according to Quddus Mirza, artist, art critic and educator, was a 'search for forging an identity in response to Western influences in realms of politics, culture, economy and science.'

. Miniature was viewed as an authentic aesthetic practice of the South Asian region. Mirza agrees that there was an element of exotica at work.

'Foreign visitors preferred to purchase miniature for its size, made with exquisite skill and labour,' he says. With an increased attention of the outside world, 'local collectors also picked miniature as the most suitable art form'. The local and global intertwined over time.

But the exoticism that miniatures reproduce and reinforce, especially for the foreign market, is a matter of intense debate within Pakistani art circles.

Rizvi holds that 'allure of the miniature is embedded with shades of Orientalism' as it stirs the exotica associated with traditions of the East.

'The flattened perspective, the bright jewel-like organic colours, the architectural details, and dress reiterate the South Asian cultures of yore,' she contends.

But simultaneously, the art critic argues, many artists have climbed on to what has become a neo-miniature bandwagon as the market is not only accepting of this genre but displays all the signs of growing. While the market is currently undervalued, prices will continue to soar before they fall.

'One reason for the sale of new miniatures is that these are easy to display and transport,' Rizvi adds.

Quddus Mirza confirms that miniature for both 'practical and aesthetic reasons' is a sought-after major at the NCA as the earlier artists' successes have inspired a younger generation of students.

'The relatively easy potential for selling, storing and making, in comparison to other disciplines such as painting, printmaking and sculptures, which need larger studio space, storage, etc., makes it an attractive discipline,' argues Mirza.

But artist Imran Qureshi dismisses the 'commodification' argument and holds that 'miniatures are just like other genres – prints and paintings, etc.'

In fact, he cautions, an inordinate focus on this aspect minimizes what the movement has already achieved in terms of globalizing Pakistani cultural idiom and inspiring a generation of artists within and outside Pakistan.

For those seeking inspiration, Shahzia Sikander remains the first of the radicals whose thesis work at the NCA subverted both the formalistic pattern as well as the thematic content. Her famed work 'Scroll' incorporated elements of architecture, autobiography and contemporary art sensibilities, thereby setting into motion a new vocabulary.

Sikander credits both the rigorous training by Bashir Ahmad and a lecture by Victoria and Albert Museum, (V&A) London, scholar Robert Skelton that gave her 'a window on the diversity within the historical miniature painting genre itself.'

Nafisa Rizvi holds that the 'allure of the miniature is embedded with shades of Orientalism' as it stirs the exotica associated with traditions of the East.

After completing her MFA from the United States, Sikander started exhibiting her works across the country and gradually built an audience that was ready to converse with the complexity and range of contemporary miniature form. Others followed suit.

In 1999, Sikander exhibited at the Hirshhorn Museum in Washington DC. 'Initially there was limited interest in the miniature form and this was one of the reasons that I chose a contemporary art museum to highlight its relevance,' she says.

Sikander wanted to reach out to critics and historians outside of the miniature painting field so that they could fathom the immense potential in the form.

Another celebrated miniaturist, Imran Qureshi, holds that his training at the NCA made him discover a new language for the genre. The creative process emanating from his intimacy with the miniature form enabled him to 'break the boundaries as an independent artist.'

In 2003, Qureshi curated the Karkhana project – inspired by the Mughal court studio workshop – and its first show. This collaborative endeavour included five other artists – Aisha Khalid, Hasnat Mahmood, Nusra Latif Qureshi, Talha Rathore and Saira Wasim – who worked on twelve paintings. This avant-garde, collective work was vital to the re-imagination of

miniature form in recent times. Karkhana 'democratized' the
art form, says Qureshi.

Other notable artists who have been torchbearers of
this revivalist movement include Faiza Butt, Hamra Abbas,
Ahsan Jamal, Mahreen Zuberi, Mohammad Zeeshan, Tazeen
Qayyum, among others. As Qureshi explains, 'This is truly a
popular and robust art movement in contemporary times.'

Another artist trained in miniature craft who came to the
US to study was Ambreen Butt. 'The West knew of miniature
painting as the art of the "other", almost folksy,' says Butt. 'They
had no idea of its contemporary practice up until the early
1990s and academia had a major role in promoting it.'

She adds that such amalgamation of the past and the present
has fascinated global art viewers. 'I have been working for the
past twenty-two years in the US but my connection with this
genre keeps on redefining itself,' she adds.

Imran Qureshi's decade-long exhibits in Sharjah, Europe
and the US popularized the form and found a receptive
art community of critics, collectors and galleries. His 2009
exhibit 'Hanging Fire' at Asia Society Museum in New York
and the installation commenting on terrorist violence among
other themes, at the rooftop of Metropolitan Museum of Art
in 2013 testified to the adaptation of scale and drama within
the genre of the miniature.

Meanwhile, Mirza believes that the practitioners of neo-
miniature did not restrict themselves to the form, but created
works in multiple mediums, formats, imagery and concerns.

Rashid Rana who is another globally renowned
contemporary artist, was also trained at the NCA in similar
traditions that Zahoor ul Akhlaq set during his teaching and
art-practice. Rana works with the new media and even in

his digital style, one of his 2002 works is entitled 'I Love Miniatures'.

This poignant production weaves a Mughal emperor's profile through countless billboards for products and films. Rana's work is both an extension and a critique of the tradition where structure of a miniature and its micro details can be explored and reinvented.

The immersion of neo-miniature in the academy and global art dynamic continues.

Sikander recalls that her decision, in the initial years, to work with the academic institutions across the US was 'instinctive'. It has enabled the inclusion of contemporary miniature painting into textbooks and academic art schools.

'Art 21 documentary in 1999–2000 focusing on my work at that time was reaching out to more than 5,000 high schools,' says Sikander.

Qureshi was commissioned by London Underground and is currently working on a major show at Barbican London. In fact, his public installations in many countries have contributed to furthering the possibilities of this form.

Iftikhar Dadi articulates a similar view: 'Global patronage is not limited to art galleries or collectors. Private foundations, not-for-profit organizations and such other academic institutions have also espoused the extraordinary work coming out of Pakistan. When did art not need legitimating by the state or market? One can find individual artistic paths, but the terms of recognition are no longer national in today's world.'

Any art form to flourish requires a frame of recognition. The global patronage to the neo-miniature movement is constructing a new framework for Pakistani artists, both within and outside the country.

In fact, artistic experiments beyond the national boundaries have liberated artists, including the miniaturists, from the constraints of cultural and political environment in Pakistan. Without a doubt, this is another testament to the possibilities inherent within the Indo-Persian miniature art form that finds revival centred in Pakistan.

Published in *Dawn*, Pakistan, 10 January 2016.

17

About Suffering They Were
Never Wrong

Pakistani art going global is a remarkable story for it typifies the ineffable contradictions of the country. In part it is a testament to the country's creative expression, an explosion of sorts; and partly a mode of resistance to the anti-art ideology that is permeating the social fabric. It's not just paintings or the booming art galleries, there is a revival underway of the moribund television drama, the resuscitation of cinema and continuous experimentation with music.

Salima Hashmi, a leading arts academician and practitioner noted in a recent essay that the 'proverbial worst of times are certainly the best of times for contemporary Pakistani art.' Our foremost historian, Ayesha Jalal in her latest book *The Struggle for Pakistan* views the creative expression as a resistance to Pakistan's forced Islamization. Jalal writes: 'The globalization of Pakistani music has been accompanied by a remarkable leap in the transnational reach of the creative arts…a younger generation of painters are making creative uses of new ideas and technologies to both access and influence a diverse and dynamic transnational artistic scene. The dazzling array of new directions in the contemporary art, literature and music of Pakistan displays an ongoing tussle between an officially constructed ideology of nationalism and relatively autonomous social and cultural processes in the construction of a "national culture".

Jalal as a contemporary historian reminds us that the domestic battle of ideas and ideologies is not over and is assuming newer shapes. At the same time, the issue of a crumbling Pakistani state haunts the future trajectory. Is the arts and literature renaissance of sorts an antidote to a state unable to fulfil its basic functions such as securing the lives of its citizens? There are some immediate examples from the subcontinent that come to mind: the reigns of Wajid Ali Shah and Bahadur Shah Zafar in nineteenth-century India were also remarkable for their artistic endeavours before the final takeover of the British. Not entirely relevant, these are important phases of our recent history to be remembered.

Pakistan's blossoming arts scene, literature festivals and musical innovations notwithstanding, the country is bleeding; and not-so-silently imploding. Other than its global image problem, not entirely as fabricated as Pakistanis have been made to believe, the country is mired in a culture of denial. The delusions nurtured by its state, its intelligentsia and citizens are stuff that mythologies are made of. The greatest of such maladies is negotiating an identity for itself. The 'Islamic' identity is now giving way to a sectarian one. No longer is it enough to be a Muslim, as the contest over who is a Muslim remains unresolved. In the 1950s, a judicial commission composed of Justices Munir and Kayani had highlighted this cleavage:

Keeping in view the several definitions given by the
ulema, need we make any comment except that no two
learned divines are agreed on this fundamental? If we
attempt our own definition as each learned divine has
done and that definition differs from that given by all
others, we unanimously go out of the fold of Islam.
And if we adopt the definition given by any one of
the ulema, we remain Muslims according to the view
of that alim, but kafirs according to the definition of
everyone else.

Despite this clarity of thought, the political elites and military
continued to use religion as a tool of politics and maximization
of power. By the late 1960s, as enunciated by General Sher
Ali Pataudi, a minister in Yahya Khan's cabinet, the ideology
of Pakistan (a vague concept) turned into a cornerstone of
Pakistani nationhood. Citizenship and faith gradually became
synonymous and the rights of Pakistani people became more
and more nebulous.

Pakistan's parliament, in a rather dramatic move, declared
the Ahmadi community non-Muslim in 1974. In the 1980s,
following the Iranian revolution, the official patronage of
anti-Shia militias started. Since then, targeting of Shias has
been on the rise and now the term 'Shia genocide' – earlier
frowned upon by experts – is entering into popular discourse.
Iran, according to Pakistan's official quarters, also sponsors
groups in Pakistan but the majority-minority dynamic sets an
unfavourable balance of power in this deadly game.

By the early 1990s, in the relentless wave of Islamization,
the country also amended its blasphemy laws and made them

even more draconian. The Christians, among others, have borne the brunt of this law.

This trajectory of the country's history has found resonance in contemporary art as well. Saira Wasim, a gifted artist from Pakistan, now based in the United States, has continued to depict the state of her homeland (and its position in the world) through a candid and allegorical lens for the past decade and a half. She has, rather remarkably, taken up taboo themes such as the naked hypocrisy of Pakistan's leaders, the mullahs, and 'honour' killings of women. Wasim has not spared the contradictory imperatives of global politics either and employed satire to lampoon US policies, especially under George Bush. This trajectory of the country's history has found resonance in contemporary art to create a new kind of postmodern miniature.

Wasim graduated from the National College of Arts in 1999 and not surprisingly found international recognition soon enough. In 2003, her works were featured in a show at the Whitney Museum of American Art. In the same year, she undertook a residency at the Vermont Studio Center. Since then the US has been her home.

Wasim's artistic expression is also influenced by her personal story. An Ahmadi by faith, she has experienced persecution and knows the intricacies of marginalization, and the hysteria for a puritanical patriotism. Her monumental work 'Patriotism' set the trend of making art a powerful mode of resistance. This was before she migrated to the US. The miniature challenged the construction of religious nationalism by depicting a motely crew of Mullahs – of almost all creeds and varieties – waging jihad, and a group of armed young men following their creed.

This painting was completed before 9/11 and many in Pakistan who consider Pakistan's predicament to be a result of the US War on Terror must see this chilling expression of national 'identity'. The young artist, barely out of college then, was seeing it all and had the gift to document it in miniature format. Fifteen years later a good number of young Pakistanis have been confused by Pakistan's rulers to the extent that violence always has a 'justification' and the perpetrators are almost always 'foreign'.

Wasim therefore is in exile, a marginalized citizen of Pakistan and of course a woman who has come a long way. She had to challenge family conventions to become an artist. These layers of exclusion and struggle are evident from her choice of themes and ability to unpack exploitative coatings of contemporary politics and society.

Throughout her work, Wasim has employed allegorical references, almost like a traditional Persian and Urdu poet. But she told me that her familiarity with Western art gave her the thought to fuse ideas. Her meticulous craft and the virtuosity of portraits and scenes make her miniatures a visual delight. In the post-9/11 world, Wasim's work turned comical but hid tragedies under that thin veneer of comedy. These tragedies were global, local and personal but never morose, as comic relief kept a little door open -- for hope and for redemption. The 2004 series, 'Passion Cycle', in minimalist terms, depicts a group of extremists who are both the leaders and the led, commenting on their version of jihad.

The evidently Mughal narratives in her work are re-crafted with a touch of photo-realism. Her works have lampooned Musharraf and his alliance with the West and well-known clerics in Pakistan are often framed in carnivalesque farces. The

American version of globalization gets a critique and so does its reaction: the various shades of Islamic extremism. In *Ronald McDonald Comes to Your Town (2009)*, Wasim depicted the McDonald's clown holding the American flag while riding on a liminal deity. Another important painting of hers in my view is called 'Identity?' that narrates the tale of a global Muslim in the contemporary age. The miniature was completed after a Pakistani-American, Faisal Shahzad, tried to carry out a terror attack at Times Square in New York in 2010. Wasim plays on the theme of identity as an American, Pakistani and Muslim. This painting is a reinterpretation of the sixteenth-century Mughal painting, 'Nasrat-e-Jang' (victorious in War). The figure 'Khan Dawan' participated in and led major battles of his time to protect his country but spent much his life in spreading peace and shunning wars. The painting hints at American-Muslims' patriotism and is also a humble plea to the 'social injustice', as Wasim told me.

For me it is also a comment, a parable for the majority of Pakistanis who want peace but are viewed as violent. The 'image problem', as we say back home!

The most recent works by Wasim are a departure from the earlier trend. Perhaps jolted by the 'bad news' from Pakistan, her series entitled 'Ethereal' comes as the most vivid and fluid narration of killings that religious minorities face in Pakistan. In the three-part series, Wasim uses bright human figures in a fleshy tone against a dark background, representing the senseless murder of innocents. Colourful clouds hovering over distorted bodies bring out the silent madness inherent in the situation. Wasim says, 'The skin tone was highly important for me which represented the insane murder of all of humanity.'

Other than the obvious political commentary, Wasim's technique plays with the use of Bouguereau's 'The First Mourning' painting, French neo-classical styles and even underwater photography.

In the tradition of miniature documentation, the historians of tomorrow would refer to these works as perhaps the testament of what was happening in the early part of the twenty-first century in a country battling with itself. In the past decade when the confluence of global and local extremist ideologies took place in Pakistan, the minorities have suffered immeasurably. Since 2009, over 12,000 members of minorities have fled Pakistan in search for security. In its recently released annual report, Amnesty International says that in Pakistan, 'Religious minorities continued to face laws and practices that resulted in their discrimination and persecution...'

Shia Muslims have been the central target of militant groups. Only in 2013-14, fifty-four attacks against the Shia community were recorded, resulting in the killing of 222 Shias. There were twenty-two attacks on the Christian community, resulting in 128 deaths. The persecution of Ahmadis, widely condoned in Pakistan, is a harrowing tale of marginalization. Each year, dozens of attacks lead to target killings and the burning of homes. After the deed is done, there is little or no condemnation in the country. Wasim is their artistic oracle, fusing the sublime with the violent and the ethereal with the ordinary.

While she was musing 'Ethereal', her tragicomic style expressed itself in the form of the Divine Comedy series. The most iconic of these included the reference to a Canadian-Pakistani cleric leading a political movement. The symbolism of that miniature cannot be lost on us. The antics of the so-called movement in the summer of 2014 brought Pakistan to a standstill, exposing all the contradictions of the message, the leader and the rhetoric that was televised. While compromised sections of Pakistani 'opinion' were branding a new messiah, miles away Wasim chronicled in a small frame an otherwise complex and lingering story.

For all its finesse and stylistic innovation, Wasim's art transmutes into a powerful form of resistance to the mainstream ideology recycled by Pakistan's power elites. The key question is, could she have done all of this while in Pakistan? It is true that many artists are doing that in Pakistan too. Imran Qureshi for instance has been producing brilliant critiques of society and its cultural symbols and Rashid Rana has taken his commentary to the global level by directly confronting globalization and its uneasy relationship with Pakistan.

Yet a blasphemy case against an art magazine, its editors and writers and of course its painters, hangs in the air. Artistic freedoms in Pakistan are curtailed but also perennially resisted. Not unlike its history and genesis, Pakistan's future remains open to interpretation. One thing is clear: the creative spirit of Pakistanis, at home and abroad, is not giving up. Not anytime soon.

Published in The *Friday Times*, Pakistan, 6 March 2015.

18

The Musical Genius of Mehdi Hasan

୭

From Khyber to Dhaka, and from Skardu to Deccan, wafts a lilting and profound voice that binds discerning lovers of music. The highly trained vocals are none other than Mehdi Hasan's, which leave music buffs like this writer to wonder how Mian Tansen may have sung Raga Darbari, his own innovation, with full-throated ease and absolute perfection in Emperor Akbar's court, be it in Agra, Lahore or Fatehpur Sikri. Listening to Mehdi Hasan's flawless exposition of what is often referred to as most royal of the ragas on which is based his composition of Perveen Shakir's ghazal *Ku baku phael gayi*, one feels privileged to be living in the melodious age of Mehdi Hasan. But it is not merely Darbari that he excels in. Name any other raga that he has garbed his ghazal in and his flair for classical music will shine unmistakeable.

While the melody queen Noor Jehan, reigned over the world of Pakistani film music, Mehdi Hasan retained his status as *Shehanshah-e-Ghazal* – an icon, a cult in the Pakistani musical universe. His gift and skill are matchless. Alas, the voice remained silenced for over a decade, due to his protracted illness, until finally the 'King of Ghazal' passed away in 2012. The man behind this soulful, mellow and earthy voice has been an enigma, due, in part, to our general proclivity not to document the lives of the outstanding characters in our cultural life. On Pakistan's culture, or lack thereof, the less said the better. Even at the best of times, we have been confounded by debates on whether music is *haraam* or *halaal* and where the glorious tradition of subcontinental Hindustani ends and the new Islamic state's cultural ethos begin.

Instead of steering towards a resolution, the debate has worsened with the rise of fully armed hordes of obscurantists, which are not just anti-culture, but a threat to Pakistan's existence as a pluralistic and vibrant society.

Therefore, writing on music and tracing the footprints of a legend are an act of defiance in itself, challenging the orthodoxy and those who wish to remove melody from our lives. Rejuvenation and preservation of our fading cultural memory, needless to say, is essential to our survival.

Rajasthan is known for its haunting melodies celebrating the relationship between the earth and the soul. The echoes of nomads and *banjaras* roaming its deserts are said to merge into sand dunes and shining stars. And it was in the town of Luna, of district Jhunjhunu in Rajasthan, where Mehdi Hassan was born in a family of musicians in 1927 (Luna is close to 100 miles from Jaipur). His father Ustad Azeem Khan and uncle Ustad Ismail Khan were well known classical singers and they also became his mentors and role models. Reportedly, Hasan's first public performance took place when he was eight years old at the Maharaja of Baroda's darbar.

After Partition, Mehdi Hassan moved to District Khushab in the Sargodha region in Pakistan and took a job as an automobile mechanic, perhaps explaining the scientific precision of his skills. However, the immense talent refused to be marginalized in the wilderness of the central Punjab. Within years Radio Pakistan glowed with his melody in 1952. This was the time when he sang the immortal ghazal *'Gulon mein rung bharay baad-e-naubahar chalay'* by Faiz Ahmed Faiz. His elder brother, Pandit

Ghulam Qadir, composed that ghazal and two other classics: Hafeez Hoshiarpuri's ghazal *'Mohabbat karne waale kum na honge'* and Razi Tirmizi's *'Bhooli bisri chand umeedein'*.

A formidable icon had emerged whose voice and mastery led the subcontinental diva, Lata Mangeshkar, to remark that Mehdi Hasan's voice was divine: *'Jo baat unki awaaz mei thi who kisiki awaaz mei nahi hai.* He was blessed by God.' With his credentials as a maestro established in a short span of time, Mehdi Hasan moved to film music where he was to enjoy a unique position as a playback singer. He was neither a pop star nor a film singer, as we understand today through the Bollywood lens. His was a musical soiree that was a blend of the popular and the courtly, of the sublime and the banal resulting in some of the best film music of Pakistani history. Perhaps, one of the cultural bonds in pre-1971 era – the eastern and western wings – was Mehdi Hasan's music.

I have met several men and women in Dhaka who, while struggling to locate some positive memories of their united Pakistan experience, point towards Mehdi Hasan's songs and ghazals. The repertoire of his film music was also wide ranging and continued through the decades.

Earlier songs, *'Aye roshnian ke sheher bata'* from film *Chinagri* (composed by Khwaja Khursheed Anwar), *'Tu laakh chahe ai jaane baharan'* from *Najma* (composed by Master Inayat), *'ik naye mod per le ayen hai halat mujhe'* from film *Ehsan* (music Sohail Rana) and the experimental *'Mein hoon yahan tu he wahan from film Gharnata'* (composed by A. Hameed) set new standards for film music not only in Pakistan but throughout South Asia.

The songs memorable for their soulfulness among others were: *'Jab koi piyar se bulaye ga'*, *'Yoon Zindagi ki rah se takra gaya koi'*, *'Mujhe tum nazar se gira tau rahay ho'*, and, the ultimate piece of complete music, *'Ik husn ki devi se mujhe piyar hua tha'*. Small wonder that Mehdi Hassan's oeuvre is ever popular and rendered even today by young and new artists to make them accessible to the youth.

The list is endless, almost like a mythical, boundless sea. For any geet touched by Mehdi sahib's intonation has something special, otherworldly to offer: the utterly romantic *'Zindagi mein tau sabhi piyar kiya kartay hain'*, the sultry number *'Tere bheegay badan ki khushbu'*, and again a love paean *Piyar bharay do sharmeelay nain* will always be remembered. Millions who understand Urdu and Hindustani must have wondered with Mehdi Hasan, *'Kyon ham se khafa ho gaye'* and celebrated the joyous *'Duniya kisi ke piyar mein jannat se kum nahi'*.

Pakistan's perennially popular film *Aaina* (with a lilting score by Robin Ghosh) acquired another dimension with the soft tunes and notes rendered by Mehdi Hasan. From the modern *'Kabhi mein sochta hun kuch na kuch kahoon'* to the anguished cry *'Mujhe dil se na bhulana'*, his film music rises above the commercialism of cinema.

Even later, his film melodies were always in public demand and a dream project for any composer. A later film released in early 1980s *Bandish* had a brilliant song *'Do piyasay dil eik huay hain aiasay, bichrain ge ab kaisay'*.

The film journey — majestic and fulsome as it was — benefited greatly from the parallel streams flowing in our cultural veins in the form of ghazals and semi-classical pieces. The two reinforced each other and even merged at many points. When the film music genre interacted with the ghazal idiom, the results were absolutely astounding. Two examples are the ghazals composed by Ahmad Faraz which were rendered with extreme sophistication and the adroitness of a miniaturist: 'Abke ham bichray tou shayed kabhi khawabon mein milain', and the masterpiece Mehdi Hasan based on the evergreen raga — Aiman — 'Ranjish hi sahi, dil hi dukhanay ke liye aa'.

Be it Mir, Ghalib, Faiz or any of the long line of contemporary poets such as Parveen Shakir and Faraz, Mehdi Hasan had the innate art to bring out the best from Urdu's versified poetry and its tender images. The ultimate of ghazals, a piece-de-resistance, is Mir Taqi Mir's 'Patta patta boota boota, haal hamara jaanay hai', (composed by Niaz Hussain Shami) which remains an outstanding chapter of ghazal singing. Parveen Shakir's first book Khushbu received its greatest tributes in the form of Mehdi Hasan's extraordinary rendition of 'Ku baku phel gayee baat shanasai ki'.

His exposition of Raga Tilak Kamod in 'Dukhwa mein kaase kahoon mori sajni' is a sample of highpoints of semi-classical music. This composition testifies to the virtuoso's genius for its effortlessness and sheer beauty. As if this incredible dexterity, range and diversity are not enough, Khan sahib's essential command over the folk genre has been a spectacular treat. In particular, 'Kesariya balama', the eternal Rajasthani song delivered amazingly with the range and vastness of the Thar desert, is an imprint on our collective memory that refuses to fade away.

Mehdi Hasan's richness of expression and superb career is a matter of our pride. His voice is what I grew up with. I remember my childhood when the radio, television, cinema and *mehfils* were nothing but revered spaces devoted to Khan sahib. His popularity cuts across ethnic, provincial and linguistic divides.

However, what did the state do? A mammoth entity inhabited by vested interests and anti-culture elements, the state initially showed minimal interest in the treatment of Mehdi Hasan's prolonged illness to the extent of being cruel. The least that Pakistan's officialdom could have done was to take care of its brilliant performer who added music to a turbulent and tumultuous country. But what came was only after the media picked up this story and forced the powerful lords of our destiny to give some attention to this issue. The voluntary response of our officials makes us ashamed of our larger, national conduct.

But this has been our tragic tradition. Our greatest artists, singers, poets and intellectuals have suffered at the hands of a conformist society and state captured by puritans especially since late 1970s. It is never too late for the intelligentsia of this country to mobilise public pressure on the state machinery so that it learns to respect cultural diversity and the imperative to nurture a creative, healthy and civilised society.

Tansen taught us how music is a route to immortality. An ailing Mehdi Hasan lost his fight to survive in 2012. But his longevity is ensured. Tansen must be proud of his new age prodigy.

Published in *Mehdi Hasan: The Man and His Music*, edited by Asif Noorani, Liberty Books, 2010.

19

Pioneers of Pakistani Pop - Alamgir and Runa Laila

❦

The decade of the 1970s in Pakistan was tumultuous to say the least. The cataclysmic events of 1971 led to the birth of Bangladesh and the emergence of Bhutto's Pakistan. The contradictions of Bhutto's politics and the consolidation of a national security state took place during this decade. After the 1971 debacle, Pakistan's first civilian martial law administrator, and later Prime Minister Zulfikar Ali Bhutto, whipped up nationalism. However, his secular and liberal politics opened up space within the country and cultural expression blossomed. It was also a country eager to forget the trauma of 1971 and leave it behind. But Pakistan was not isolated as the seventies were a decade of transition in many other countries and towards the end of the decade the rise of neoliberal conservatism resulted in a shift towards conservatism even in advanced countries.

Bhutto nationalized many industries, launched redistributive programmes such as land reform and other changes, and also worked towards a consensus constitution that the country had been aiming to achieve since its creation in 1947. The cultural institutions received state patronage and Pakistan television emerged as a major platform for an unprecedented era of openness. Faiz Ahmad Faiz was assigned the task to devise a new cultural policy that remains one of the most relevant, yet neglected documents of our recent history. PTV was also a vehicle for propagating democratic and socialist ideas, while playwrights such as Enver Sajjad, Safdar Mir and others found ways to articulate their ideology through popular culture.

Concurrently, the global trends such as the rise of pop music, new movements in art and fashion also influenced urban Pakistan. Some of these symbols were state-led such as when Bhutto popularized both the *shalwar kameez* and the Mao jacket as formal apparel. But experimentation by musicians fused the folk with the changing contours of technology and Western trends. Initially, film music played an important role in hybrid forms and this is how Pakistan's pop revolution commenced during the 1970s.

The seventies were also the peak years of Pakistani cinema. By the arrival of 1980s and the conservative dictatorship of General Zia-ul-Haq, the film industry declined and only in recent years has it been trying to re-emerge from the ashes. The 1970s pop was an offshoot of a vibrant film music scene and the thriving cinema culture. Pakistani urban–middle classes adopted fashion, lifestyle and listened to music from the Pakistani films of those years. Pakistani filmstars like Waheed Murad and Shabnam popularized long hair for men and short-shirts for women in the country. A certain 'hair dance' also became popular in which, shedding all their inhibitions, young Pakistani dancers used to shake it literally.

The film industry provided directors and musicians a platform to fuse western sounds with the local culture and

Pakistani art. This synthesis gave way to new innovations by Pakistani musicians. Ahmed Rushdi and Runa Laila became the voices of that era. Later, Alamgir emerged as the torchbearer of a new musical sensibility, which continues in one form or another even today. These feisty singers and their composers attracted younger Pakistanis.

The seventies, in terms of global pop, music were a decade of new, thriving trends and inventions resulting in the emergence of fresh genres and sub-genres. Disco emerged during this decade, as did multiple variations of rock music such as punk and soft rock, glam rock, hard rock, etc. The origins of hip-hop can also be traced to this time. Pakistan slowly absorbed such trends.

The Pakistani music scene witnessed a gradual transition from popular film music to our own version of pop. Initially, the film industry absorbed pop influences but the focus and individualism of the performer makes this genre distinct from its cinematic variety. Alamgir's performance of '*DaikhanaTha*' on PTV with a Turkish pop singer symbolizes the turning point in terms of musical expressions of this decade. This was foreboding as the decline of the film industry, and the music, in 1980s gave more space to the blossoming of pop as a genre.

The Magical Runa Laila

But even before Alamgir turned into a pop idol, the Bengali singer Runa Laila had made her mark and set many a trend. As the trailblazer of her particular genre, Laila remains unmatched for her versatility in rendering geet, ghazal and club numbers (to be called disco in the eighties).

Runa Laila, born in 1952, started her career in late 1960s as a playback singer in Pakistan's film industry. She grew up in Karachi and received training in music at an early age. She received early music instruction from many teachers including Ustad Qadeer, also known as Piya Rang Habib Uddin Ahmed, and Ustad Ghulam Kader, the elder brother of Mehdi Hassan. She even trained in the art of *ghazal gayeki*. Her parents wanted her to be an acclaimed dancer and ensured that that she was schooled in Kathak and Bharatanatyam styles. However, her voice was soon recognized as her forte.

Laila started rather early and as a young child performed on a stage show, inter-school competitions and won many prizes. As she grew up, Radio Pakistan and Pakistan Television (PTV) recognized her extraordinary talent and made her debut as playback singer for the movie *Jugnu*. As a teenager she sang '*Unki naz ron sey mohabbat ka jo paigham mila*' in the film *Hum Dono* (1966). Later, Laila performed on PTV as well and made several memorable appearances including in the '*Zia Mohiuddin Show*'.

What made Laila distinctive from her peers was the fluidity of her voice and style. From the conventional film geet to spirited songs such as '*Mera babu chayl chabeela*', she covered a wide range. Two songs of that era '*Tune kiya shay mujhe pilaadi hai*' (what have you made me drink) and '*Dil dharke mein tum se yeh kaise kahoon*' (my heart flutters when I wish to tell you something...) are memorable for they changed the future direction of film music as a whole.

'*Tune kiya shay*' as included in *Tehzeeb* (1971) was picturized on the Lollywood diva Rani. It was playfully inventive and the situation of a young woman getting drunk in her bedroom and celebrating it was unthinkable for decades to come. Laila's other hit *Dil Dharke* which continues to inspire covers and pop culture today was again filmed in a bedroom setting where Rani seduces Waheed Murad. The film *Anujuman* released in 1970 and was an all-time blockbuster that established Laila as a formidable playback singer. There was no looking back.

In early seventies, Laila became a threat to established singers such as the maestro Madam Noor Jahan. There are many oral accounts as to how the evergreen Noor Jahan kicked her out of one of the studios while singing a duet.

After 1971, Laila stayed in Pakistan for a few years, eventually moving to Bangladesh. Her legacy has been permanent as no discussion on modern Pakistani film music is complete without her reference.

In 1974, Laila sang for Bollywood and gained much traction but it was in her new home in Bangladesh that she found another illustrious period of fame and experimentation. In India she made her debut with the film *Ek Se Badkar Ek* (1974) and worked with eminent composers such as Jaidev, Kalyanji Anandji, Laxmikant-Pyarelal and Bappi Lahiri. In Bangladesh she continues to sing and is very much an iconic figure. Her versatility became the hallmark of post-1971 Bangladeshi film music as well as pop music. In the world of Bengali pop her songs *'Sadher laubanailo morey'* and *'Bondhu tin din tor barite gelam'* are extremely popular among others.

Few vocalists have crossed regions and boundaries with ease. Laila has been honoured with multiple awards in Bangladesh, Pakistan and India. Her exit from Pakistan, however, means more than a physical departure. It also ended an era of the hybridized Pakistani culture, the influences of East Bengal spelling a more religio-nationalistic identity that also affected popular culture.

Alamgir, the King

It is not surprising that the other icon of the seventies and beyond was also of Bengali descent. Alamgir studied in Dhaka and moved to Karachi for higher education. He was born in modern-day Bangladesh and completed his early education in Dhaka. As a talented artist, he became a major figure in Karachi's pop scene. It was PTV that brought him a mass following. His first song for PTV was 'Albela rahi' featured in Pakistan's first pop musical series 'Sunday ke Sunday'. His second song 'Pyar hai zindagi ka gehna' was inspired by an English song. Alamgir earned the title 'Elvis of the East', given his style and the global context of the times. His music earned him wide popularity within Pakistan, notably amongst the younger generation.

In Karachi, he started singing at a small café called Globe Hotel on Tariq Road where his vocals and guitar skills were noticed, taking him to PTV. This is where he met the finest of our composers and another avant-garde artist Sohail Rana who chose him as a guitarist for the children programme's Hum Hi Hum, which he presented every week. By the early 1970s, Alamgir was a heartthrob and crowds would gather on Tariq Road just to catch a glimpse of our own Elvis.

Alamgir, though inspired by Western pop, set his own style. He transformed the older modes of presenting music, and by dancing and engaging his audience, he set a new culture into motion. He was even ahead of the Western trends in those times as he chose his costumes, the stage ambiance and, well before the music video generation, presented a theatrical package along with music.

Alamgir merged the local influences such as Kishore Kumar, Manna De, Abbasuddin, Hemanta Mukherjee, Mehdi Hassan with the music of The Beatles, The Rolling Stones, Englebert Humperdink and Simon and Garfunkel, among others.

Film music was not where Alamgir could make inroads. Whatever little he sang for films was widely appreciated and acclaimed. In 1978, he received the Nigar Award, along with Mehdi Hassan and Noor Jehan for the song *Mujhe dil say na bhulana* from another outstanding film of that time *Aina*. All in all, he sang over 400 songs on PTV, that too in many languages.

Alamgir later migrated to the United States where the rest of his family was located but he had also internationalized his oeuvre. Since the 1970s, he has performed in nearly forty-five countries around the world.

The trend-setting work of Alamgir is less known today. He individualized pop music, taking it out of the cinema screens onto private spaces and later the television screen which as a mass medium had a far greater reach than even cinema. Aside from his individual performative experimentation, Alamgir collaborated with local and foreign artists and became a bridge, the harbinger of transition. The political environment unwittingly helped him. As more and more Pakistanis switched to television and video cassette recorders from late 1970s, the pop acquired a more discrete and widely acceptable shape.

In recent years, the music revolution which is aided by the youth bulge and an explosion of creativity across the country can be traced back to Alamgir, his style and his ability to carve a niche within the conventional parameters of Pakistani music.

Towards another Pakistan

The Pakistan of seventies was another country. Partying, dancing, drinking alcohol, and horse racing were not taboos. Cinemas thrived across the country. Pakistan also straddled the 'hippie trail' from Turkey to India, frequented by western tourists. It interacted closely with the Western culture. Hippies were common sight near hashish shops in Peshawar. Bars were commonplace in major urban centres. Musical fanfare at the shrines of Sufi saints defined the cultural outlook of the country. The urban middle classes also sympathized with radical politics and comprised perhaps the most politically active generations in Pakistan. But this changed all too soon.

Zulfikar Ali Bhutto, as a powerful prime minister, steered the country towards a global Muslim identity. The new constitution included several 'Islamic' clauses, and Pakistan hosted the second OIC Summit in 1974 to showcase solidarity with the Muslim world. In the same year, the Ahamdiyya community was declared 'non-Muslim' by the Parliament through a constitutional amendment. In a move to appease the right-wing religious lobby, Bhutto started the Islamization process towards the end of his rule. This state action unleashed a never-ending process, which was appropriated by General Zia-ul-Haq who took over the reins of power in 1977. From that date onwards, the wave of Islamization changed the institutional and social landscape of Pakistan with serious consequences for the arts, culture and popular imagination of Pakistan's identity.

Essay for *Pakistan's Radioactive Decade: An Informal Cultural History of the 1970s*, OUP, Pakistan, forthcoming.

20

Asim Butt's Activism Through Art

❧

The axiom that art is located in, and is an expression of societal labyrinths, is best reflected in the case of Pakistan. For decades, the construction of 'Pakistani art' has taken place in exclusive art schools and studios. Perhaps, there is nothing peculiar about this trajectory. After all, art is inextricably linked to patronage and is now a commercial endeavour with the market defining standards and setting benchmarks of 'greatness'. Within this perspective, Asim Butt, the semi- bloomed flower, to use a metaphor from the legendary Urdu poet Ghalib, set a new direction and renegotiated the relationship between art and public spaces in a radicalized country.[1]

Pakistan's public spaces have been vandalized and twisted by the state and powerful elites in a futile search for an Islamic identity. This identity has also been located and re-imagined within the context of militarization, jingoism and the pernicious displays of nuclear prowess. Since the advent of Islamo-fascism in the late 1970s – a defining moment in the political history of Pakistan – the concept of public space in Pakistan has been reinterpreted and redefined by a predatory, yet failing state trying to assert its weakening grip over the millions it purports to serve and protect. The most common displays emanate from religious symbolism. In every town and city, a sign of the Arabic name for God Almighty – Allah – is the neo-aesthetic of post-1971 Pakistan. Similarly, public spaces are also adorned with Arabic verses, Quranic names for God and the Prophet (Peace Be Upon Him) and a bizarre combination of commercial advertising and religious zealousness. Sadequain would perhaps the only exception here for his public art crossed several boundaries of state-set limits.[2]

Many would argue that there is nothing wrong with this public aesthetic. However, in a vibrant, plural society and culture such as Pakistan, this homogenous hegemony has led to various forms and modes of resistance. A common expression of resistance has been the proliferation of poster art, especially in the subaltern terrains of Pakistani mindscape. From the flourishing truck art forms, to irreverence engraved on the 'backsides' (another popular cultural connotation in contemporary Pakistan) of rickshaws and vans to the representation of Sufis, saints and religious figures on posters, all have been a concurrent representational stream.

The second and more meaningful symbolism which has now captured the larger public imagination of Pakistan pertains to the assertion of military might. The strategic placement of missile replicas is an omnipresent and patently visible urban aesthetic. Across the country, various missiles named after the Islamic heroes of Pakistan's imagined past are the tottering national discourses on the construction of a Jihadist ideology that has gripped the Pakistani state and society, perhaps beyond redemption. Since the nuclear tests carried out by the state in 1998, the bleak, barren and quite significantly fake replicas of the Chagai Mountains (home to the nuclear explosions) were also littered across the public-cultural-psychological space of Pakistani consciousness.

That the Pakistani studio art attempted to resist these cultural impositions and revolutions is a story marred by signs of retreat, defeat and ignominy. The National College of Arts in the 1980s prepared a charter for artists and as a textual entity it was perfect. It called for resistance, action and reinvention, but significantly in the confines of studios and galleries often inaccessible to the 'masses'. The critical path of this collective movement is a subject of a separate and perhaps, much wider study than this communiqué allows for. Suffice it to say, very few artists ventured into the public domain. Those who did were either 'commissioned' artists and architects, or extensions of statist conceptions of public art.[3]

Lahore, the uber-capital of the mythical Punjab however, narrated a somewhat different story. Its recent rulers have erected replicas of fading Mughal glory as an advancement of their political ambition and perhaps a means to reinterpret Lahore's heritage. The famous Liberty roundabout in Lahore's posh Gulberg area showcases a figment of the fountains erected in the beatific Shalimar Gardens. However, this was a politically convenient venture for the Shalimar Gardens testify to both the glories of the medieval Mughal Islamicate, as well as echo the pursuit of Paradise through the Islamic garden layout. Ultimately, all of this fits in with the meta-narratives of Jihad and Jihadism where attainment of the eternal garden and *houries* is a widely noted ambition of the twenty-first-century suicide bomber.

Challenging these public narratives and aesthetics therefore, has been a fairly impossible endeavour for any Pakistani artist. The binary of studio versus popular art prevented a convergence of the scattered streams of resistance. It is in this peculiar context, that Asim Butt emerged from nowhere and made perhaps the seminal efforts to shun the studio art and find a cultural home on the streets, paths, shrines and other public spaces of Pakistan. As a young art student, Asim Butt had already charted a course for himself by working on the murals around the shrine of Abdullah Shah Ghazi.

As a twenty-three-year-old art student at the Indus Valley School of Art and Architecture in Karachi, Butt began with his explorations of the cityscape. His murals at the Abdullah Shah Ghazi shrine in Karachi were electric and involved intense engagement with the transitional communities of beggars, prostitutes, junkies and other dreads of society who had been rejected by convention and were in turn extremely eager to reject convention themselves. This was also a space where Asim discovered many soul mates -- ordinary, nameless people -- and engaged in a collective artistic dialogue. Not unlike the archetype of a Sufi Khanqah, he replicated a parallel space outside the formal confines of a Sufi shrine.

5 Ways to Kill a Man was Asim's first mural near the shrine -- an intense, provocative and political reaction to the US invasion in Iraq that underlined the eternal futility of war and violence. It is noticeable that Karachi was also the playground for the religious right to assert its opposition to the Iraq war on a regular basis. However, the resistance to the Iraq war by the right-wing parties of Pakistan was located in the Islamist context. Butt's mural on the other hand, was a collective endeavour within the parallel Sufi space outside the formal shrine. His was a secular, historical and interiorized expression of resistance to war. The 'five ways to kill' coincided with the five senses, thereby, asserting the essential humanist overtones of this mural. The second major artwork entitled *Glue*, emerged from the community of glue sniffers that is also commonly found outside Sufi shrines. The mural depicted the pervasive addiction to glue sniffing, an unchecked, deadly path for the disillusioned youth of the country who are in need of appropriate role models and mentors. A more direct engagement emerged in the form of *American Rage*. In this mural, American military hysteria and brutality is captured in its entirety; a sordid chapter in US military strategy which used incisive intervention, torture, subversion and an all-out assault against the self-created, hydra-headed demon that is 'terrorism'.

Throughout his formal training at Indus Valley, Asim's foray into public art continued as a parallel learning process in direct contrast to the formal training imparted at the school. In 2005, Asim Butt initiated the Karachi Stuckists group and indigenized the global notions of stuckism[4] in the Pakistani context. Between 2005 and 2007, the growing corpus of his public arty, attracted wide attention from critics, the media and citizens of Karachi.

By the time Pakistan witnessed yet another upheaval in its political history – the so-called Lawyers Movement in 2007 that coalesced into an anti-Musharraf movement – Asim had set a direction for activism through art. This unique moment in the country's otherwise tumultuous history came as a godsend for a public art practitioner such as Butt. In the months that followed, the dismissal of Pakistan's Chief Justice by the military ruler and the growing momentum of citizen resistance provided an unprecedented boost to Asim's artistic energy. The political transformation of the Pakistani state and society coincided with the blossoming of Asim's personal direction and artistic endeavours, and his public art-activism grew beyond the urban metropolis of Karachi. Very soon, the walls of Karachi were sprayed with 'eject' signs and graffiti, which were soon picked up by the civil society groups as an instrument for non-violent protest across the country, calling for the military dictator to abdicate his grasp over the body politic. For those tense months after Musharraf imposed the emergency, Karachi witnessed the number "420" repeated to create large arrows at the Supreme Court, Karachi Bench.

The iconography emerging out of Asim's unwavering passion was a trend-setter and would inform public art debates and practices in the years to come. Sadly, the anti-Musharraf movement was compounded by the return of Pakistan's enigmatic icon of those times, Benazir Bhutto on 18 October 2007. The capture of Pakistan's political space by Islamism and militarism, however, meant little scope for a public figure such as Benazir Bhutto to mobilize public opinion freely and without violence. Less than three months after her return to Pakistan, she was murdered in the symbolic town of Rawalpindi, which continues to denote the real power center of the country. Immediately after her murder, Karachi and Sindh were in flames and several days of violent upheavals paralyzed the entire country. Asim's work in these days was also significant. The 'eject' sign was replaced by symbols of 'STOP'. The use of burnt vehicles as the metaphors of a brutalized polity was extremely inventive. Butt used spray paint as the medium in familiar sites to advocate peace. Perhaps, this signified the ultimate profundity of public art in traversing dimensions and meanings in the public arena.

In the last years of his rather short life, Asim travelled across the length and breadth of Pakistan, and dabbled in more serious and iconoclastic public art. He had perhaps started with his Karachi ventures and his direct critique of the largest urban party soon brought him under the radar of secular vigilantes. Risk-taking is inherent in public activism, so Asim remained undeterred.

Perhaps, the most layered of Asim's activism related to the three public expressions: first, the wordplay resulting in a public statement – *Shariat ill;* the confrontational statement 'Bad idea' on a bench outside Minar-e-Pakistan, Lahore; and graffiti cigarette pack of '*Marchoro*'.

Beyond the time-bound political turmoil, Asim's work touched upon the fundamental issue of state ideology as demonstrated by the populist political card of introducing a Shariat Bill in Pakistan. It is widely acknowledged that there is no consensus on Shariah and therefore all such slogans end up being sectarian impositions of a Sunni worldview now appropriated by the Wahabi-Salafi Islam (with heavy financing from the Middle East). Thus, Butt's most pertinent graffiti represents the latent ills of an imagined ideological legislation with the potential of damaging the society further. Shariat 'Bill' therefore in a simple expressive stroke turns into an 'ill'. It is difficult to imagine how many artists would dare to do that in a country infested by murder-brigades.

The most daring of Butt's ventures *I Have a Dream* experimented with Pakistan's identity and the bloodline of Partition that refuses to dry up even after six decades. In a carefully laid out public park around the symbolic, Jungian, Minar-e-Pakistan, a bench was used by Asim to critique the project. This iconoclastic foray locates itself in the physical space where the Lahore Resolution of 1940 was passed. 'Bad idea' is what graffiti says while exploring and subtly subverting Muslim and Hindu identities (as the colours red and green, locked in battle are represented by a Hindu trident and a Muslim arrow). To do this outside the contours of studio space and in the middle of a public space required courage, inventiveness and manifested the desire to reach out. Butt challenged the sacred cow of Two Nation Theory in contemporary Pakistan through his simple and effective explorations.

Another offshoot of this theme earlier played out on cigarette packets and inverted the literal warning signs printed on such packets. Thus Malboro Lights converts in the Pakistandom as 'Mar Choro Fights', expressing the complexity of contemporary Pakistan in as much its foundations were soaked by the blood of the victims of the violence of Partition and mass migration, dishonoured by political and religious bigots. The embedded violence in a national imagination and its recurrence was captured and relayed out in the public domain by Butt through his several activist ventures.

Perhaps the first theme of its kind to be exhibited in the public arena was sexuality. Many public artistic expressions by Butt had homoerotic overtones, but more importantly, they defied the conventional view of representing the human body in the Islamic Republic. The hallmark of post-1947 decades has been the gradual deletion (to use a Butt-esque term) or the near-invisibility of public sculptures, and Butt's work reinvented the form through his murals at various public sites. Male figures, sexual politics and even gender relations feature heavily in these representations. There was a political dimension to even the representation of human form(s) as the phallic imagery was covertly played out to represent both the beauty and ugliness of machismo as the driver of violence, war, hunger and exploitation.

Asim's art activism on the metaphorical Pakistani street, however, did not impede his expansion as a studio artist. If anything, engagement with the political provided further layers to his studio art. There was a deeper penetration of the political into the personal, thereby detaching and undoing the existential from the hazards of nihilism. The lines were less anguished and more controlled in the later works; and the medium of oil on canvas acquired political tones conversing with the inner apparitions of the artist.

It would be difficult to summarize Butt's scope and range of art-activism. It delved into the personal and the political with relative ease. More importantly, it challenged orthodoxies and defied the Islamism and militarism of the Pakistani public spaces and raised the forgotten questions of identity of the artist in the political milieu in which he/she operates. For this very reason it is vital to remember Butt's work and celebrate it as heralding a new sensibility — a unique artistic sensibility espousing the common, breaking studio walls and expanding its frontiers to imbibe the wider social and political traumas. Butt's personal traumas could not have found a better, grander arena than the polarized cultural territories within Pakistan.

A tragedy greater than Asim's death was that he lived in a society that had yet to begin its search for identity; and turn the internal chaotic dynamic into a more conducive space for creativity. In a small span of time he carved a niche for himself and for generations of younger artists who aspire to follow him in spirit. This is the greatest of legacies that Asim's public art has bestowed an anguished country like Pakistan.

PERSONAL ESSAY

21

That Easy Intimacy: A Pakistani Rediscovers Bangladesh

❧

As a Pakistani, there is a part of you that reacts instantly to the word Bangladesh: guilt, remorse or, in some cases, nostalgia can suddenly take over. I am from the generation that was spared the horrors of Pakistan Army actions, of information blackouts on the massacre of Bengalis in the name of Pakistani nationalism. But what does it mean to be half a Pakistani, without East Bengal – especially when you know a bit of history and have managed to see through the falsities of the textbooks? It means nothing or it means a lot; it depends on which way you want to look at the other half, now a proud, vibrant country.

Working in international development is what took me to Bangladesh for the first time, many years ago. Prior to that, I had been familiar with the country's mythical music, rich poetry and tales of its golden sunsets and singing rivers, but had never touched its soil. Bengal's magic is embedded in the Subcontinental imagination, and these images and literary references long shaped my view of the country. However, my romantic notions were severely jolted when I arrived in Dhaka — at first glance, an overcrowded concrete jungle typically lacking in urban planning. More of the same, I concluded: big cities, despite their buzz, can let you down.

Still, my disappointment did not last, as I soon undertook to seek out the city's various corners, its hidden spaces of beauty and comfort; above all, what I found was an engaged citizenry marching on. Discovering the University of Dhaka and its surroundings came as a much-needed connection, though older parts of Dhaka are also quite mesmerising. The gulmohar (or krishnachura) trees, almost on fire, greet a visitor on nearly every street, as does a tremendous volume of rickshaws.

Then there is the Shaheed Minar, the monument marking Bengali resistance founded on linguistic identity. The physical monument is modern, and by itself is not particularly exciting. However, its significance is truly monumental, marking as it does Bengali nationalism from 1948 to 1971 under the misrule of West Pakistan elites. Given movements for ethnic, linguistic and provincial identities ongoing in today's Pakistan, the Shaheed Minar is a powerful reminder of how centralized rule and marginalization of cultural identities lead to festering problems.

A colleague who took me to see these sites was most polite with me. He was fervently nationalistic but chose his words carefully — at least until I asked him to drop the formalities and just say what he wanted. Then the floodgates opened, and out came his personal memories and renditions from Bengali oral histories. I even found myself apologizing, though I then laughed at myself for such a delusional gesture — my few words of apology meant nothing against the horrors of Bengali suffering. Luckily, the charms of the place and the krishnachura trees came to my rescue. And so, I brushed the dark side of our shared histories under the proverbial carpet, just the way that Pakistan has done. For many people in Pakistan, 1971 is today an invisible event, a deliberately ignored footnote in our collective memory, despite being one that should remain understood as a moment of reckoning for the entire country. After all, majority provinces seldom secede; it is usually the other way around.

'Our' Iqbal

Another day I spotted the majestic colonial building known as Curzon Hall, an architectural gem. This time I was on my own, daring to explore the city on a Sunday when some time was available. A student near the hall was curious to know who I was, and immediately took it upon himself to be my guide, host and friend. Curzon Hall is also a part of the university and has adjoining hostels where my new friend, Shaheen, lived.

Named after the former viceroy of India, Curzon Hall was renamed Iqbal Hall under Pakistani rule. Muhammad Iqbal is Pakistan's national poet, regarded as the one who first 'dreamed' of Pakistan. In his famous Allahabad address of 1930, Iqbal mentioned the need for local autonomy, which the state of Pakistan and its loyal historians subsequently interpreted as a demand for Pakistan. In fact, the poet is on record saying – immediately after his address – that he never asked for a separate country. Iqbal died in 1938, nine years before the creation of Pakistan. So the links are at best tenuous, but of course nation states have to create heroes and histories.

Still, the real irony surrounding Iqbal is that his famous tarana (anthem) is India's unofficial national anthem, which begins with the mellifluous lines:

Sare jahan se acha hindustan hamara
Ham bul-bulen hain is ki ye gulistan hamara
Our Hindustan is better than the entire world
We are the nightingales and this is our garden.

In 1971, of course, Iqbal Hall had to go (renamed again as Curzon Hall), as did several other reminders of the immediate past. 'Our' Iqbal composed poetry in Persian and Urdu, and the latter's imposition by West Pakistan had been a perennial source of conflict. Earlier, at the Shaheed Minar, I had also remembered Muhammad Ali Jinnah and his controversial speech of 1948, in which he pronounced Urdu the state language. That speech was delivered right here in Dhaka, at Curzon Hall, and Jinnah had said, 'There can be only one state language if the component parts of this state are to march forward in unison, and that language, in my opinion, can only be Urdu.' Jinnah died in September 1948 and if he had known that his remarks were going to spark such a controversy, he might well have changed his mind.

It is only by travelling in the interior that one realises the deep love that Bengalis have for their language and culture. Bangla is rich, and the eighteenth-century renaissance developed strong traditions of poetic and literary expression culminating in the emergence of Rabindranath Tagore in the late nineteenth century. Bengali folk art, its folk songs and tales are all part of the lived culture. Yet the state of Pakistan took Jinnah's words on language a bit too seriously. Muslim, Islam, Urdu and a linear view of Pakistan became the key divider between the two wings. The religious right continuously undertook propaganda against the inherently secular and plural culture of East Pakistanis. Bengali women wore bindis regardless of their religion, and all Bengalis, irrespective of their faith or creed, love and worship Tagore, who was not a Muslim.

These cultural differences were apparent despite the commonalities. Today, these differences remain, again despite the commonalities – such as dynastic politics, corruption, use of religion as a political 'card' and chaotic governance. When I visited Dhaka, Bangladesh was also ruled by a technocratic and army-backed regime, and was professing to clean up the country of corrupt politicians and officials. This was hauntingly similar to what General Pervez Musharraf had likewise announced and attempted to undertake.

Technocrats were being called clean in both the countries; there was a high profile Anti-Corruption Commission in Bangladesh and a high-powered National Accountability Bureau in Pakistan. But military men were heading both institutions! In due course, the 'caretaker' government of Bangladesh gave way to a return of democracy, where one of the dynastic politicians went back into power – and another into opposition. General Musharraf also had to give up power in 2008 when he resigned, handing over power to the very politicians he had tried to oust.

Still, the commonalities ended here, jammed in the technical details. Bengalis are not known for their patience with authoritarian rule. Pakistanis on the other hand have learned to live with long spells of army rule. Many say that this has now changed, that it would be difficult for any future coup to sustain. Of course, only time will tell.

Old Model

One of the more stunning sights in Dhaka takes place each evening, when the garment factories shut down and long lines of women workers leave for home. At that time, the major roads suddenly become buried under energy and colour, with tens of thousands of women dressed in saris and shalwar kameez. It is a surreal sight indeed, and highlights a palpable difference between Bangladesh and Pakistan. In Dhaka, women appear to be far more mobile and, apparently, safe in the urban jungle. To my eyes, such visibility in the public sphere was a great slap to the Islamists who want women to be veiled and, ideally, locked in their homes.

In 2010, jute-producing Bangladesh exported garments worth USD 12 billion, leaving the cotton-producing Pakistan far behind. Bangladesh has also made great progress in terms of population planning, while higher levels of literacy and secondary education for women have brought down the fertility rates by half in the past two decades. Pakistan, the former compatriot, has yet to make a noticeable advance in this area.

Being a Pakistani visitor in Bangladesh invites much curiosity. Most people I met had a story to relate: many had parents or grandparents who had lived in (West) Pakistan. Thanks to Bollywood and Indian soaps, Hindi/Urdu is widely understood, especially by the young population. And so Bollywood helps the young Bangladeshi understand me, a Pakistani. This is the irony I pointed out to my friend, Nazrul, a lawyer and academic, who laughed in response. His wife, Prachee, is a well-known actor who has received several awards for her performances in off-beat cinema productions.

Nazrul insisted that I visited Old Dhaka, where the influence of the nawabs of old and their hybrid culture continues to survive. The best biryani is available in this area. Developed by the Mughals, the area has typical features for anyone familiar with Lahore or Delhi, albeit on a smaller scale. Nazrul wanted me to taste something familiar, but my real discovery was the Bangla cuisine. I ate the best fish – from the iconic hilsa to the regular pomfret. However, such is the beauty of the language that even fish have most romantic names: pomfret, for instance, is roop chada (moon-faced). Bengali sweets are also notably subtle and light, not dripping with oil -- shondesh, roshogolla and chomchom are, in my opinion, superior Bengali cousins of what we prepare in Pakistan (or the western parts of North India).

In Chittagong and Kushtia (a rural district), the cuisine got even better. The fish varieties grew in number and I tasted the most delightful sweets, either at people's homes or in small eateries where Hindi and Bangla songs keep diners entertained. In fact, it was during travels in the countryside that I finally met my constructed image of the verdant Bengal. The rice fields, the numerous rivers and lush green fields are breathtakingly beautiful. In the villages are ponds where men and children bathe, and narrow dirt roads snake through the jungle and fields. The infrastructure is not as developed as, say, in Punjab province, and the major highways are narrow and can be quite frightening due to heavy traffic.

But in this populous country, one cannot help but notice the dynamism. The economy has grown by six percent annually over recent years, and a huge private sector keeps the country moving despite the inefficiencies of the public sector. Akbar Zaidi, Pakistan's accomplished economist, has observed that Bangladesh was 'considered to be a basket case in 1971, (but) is today offering a mirror to others on how developing countries can become a development state'.

Those Many Encounters

I did not feel foreign enough, and will be back. The Bengalis struggled for the country where I live. In fact, Zaidi himself recently published an article that stated, 'In many ironic ways, it is Bangladesh which has become Jinnah's Pakistan – democratic, developmental, liberal, secular – while Pakistan has become his worst nightmare – intolerant, authoritarian, illiberal and fundamentalist.'

An action by the Supreme Court of Bangladesh had revered the country to being a secular republic. In addition, radical Islamist literature has been banned, while in Pakistan there is an exponential growth in the influence of the fundamentalists. Thus, for me travels to Bangladesh evoke thoughts of lost opportunities, of war, violence and separation.

I am not a fan of partitions, but Bangladesh feels as though it was meant to be. However, this should not preclude the two countries reviving and strengthening their trade and cultural ties. It is a true pity that Pakistan's elites are yet to properly apologise to the state and people of Bangladesh.

All I have experienced, meanwhile, is hospitality, warmth and generosity of spirit, and minimal bitterness. The Pakistani cricket team is much appreciated in Bangladesh; Atif Aslam, our pop idol, is a huge favourite of the youth; and Pakistan is no longer an entity to resent, even as the memories of 1971 are kept alive. There must be many roads that can help us reset the trajectory of the last four decades, and to heal the wounds.

After those many encounters, that easy intimacy, we are strangers now – After how many meetings will we be that close again?

— FAIZ AHMED FAIZ, TRANSLATED BY AGHA SHAHID ALI

22

Loharwana: A Lahori Rambling

❧

There was a Lahore that I grew up in, and then there is the Lahore that I live in now. Recovering from an exile status for two decades, I find myself today turning into something of a clichéd grump, hanging desperately on to the past. Yet I resist that. Writing about Lahore is a sensation that lies beyond the folklore – *Jinne Lahore ni wekheya o janmea nai* (The one who has not seen Lahore has never lived). It has to do with an inexplicable bonding and oneness with the past, and yet a contradictory and not-so-glorious interface with the present.

Lahore is now the second largest city in Pakistan, with a population that has crossed the 10 million mark. It is turning into a monstropolis. Had it not been for Lahore's intimacy with Pakistan's power base – the Punjab-dominated national establishment – this would be just another massive, unmanageable city, regurgitating all the urban clichés of the Global South. But Lahore retains a definite soul; it is comfortable with modernity and globalization, and continues to provide inspiration for visitors and residents alike.

Over the last millennium, Lahore has been the traditional capital of Punjab in its various permutations. A cultural centre

of North India extending from Peshawar to New Delhi, it has
historically been open to visitors, invaders and Sufi saints alike.
Several accounts tell how Lahore emerged as a town between
the sixth and sixteenth centuries BC. According to commonly
accepted myth, Lahore's ancient provenance, Lohawarana, was
founded by the two sons of Lord Ram some 4,000 years ago.
One of these sons, Loh (or Luv), gave his name to this timeless
city. A deserted temple in Lahore Fort is ostensibly a tribute to
Loh, located near the Alamgiri gate, next to the fort's old jails.
Under the regime of Zia ul Haq, Loh's divine space was closed
and used as a dungeon in which to punish political activists.

Later records, such as Ptolemy's *Geographia*, written
around 150 AD, refer to Lahore as 'Labokla', and locate it with
reference to rivers Indus, Ravi, Jhelum and Chenab. Another
readable account from the past is that of Hiuen Tsang, the
famous Chinese pilgrim who visited Lahore during the early
seventh century AD. He described it as a large Brahminical
city – mullahs beware! There is many a contradiction within
these accounts, of course, but the important point is that
Lahore was not built yesterday. Its ancient moorings explain
its indomitable will, ability to survive the upheavals of time,
and an innate life beyond the limits of recorded histories,
fancy notions of urbanity and cultural evolution. Lahore is also
about its centuries of residents. The mystique of the city thus
is a personalized experience, as if a city were in permanent
dialogue with its residents even while speaking to a newcomer.

Little Ghazni

I spent my early years in a Model Town colonial bungalow,
which was originally the creation of a Hindu doctor who had
to leave the city at Partition. This was an age when birds were

an integral feature of Lahori skies, and the seasons played out their glory. As the name suggests, Model Town was an 'ideal' suburb, created during the Raj by the advanced citizenry on the idea of 'cooperative urban life'. Established in 1922, Model Town was the fruition of advocate Diwan Khem Chand's unshakeable belief in the values of self-help, self-responsibility and democracy, loosely the principles of cooperative societies. This was the reason why Model Town was established as, and still is, a 'cooperative society'. What fewer people know is that these values of cooperation were first popularized by George Jacob Holyoake, a nineteenth-century English social reformer responsible for the cooperative movement. Incidentally, Holyoake was also infamous for the distinction of having invented the phrase 'secularism', for which he was the last citizen to be convicted for blasphemy in England.

Khem Chand and the renowned engineer and philanthropist Sir Ganga Ram (founder of the two famous Ganga Ram Hospitals, in Lahore in 1921 and Delhi in 1954) together created Model Town. As a child, I would hear these stories from my father, also a lawyer, connecting his surroundings with his profession and middle-class dynamism. The importance of Model Town is such that it became the twentieth-century standard for urban living in Pakistan. In every city in the country, you can find a Model Town or its close relative. As Ranjana Sengupta writes, 'Many of the elements of Model Town, Lahore, were followed in the colonies that came up in post-1947 Delhi, including one also named Model Town.' Lahore and its trends can be infectious.

But this suburban delight was not the Lahore with which my grandmother was acquainted. She called it a jungle, and returned to the walled city on any given pretext. The journey involved a bus ride, hopping tongas and walking along the ancient streets of surreal Old Lahore. I would accompany her on each of these visits. We would move through the gates of Old Lahore, which sported no signage or self-conscious tourism-promotion gimmickry. Rather, passing through these gates was entering into a domain of lived history. And this is what Lahore remains – a lived and a living city.

Under the early Sultans of Delhi, especially during the eleventh and twelfth centuries, Lahore assumed considerable importance as the easternmost bastion of Muslim power, and an outpost for further advance toward the riches of the East. Apart from being the second capital, and later the only capital, of the Ghaznavid kingdom, Lahore had great military and strategic significance: whoever controlled it could look forward to sweeping the whole of East Punjab to Panipat and Delhi. Long known as 'Little Ghazni', Lahore attracted mystics and scholars from Central Asia. Ali Hajweri (who died in 1077), also known as Data Sahib, was one such luminary of that age, whose primal book Kashf-al-Mahjub (the Unveiling of the Hidden) remains an authentic treatise on an Islamic variant of mysticism, and whose shrine is today busier than ever.

My Old Lahore visits were never complete without a salaam to the great saint, and this habitual halt continues even three decades later. The value of Kashf-al-Mahjub lies not only in the experiential accounts of contemporary mystic orders, but also in the fact that it is a seminal, systematic exposition of personalised mysticism. Over time, Kashf has become a standard textbook for Sufis. In popular lore, Ali Hajweri is also the protector of Lahore. During the Indo-Pakistan war of 1965, many a Lahori attributed the city's survival to the saint,

and to his fantastic ability to catch Indian bombs in his green
fakiresque robes.

Mughal Dream

It is not that Lahore did not face devastation during what is
commonly known as the 'medieval' ages. The fearless Mongols
were there to inject fear into the Lahore-walla, and in 1241,
during the chaos following the death of Sultan Shams-ud-
din Iltutmish, the Mongols attacked and levelled the city.
Thousands were killed. Lahore was a desolate place until Sultan
Balban, who, after 1270, restored the fortifications of Lahore
and proceeded to rebuild the city. True, the sultans were more
focused on Delhi as the Islamicate capital, with Lahore being
only a strategic outpost to be protected. However, the walled
city lived on and expanded.

During the early sixteenth century, the victory of Babur and
the defeat of the last sultan, Ibrahim Lodhi, ushered in a new
era in Indian history. Babur captured Lahore in 1524, before
he was proclaimed emperor of India. This was the beginning
of Lahore's expansion and beautification, much of which can
be seen today – notwithstanding the population explosion and
atmospheric pollution that seem to put the Mongol threats of
yore to shame. The prime of Mughal rule – from 1524 to 1752
– and the special attention by Mughal emperors, particularly
Akbar, Jahangir and Shah Jahan, transformed Lahore into the
ultimate representation of Mughal aesthetics. For the two
centuries following the ascension of Akbar in 1556, Lahore
was a Mughal dream translated into architecture. Little wonder
the adulation with which the English poet John Milton wrote
in 1670:

His eyes might there command whatever stood
City of old or modern fame, the seat
Of mightiest empire, from the destined walls
Of Cambalu, seat of Cathian Can,
And Samarcand by Oxus, Temir's throne,
To Paquin of Sinaen Kings, and thence
To Agra and Lahore of Great Mogul…

The Delhi-obsession of the Muslim rulers of India was interrupted when Akbar made Lahore his capital from 1584 to 1598. The majestic Lahore Fort was rebuilt, next to the Ravi River, and the urban habitation was enclosed within a red brick wall boasting a dozen gates. Jahangir and Shah Jahan further extended the fort, building palaces and tombs, and laying out gardens, among which only the Shalimar Gardens survive today in their unkempt glory. Jahangir loved Lahore, and he and his wife, Noor Jahan, chose to be buried at Shahdara, on the outskirts of Lahore. The tomb of Jahangir and Noor Jahan is today a majestic and melancholic monument.

Shah Jahan – the most extravagant of the Mughals – was born in Lahore, and his eldest son, Dara Shikoh, also found the city enticing. Dara was a popular figure in Lahore, and it was there that he found his spiritual mentor, Mian Mir (also buried in Lahore). Dara's nemesis and Shah Jahan's successor, Aurangzeb (1658-1707), bestowed on Lahore its most famous monument, the Badshahi mosque and the Alamgiri gateway to the Fort. Even during the anarchy that followed Mughal rule, Lahore remained a city with a formidable reputation; under Sikh rule, from 1780 to 1846, it was popularly referred to as the 'Mughal capital'.

It took almost a century for the British to move towards the Punjab, from their foothold in Bengal. The annexation of the Punjab in 1849, and the successful control of the 1857 uprising in many parts of North India, resulted in the consolidation of the British Empire. Due to its strategic location, Punjab was subsequently central to the architecture of the colonial power. Lahore was to become a major outpost of the empire in the 'Great Game' that continues to be played out in Afghanistan, as the sahibs ventured to create social and cultural spaces for themselves in otherwise unfriendly and unfamiliar surroundings.

The earliest signs of colonial Lahore are found within the Lawrence Gardens (baptised the Bagh-i-Jinnah following Independence), representing the quintessential Raj ethos. Built primarily for the sahibs and memsahibs, the park has managed to maintain its dreamlike beauty for a century and a half, with halls and pavilions that play on the nostalgia for 'home'. A garden in the heart of British Lahore was essential. True to the colonial policy, the new garden was a continuation of the Mughal tradition of creating baghs as the aesthetic expression of self-indulgence. This project also reflected the expanse of the British Empire. Thousands of saplings of various exotic species were imported from colonies around the world, and by 1860, the gardens were set up as a Lahore version of the famous Kew Garden in London. During chilly winters and unbearable summers, for years I have walked in the Lawrence Gardens. Indeed, my fondest memories of Lahore are in one way or another linked to this splendid park. Whenever I have wanted to hear the sound of trees, I have not been disappointed.

The contemporary core of Lahore's architecture and spaces are rooted in the British period, with a marked emphasis on the brick-based Anglo-Mughal architecture style, a combination of the Mughal, Gothic and Victorian. The famous Young Men's Christian Association and General Post Office buildings of Lahore were built to commemorate the golden jubilee of Queen Victoria, an event marked by the construction of clock towers and monuments all over the Subcontinent. This was also a time when institutions were intrinsically linked to their buildings – such as the High Court, Government College, Forman Christian College, Lahore Museum, Governor House, National College of Arts, Tollinton Market, Punjab Assembly and the old campus of Punjab University. The latter was once considered the largest centre of education in Asia.

The 'Paris of the East' had already emerged as a cosmopolitan and cultural capital of British Punjab, where poets such as Iqbal and artists such as Amrita Sher-Gil, as well as future writers like Khushwant Singh, Amrita Pritam, Saadat Hasan Manto and Faiz Ahmed Faiz were all to emerge. But the multicultural spirit of Lahore was to be ruptured by Partition. In the new state of Pakistan, Lahore therefore became 'provincialized', while the large-scale exodus of non-Muslims inevitably worked to limit the city's secular credentials.

Layers and Layers

I studied at Aitchison College, known as Lahore's top college and one that had the dubious distinction of aiming to educate the relatives of the ruling chiefs of the Punjab. Aitchison's foundation stone was laid in 1886 by the then-viceroy, the Earl of Dufferin and Ava, and it was named after the then-lieutenant-governor of the Punjab, Charles Umpherston Aitchison. During my years at Aitchison, the quality of academics remained at best tentative, but its sprawling 186-acre campus was a veritable treasure trove of the finest Anglo-Mughal buildings. Its tree-lined boulevards and playgrounds still return to me at times in my dreams.

The most memorable of experiences was living in one of the bungalows in the Government Officers' Residences, known as GOR-1. Located in the centre of Lahore, GOR-1 is to Lahore what the so-called Lutyens bungalows are to Delhi. The verandas, little gardens next to each bedroom, and the fragrance of Lahore's monsoons and springs, all of these were best experienced in this part of the city. Others will of course have loved where they grew up as well, for each Lahori has his or her own store of memories and attachments. Beyond the annals of history, there are as many Lahores as the number of its residents. This is why those who migrated from Lahore to India after 1947 could not take Lahore out of their system. Khushwant Singh has to reconcile with his memory time and again; his writings replete with Lahore tales. Prem Kirpal, a Lahori migrant to Delhi, wrote these lines to sum it all up:

> My beloved City of Lahore
> Still standing not far from Delhi
> Within quicker reach by air or train,
> Suddenly became a forbidden land
> Guarded by a sovereign state
> Of new ideologies, loves and hates.

Kirpal's poem is befittingly titled 'Spirit's Musings'. A spirit will break free of limits. These individuals were not locating their selves in the politics of Partition per se; this was the personal that gets submerged in the cruel and indifferent political.

It was in Lahore that I met the Indian writer and former diplomat Pran Neville. He was there to launch his own book on Lahore, titled *A Sentimental Journey*. It was a monsoon evening, heavy and similar to the weather on the day when his family packed their bags for Delhi. Unusually fit and active for a man who had lived over seven decades, he appeared timeless. Sitting in Lahore, he walked various paths and cities in his conversation. Having travelled the world as a foreign-service officer, Neville had concluded that foremost, he was a Lahore native. In a conversation, he declared, 'In a way I never left Lahore, because it was always with me. I am an un-reconstructed Lahori, you could say, who never thought he would live anywhere else.'

When riots shook Lahore in July 1947, Neville's siblings moved to Delhi, but his parents were reluctant to migrate. Finally, persuaded by their Muslim friends, his parents also left, though with a fantastic certitude that they would return after the dust settled. That has been one of the foremost tragedies of Partition: many who left in the flurry of events were convinced they would return some day to their homes, villages and cities. This was never to happen. The lines instead got thicker on the canvas of history.

Today, in Delhi, Neville leads a group composed of Lahore's former residents, who meet regularly and share memories of a city that lives on within them. Memory needs a playground, seeks indulgence and reconciliation. Pran Neville, Ajeet Caur and Khushwant Singh, in Delhi, try to inject some order into the chaos of their ruptured memories. Yet in many ways, Lahore remains one of the most invisible and underappreciated cities in the region. The journalist Simon Jenkins once wrote: 'For centuries the Grand Trunk Road from Delhi through Punjab carried the history of the subcontinent streaming beneath the walls of Lahore. But while India is at least fighting to rescue what remains of its past, Lahore is left to languish.'

Despite the appearance of neglect for its monuments, however, Lahore's upkeep has not been all that bad, by South Asian standards. Under the former chief minister of Punjab and later prime minister, Nawaz Sharif, Lahore found a new builder. Sharif's interest in and fondness for Lahore has been given continuity by his efficient younger brother, Shahbaz, twice the Punjab chief minister. The upgrading of infrastructure and serious (though admittedly ad hoc) attempts at urban planning has ensured that Lahore's untrammelled growth does not become a nightmare. But no amount of goodwill can hide the fact that this wondrous city is one of the most polluted in the region.

It is a separate matter that one of the most robust citizen-led urban mobilisations in Pakistan during recent years has been the Lahore Bacaho Tehreek, the Movement to Save Lahore. Saving the trees along Lahore's canal, which cuts across the urban jungle, has been the focus of this movement, though it also laid the foundation for the 2007 lawyers' struggle for rule of law in the country.

Other groups, such as a spectrum of conservation associations, likewise testify to the electric zest of Lahoris. Indeed, since the inception of Pakistan, Lahore has been a nerve centre of political mobilisation and public opinion. I am reminded of writer S. Asad Raza's evocative lines:

The world in general has few cities that interweave so seamlessly a great vitality today (the city is about the twenty-fifth largest on the globe) with an unbroken and luxurious history (spanning the last two millennia). Only in Lahore do you find the sepulchre of the legendary Anarkali, the star-crossed dancing girl buried alive for her love of the young prince Salim (the film Mughal-e-Azam is a version), inside the dusty Archives of the Punjab Secretariat, which was a mosque that the British whitewashed, and is now decorated with portraits of British colonial governors. Layers and layers: it's that kind of place.

When a city delineates the cultural and political contours of a country, and handles the conflicting layers of past and present, it has to be out of the ordinary. And this is why Lahoris love to say: *Lahore, Lahore aye.*

Notes and Bibliography

1: The Unholy Trinity of Love: Kabir, Bulleh and Lalon

1. *Kabir: The Weaver's Songs* published by Penguin India, January 2003, Delhi.
2. *Kabir: The Weaver's Songs* published by Penguin India, January 2003, Delhi.
3. Ibid. Page 94.
4. Ibid. Page 94.
5. Ibid. Page 203.
6. Muzaffar A. Ghaffar's *Masterworks of Punjabi Sufi Poetry, Bulleh Shah Within Reach* – Volumes 1 & 2 published by Ferozsons (Private) Limited.
7. http://www. parabaas.com
8. Translated by Gautam Sengupta; *Bouls of Bengal*; available at http://www.sos-arsenic.net/english/intro/bouls.html
9. *Reading About the World, Volume 2,* edited by Paul Brians, Mary Gallwey, Douglas Hughes, Azfar Hussain, Richard Law, Michael Myers, Michael Neville, Roger Schlesinger, Alice Spitzer, and Susan Swan, Harcourt Brace Custom Books.
10. Ibid.
11. Available at http://sos-arsenic.net/lovingbengal/lalon.html

2: Devotion, Syncretism and Politics: Myth and Legends of the Indus

Bibliography

BOOKS

Albinia, Alice. *Empires of the Indus: the Story of a River*. London: John Murray, 2008.

Auj, Nurulzaman A. *Harappan Heritage*. Multan: Caravan Book Centre, 1998.

Griffith, Ralph T. H. *Hymns of the Atharvaveda*. Vol. 1. Delhi: Munshiram Manoharlal Pvt. Ltd., 1985.

Griffith, Ralph T. H. *Hymns of the Rigveda*. Vol. 2. Delhi: Munshiram Manoharlal Pvt. Ltd., 1987.

Possehl, Gregory L. *Indus Civilization: A Contemporary Perspective*. Delhi: Vistaar, 2002.

Qureshi, Samina. *Legends of the Indus*. London: Asia Ink, 2004.

ARTICLES

Memon, Altaf A. "Devastation of the Indus River Delta." *World Sindhi*. Proc. of World Water and Environmental Resources Congress 2005, Alaska, Anchorage. May 14-19, 2005. American Society of Civil Engineers, Environmental and Water Resources Institute. Web. 30 Sept. 2009. <www.worldsindhi.org/.../ Delta_Devastation_Alaska_Paper_Revised_Draft.doc>.

'Indian Mythological Rivers' from *Indianetzone*, published on 19 January 2009. Web. 14 Sept. 2009. <http://www.indianetzone. com/28/indian_mythological_rivers.htm>.

'Pak-India talks on Kishanganga Hydro Project break down,' *Daily Times*, 6 June 2009, Web. 14 Sept. 2009. <http://www.dailytimes. com.pk/default.asp?page=2009%5C06%5C06%5Cstory_6-6-2009_pg7_27>.

'The Indus Waters Treaty: A History.' *Stimson*. 2007. Web. 14 Sept. 2009. <http://www.stimson.org/?SN=SA20020116301>.

NOTES

1. Possehl, pp. 247-252.
2. Albinia, xvi.
3. Ibid, p. 106.
4. Indianetzone.
5. Griffith (1987), p. 172: Book VIII.
6. Ibid, p. 98-99: Book VII, Hymn XCV. Author's comments: Here, 'Sindhu or Indus appear to be intended under this name [of Sarasvati].'
7. Albinia, pp. 159-60.
8. Griffith (1985), p. 119: Book IV, Hymn XIII
9. Ibid, p. 288: Book VII, Hymn XLV.
10. Griffith (1987), p. 528-529: Book X, Hymn LXXV, The Rivers.
11. Albinia, pp. 107-8 for a detailed description.
12. Ibid, p. 90.
13. Ibid.
14. Qureshi, p. 44.
15. Ib   42.
16. Ibid.
17. All ni , p. 155.
18. Ibid, p. 162.
19. Queshi, p. 73.
20. Ibid.
21. Quoted in Albinia, p.79.
22. Ibid, p. 97.
23. Ibid, p. 79.
24. H.T. Sorely as quoted in Qureshi, p. 42.
25. Alibinia, pp. 94-95.
26. Qureshi, p. 49.
27. Albinia, p. 110.
28. Ibid, p. 96.
29. This section is based on the summary given at Stimson.
30. Ibid.
31. Ibid.

32. Ibid.

33. http://www.wwfpak.org/foreverindus/pdf/290409ifap_%20
annualreport_2008.pdf

34. Memon.

3: Through a Screen, Darkly

1. Arundhati Roy, *The God of Small Things*, published by Flamingo,
an imprint of HarperCollins Publishers [Special overseas edition
1997], page 27.

2. Ekta Kapoor is the Creative Head of Balaji Telefilms that
produces TV serials for all leading entertainment channels.

3. Kapoor's Balaji Telefilms is valued at over ₹230 crore; it trades
on the stock market and remains entertainment television's most
sought after company.

4. An interview with an Indian housewife, by the author.

5. An anonymous interviewee via email.

6. An interview with a senior professional at the STAR TV revealed
that demand was not always a constant and often production
houses such as Balaji were flooding the so-called, amorphous
'market'.

7. Gauri Parimoo Krishnan, senior curator at the Asian Civilizations
Museum in Singapore quoted in Salil Tripathi's 'Gods, princes
and demons' published by *New Statesman* on 22 May 2008.

8. Such as Nabaneeta Dev Sen and Madhu Kishwar.

9. For instance, in a Kannada version, Sita is Ravana's daughter. In
certain tribal renderings, Sita is unfaithful to Rama. Elsewhere,
Ravana occasionally acts in a humane way. In the Malay version,
Laksmana is the brave brother, Rama is weak, occasionally beats
his wife, and Ravana is a descendant of Adam. In some Thai
versions, Rama is Buddha and Ravana is his cousin.

10. Available at http://www.newstatesman.com/ theatre/2008/05/
rama-india-sita-epic-story.

11. In 2006, each episode production cost ₹1.8 million. Smriti Irani aka Tulsi is supposed to charge more than ₹0.8 million per month per serial, making her the highest paid Indian TV actress. Ronit Roy aka Mihir charges ₹0.8 million per month. There is no move to cut the budget, as the show gets full house even today.

12. The blog is titled Nimbus Equations. Accessed on 25 June 2008: http://embraizal.blogspot.com/

13. This famous quote remains widely applicable to postcolonial societies including the fast growing economies such as India, Pakistan and Bangladesh.

14. I am grateful to Madeiline Bunting for this befitting term. For details see, 'The middle classes have discovered they've been duped by the super-rich'published in The *Guardian*, UK, 25 June 2007.

15. The definition of these forums as 'social' denotes how the TV soaps, their representations assume a social reality, a 'truth' in themselves.

16. Courtesy a quick recourse to Madhu Kishwar, 'Yes to Sita, No to Ram! The Continuing Popularity of Sita in India', in *Questioning Ramayanas*, a book of essays edited by Paula Richman, co-published by University of California Press, USA and Oxford University Press, New Delhi, 2000.

17. Multiple discussions with the adherents of Madhu Kishwar's school of thought.

18. For an excellent discussion on related themes, see Kajri Jain, Imagined and performed locality: the televisual field in a north Indian industrial town, Deakin University; n.d. Draft available online: http://web.mit.edu/cms/mit3/papers/jain.pdf

19. Discussions with the author held in January 2008.

20. From Arundhati Roy's speech at the opening Plenary of the World Social Forum in Mumbai on 16 January 2004. Printed in *The Hindu*, online edition, 18 January 2004.

21. A Mumbai-based media professional who wishes to remain anonymous remarked in an interview: 'Viewership ratings are calculated by viewing tendencies of some 1,500 households. A sample based on 1,500 homes decides the taste of entire "India".'

4: The Cult of the Feminine: Kali and the Sindh Province of Pakistan

BIBLIOGRAPHY

AFP News report – 26 December 2008, Ayaz, Shaikh. *Shah Abdul Latif*, 228th Anniversay memorial pp. 24–25.

Akberabadi Akhter Ansari – Parwaz, Karachi, June 1948 pp. 12. BBC News Story.

Dawn, *Benazir termed new age's Marvi*.

Hasan, Syed S. Shah Abdul Latif Bhittai (Essay) Research Forum, Publications, Number 1987 p. 27.

Hussain, Dr. Fahmida. *Image of 'Woman' in The Poetry of Shah Abdul Latif*. 1st ed. Karachi: Shah Abdul Latif Bhitai - University of Karachi, 2001. Print.

International Center for Chemical and Biological Sciences University of Karachi.

Jan, Ammar A., *Tales of Women's Resistance in Pakistan* by in *News on Sunday*, 10th September, 2008.

Kalhoro, Zulfiqar A., 2009, *Rock Carvings and Inscriptions of Sado Mazo in Johi, dadu, Sindh, Pakistan, Journal of Asain Civlizations* Vol.32. No.2 pp. 94–125.

Kalhoro, Zulfiqar A., 2010. *Representations of Music and Dance in Islamic Tombs of Sindh, Pakistan*. Music in Art-International Journal for Music Iconography Vol XXXV, No.1-2. pp. 201–217.

Kinsley, David, *Hindu Goddess: Visions of the Divine Feminine in the Hindu Tradition*, New Delhi: Motilal Banarsidass, 1987, 116.

Kinsley, David, *Tantric Visions of the Divine Feminine: The Ten Mahavidyas*, Berkeley: University of California Press, 1997, p. 70.

Khalid, Haroon, *The Origination of the Bhadrakali Mandar at Niaz Beg: A Historical, Architectural and Artistic Survey*, p. 10.

Kalhoro, Zulfiqar A., 2010, *Hindu and Sikh Architecture in Islamabad and Rawalpindi, Journal of Asian Civilizations* Vol 33. No.1

Kalhoro, Zulfiqar A., *Drink deep indeed,* The *Friday Time*

Kalhoro, Zulfiqar A., *Hide not your Wine from those who Drink: Folktale and Tombs of Bar woman and Drunkards in Gadap*, Karachi (Forthcoming 2011) Journal of Pakistan Historical Society.

Kalhoro, Zulfiqar A., *Kasu Ma,* The Friday Times, published in 2009 Pakistan Hindu Council.

Samad, Rafi U., *Ancient Indus Civilization*, p. 128.

Bhutto, Benazir. *The Story of Benazir* from *Marvi of Malir* Shah Latif by 21 June 2003.

Wazir, Agha, *Tanqueed O Adab Aur Majlisi Tanquid, Ainae Adab*, Lahore 1981 p. 43.

NOTES

1. International Center for Chemical and Biological Sciences University of Karachi.
2. Pakistan Hindu Council.
3. Shaikh Ayaz, Shah Abdul Latif, 228th Anniversay memorial pp. 24-25.
4. Zulfiqar Ali Kalhoro, 2009. Rock Carvings and Inscriptions of Sado Mazo in Johi, dadu, Sindh, Pakistan, *Journal of Asain Civlizations* Vol.32. No.2 pp. 94-125.
5. Kalhoro, Zulfiqar A., 2010. '*Representations of Music and Dance in Islamic Tombs of Sindh, Pakistan.* Music in Art - International Journal for Music Iconography Vol. XXXV, No.1-2. pp. 201-217.
6. Ibid.
7. Agha Wazir. Tanqueed O Adab Aur Majlisi Tanquid, Ainae Adab, Lahore 1981 p. 43.
8. Hussain, Dr. Fahmida. *Image of 'Woman' in The Poetry of Shah Abdul Latif.* 1st ed. Karachi: Shah Abdul Latif Bhitai - University of Karachi, 2001. 46. Print.

9. *Ancient Indus Civilization* by Rafi U. Samad p. 128.

10. David Kinsley, *Hindu Goddess: Visions of the Divine Feminine in the Hindu Tradition*. (New Delhi: Motilal Banarsidass, 1987), 116.

11. (David Kinsley, *Tantric Visions of the Divine Feminine: The Ten Mahavidyas* (Berkeley: University of California Press, 1997), p. 70.

12. The origination of the Bhadrakali Mandar at Niaz Beg: A historical, architectural and artistic survey By Haroon Khalid p. 10.

13. Zulfiqar Ali Kalhoro 2010. *Hindu and Sikh Architecture in Islamabad and Rawalpindi, Journal of Asian Civilizations Vol 33.* No.1

14. Deval Devi is the Kuldevi (family goddess of Detha Charans living in Sindh, Rajasthan and Gujarat). She is an avatar (incarnation) of Hinglaj Mata and cousin of Karni Mata whose temple is situated at Deshnoke near Bikaner in Rajasthan. Deval devi was born into Charan family. Deval was a cousin of Karni Mata. Deval Devi was Shakti not Sati. There are two forms of Devi worship in Sindh: Shakti and Sati. Major Sati temples are located in Tharparkar region of Sindh. She played a very important role in the epic of Pabuji Rathor. Pabuji is the deified god and he is widely worshipped by pastoral communities living in Rajasthan and Gujarat in India and Tharparkar in Sindh.

15. Hussain, Dr. Fahmida. *Image of 'Woman' in The Poetry of Shah Abdul Latif.* 1st ed. Karachi: Shah Abdul Latif Bhitai - University of Karachi, 2001. 430. Print.

16. Sibte Hasan, Shah Abdul Latif Bhittai (Essay) Research Forum, Publications, Syed Sibte Hasan Number 1987 p. 27.

17. Hussain, Dr. Fahmida. *Image of 'Woman' in The Poetry of Shah Abdul Latif.* 1st ed. Karachi: Shah Abdul Latif Bhitai - University of Karachi, 2001. 227. Print.

18. Ibid.

19. *Drink Deep Indeed* by Zulfiqar Ali Kalhoro – Published in *The Friday Times.*

20. Hide not your Wine from those who Drink: Folktale and Tombs of Bar woman and Drunkards in Gadap, Karachi (Forthcoming 2011) Journal of Pakistan Historical Society.

21. *Kasu Ma* by Zulfiqar Ali Kalhoro in *The Friday Times,* published in 2009.

22. *Tales of Women's Resistance in Pakistan* by Ammar Ali Jan in *News on Sunday,* published on 10 September, 2008.

23. Hussain, Dr. Fahmida. *Image of 'Woman' in The Poetry of Shah Abdul Latif.* 1st ed. Karachi: Shah Abdul Latif Bhitai - University of Karachi, 2001. 195. Print.

24. Ibid. 206.

25. Ibid. 215.

26. *Benazir termed new age's Marvi* by Dawn correspondent.

27. *The Story of Benazir* from *Marvi of Malir* Shah Latif by Benazir Bhutto, 21 June 2003.

28. Hussain, Dr. Fahmida. *Image of 'Woman' in The Poetry of Shah Abdul Latif.* 1st ed. Karachi: Shah Abdul Latif Bhitai - University of Karachi, 2001. 178. Print.

29. Akberabadi Akhter Ansari – Parwaz, Karachi, June 1948 p.12.

30. Hussain, Dr. Fahmida. *Image of 'Woman' in The Poetry of Shah Abdul Latif.* 1st ed. Karachi: Shah Abdul Latif Bhitai - University of Karachi, 2001. 411. Print.

31. BBC News Story.

32. AFP News report – 26 December 2008.

5: The Enigma of Dual Belonging: Qurratulain Hyder's Enduring Popularity in Pakistan

1. The authors interviewed are Dr. Enver Sajjad and Mustansar Hussain Tarar. In addition, Afzaal Ahmad of Sang-i-Meel publications, Lahore, Pakistan, was interviewed via telephone. Inputs from a small sample of readers were also collected for the arguments developed in this paper. Thanks are also due to

Sadia Dehlvi, India, for anecdotes on Pakistani visitors rushing to meet Qurratulain Hyder during their visits to Delhi.

2. It is somewhat disquieting that Hyder's self-translation of AKD as *River of Fire* did not become in the words of Khushwant Singh, '*the rage in English that it is in Urdu*'. Singh also said that '*she'll have only herself to blame*'. This is also a view held by others as the English version was abridged and could not do justice to the depth of the original in Urdu.

3. Javed Akhtar, Indian poet and lyricist's audio tribute to Hyder published by the Rediff website.

4. Asif Farrukhi, *The Diva of Urdu Fiction, Dawn*, 26 August 2007.

5. Comparison between the two great elegists in Urdu poetry: Anis and Dabeer. This has been a favourite theme in early Urdu literary criticism. Hyder mocked this in several interviews published in, Syed Aamir Sohail et al., *Qurratulain Haider—Khasoosi Mutal'a*, Multan Arts Forum, 2003.

6. Hyder in a 1998 interview given to NDTV's Radhika Bordia.

7. H. M. Seervai, *Partition of India – Legend and Reality*; monograph in the Constitutional History of India, 1989.

8. For some engaging discussion in the Indian context see Partha Chatterjee, *History and the Domain of the Popular.*

9. While proponents of history from below and the French Annales school of historians have considered themselves part of social history, it is seen as a much broader movement among historians in the development of historiography.

10. Translated by the author from Urdu, *Aag Ka Darya*. Sang-i-Meel Publications, 2007 edition, page 128.

11. Translation found in 'The Vision of Qurratulain Hyder' by Khalid Hasan, *The Friday Times*, December, 2008, Vanguard Publications, Lahore, Pakistan.

12. M. Asaduddin, *The Exiles Return – Qurratulain Hyder's Art of Fiction*, Manushi

13. Editorial, *Daily Times*, 17 January 2008.

14. Kumkum Sangari, 'Qurratulain Hyder's Aag Ka Darya', *Muse India*, Issue 14 Jul-Aug 2007, p. 2.

15. C. M. Naim, *Annual of Urdu Studies*, vol. 1, 1981 p. 107. <http://dsal.uchicago.edu/books/annualofurdustudies/pager.html?objectid=PK2151.A6152_1_113.gif>

16. M. Asaduddin, *The Exiles Return – Qurratulain Hyder's Art of Fiction*; Manushi.

17. Translation found in *The Vision of Qurratulain Hyder* by Khalid Hasan, op cit.

18. Ibid.

19. Ibid.

20. William Dalrymple, *White Mughals: Love and Betrayal in Eighteenth-century India.*, Harper Perennial, New Edition (2 May 2003). Set in and around Hyderabad at the beginning of the nineteenth century, *White Mughals* tells the story of the improbably romantic love affair and marriage between James Achilles Kirkpatrick, an East India Company official, and Khair-un-Nisa, a Hyderabadi princess. The novel explores 'cultural intermingling and hybridity that defines both eastern and western cultures, and a convincing rejection of religious intolerance and ethnic essentialism'. (Jerry Brotton – this text refers to an out of print or unavailable edition of this title).

21. In my meeting with her, she elucidated how modern this novel is in terms of its characterization, mood and technique. There were traces in it of what was to be known at least a century later as the stream of consciousness technique.

22. Kumkum Sangari, Qurratulain Hyder's *Aag Ka Darya*, op cit.

23. Ibid.

24. Ibid.

25. Translation found in *The Vision of Qurratulain Hyder* by Khalid Hasan, op cit.

26. Ibid.

27. Foreword to *Aag Ka Darya*, Qurratulain Hyder, New Delhi, 21 December 1988.

28. Ibid.
29. C. M. Naim, translation Outlook India Web version, 21 August 2007, Delhi.
30. Interview with the author.
31. Hyder in a conversation with the author remarked that while she loved Oxbridge and London, she decided that her sources for literary inspiration rooted in the sub-continental culture and history were missing.
32. Interview with the author.

6: Reclaiming Humanity: Women in Manto's Short Stories

1. From 'O Lord, Return My Prostrations!': *On the Poetics of Manto*, by Syed Noman ul Haq, Daily Dawn (Books & Authors), 5 August 2012.
2. Jalil, Xari. (2012). 'Manto's kahani lives on.' Dawn, 12 May 2012.
3. An exhaustive review of male writers and their works can be found in *Adab ki Nisai Rad-e-Tashkeel*, edited by Fahmida Riaz, February 2006, Wada Kitab Ghar. Karachi.
4. Wadhawan, J. C. (1998). *The Life of Saadat Hassan Manto*, Lotus Collection (Roli Books).
5. Zehra, A.S. (2012). *Manto: The Unmatched Craftsman who Strips Life of its Illustions*, Express Tribune.
6. From 'O Lord, Return My Prostrations!': *On the Poetics of Manto*, by Syed Noman ul Haq, Daily Dawn (Books & Authors), 5 August, 2012.
7. Hassan, Khalid. (2002), *Memoirs of Manto*.
8. Kumar, Sukrita Paul. (1996). *Surfacing from Within: Fallen Women in Manto's Fiction*. Annual of Urdu Studies Vol. 11.
9. 'He saw women the way he saw men'. Dawn. 6 May 2012.
10. Shafique, K. A. (1999), *Portrayal of Women in the Stories of Saadat Hassan Manto*.

11. Translation by Hamid Jalal found in *Manto: Centenary collection*, edited by Ayesha Jalal and Nusrat Jalal; Sang-i-Meel Publications, 2012. Lahore.

12. Riaz, Fahmida. (2012). 'His woman is a human being'. The News.

13. 'Manto saw women the way he saw men'. Dawn, 6 May 2012.

14. Ibid.

15. Hasan, K. (2002). *Memories of Manto*. The *Friday Times*, Lahore.

16. Najma Manzoor, 'Manto, Aurat Aur Waris Alvi' found in Fahmida Riaz (ed.), 'Adab ki Nisai Rad-e-Tashkeel', February 2006, Wada Kitab Ghar, Karachi.

17. Kumar, Sukrita Paul (1996) *Surfacing from Within: Fallen Women in Manto's Fiction*. Annual of Urdu Studies Vol. 11.

18. Shafique, K. A. (1999) *Portrayal of Women in the Stories of Saadat Hassan Manto*.

19. Kumar, Sukrita Paul (1996) *Surfacing from Within: Fallen Women in Manto's Fiction*. Annual of Urdu Studies Vol. 11.

20. Shafique, K. A. (1999) *Portrayal of Women in the Stories of Saadat Hassan Manto*.

21. A legendary Urdu novel by Mirza Hadi Ruswa published in 1899 portrayed the travails of a young girl Ameeran from Faizabad, UP who is abducted and sold at a Kotha in Lucknow. In the cinematic renditions of this work, Umrao Jan has been shown as the 'innocent victim' thus playing to (conservative) middle class imagination of North India and Pakistan.

22. From 'Literary notes: Intizar Husain discusses realism in Manto', Daily Dawn, 6 May, 2012; Pakistan.

23. Shafique, K.A. (1999), *Portrayal of Women in the Stories of Saadat Hassan Manto*. In Dawn, 13-19 May, 1999.

24. Kumar, Sukrita Paul (1996), '*Surfacing from Within: Fallen Women in Manto's Fiction*,' Annual of Urdu Studies Vol. 11.

25. Ibid.

26. Riaz, Fahmida (2012), 'His woman is a human being.' The News.

9: 'Who Will Listen to the Tale of My Woeful Heart?' The Portrait of 'Nautch Girls' in Early Urdu Literature

1. Mirza Muhammad Hadi Ruswa, *Umrao Jan Ada: Courtesan of Lucknow* tr. Khushwant Singh and M. A. Husaini, reprint ed., (Hyderabad: Disha Books, 1993).
2. Vinay Lal, 'The Courtesan and the Indian Novel' *Manas*.
3. Ibid.
4. Ruswa, 151.
5. Ibid, 152.
6. Hasan Shah, *The Nautch Girl: A Novel* tr. Qurratulain Hyder (New Delhi: Sterling Publishers, 1992).
7. The author interviewed her in 2005 and Hyder forcefully argued why *Fasana-e Rangin* had all the elements of a modern novel.
8. Asif Farrukhi, comp. *Dastan-e 'ahad-e gul* (Karachi: Maktaba-e Daniyal, 2002).
9. Vikram Sampath, *My Name is Gauhar Jaan! The Life and Times of a Musician* (New Delhi: Rupa Publications, 2010).
10. Found in Sampath, 183.
11. Ghulam Abbas, 'Anandi,' tr. G. A. Chaussée *The Annual of Urdu Studies* 18 (2003): 324.
12. Abbas, 339.

11: Silhouetted Silences: Contemporary Pakistani Literature in the 'Age of Terror'

1. This paper was presented at the SAARC Literature Festival held in Agra (March 2009) by the Foundation of SAARC Writers and Literature. The author is grateful to Ajeet Caur (India), Irfan Javed, Dr Asif Farrukhi and Fahmida Riaz (Karachi); Syed Aadil Shah (Islamabad); Umair Javed (Lahore); and Shah Jahan (Peshawar) for their contributions, comments, advice and encouragement.

2. *Terrorism and modern literature from Joseph Conrad to Ciaran Carson*, by Alex Houen, Published by Oxford University Press, 2002; 310 pages.

3. *The Reluctant Fundamentalist* by Mohsin Hamid. Published by Doubleday Canada, Limited, 2007; 192 pages.

4. Ibid.

5. *No space for further burials*, by Feryal Ali Gauhar. Published by Women Unlimited, 2007, Original from the University of Michigan, Digitized 28 June 2008, 192 pages.

6. *A Case of Exploding Mangoes* (E-Book), By Mohammed Hanif. Published by Knopf Publishing Group, 2008, 320 pages.

7. Translated from Urdu by the author.

8. Translated from the Urdu by Asif Farrukhi. The author is grateful for his guidance and sharing this translation.

9. The poem was composed in the backdrop of a brutal tragedy. Bajaur is a small city near the border of Afghanistan that was bombed during the search for terrorists, resulting in the death of many students.

10. Translated by Syed Aadil Shah and adapted by the author.

11. Adapted from Karthigesu Sivathamby fifty years of Sri Lankan Tamil literature TAMIL CIRCLE magazine http://tamilelibrary. org/teli/srilitt.html

12. This statement is equally valid for other South Asian countries.

14: Public Spaces, Architecture and National Identity

1. Apoorva Shah, (May/June 2011), *The Most Dangerous Place: Pakistan's Past, Pakistan's Future*, World Affairs. <http:// www.worldaffairsjournal.org/article/most-dangerous-place-pakistan's-past-pakistan's-future >

2. Remembrance: The man Behind the Masterpiece, 22 March 2009, Dawn, <http://www.dawn.com/news/859634/ remembrance-the- man-behind-the-masterpiece>

3. 'Qutb Minar and its Monuments, Delhi-UNESCO World Heritage List,' World Heritage Convention – UNESCO, <https://whc.unesco.org/en/list/233>

4. 'Mausoleum complex' Quid-e-Azam Mazar Management board, <http://qmmb.gov.pk/mausoleum-1.html>

5. Ibid.

6. cda.gov.pk   <http://www.cda.gov.pk/about_islamabad/history/#ad-image-0>

7. Ali Arsalan, *Bordering Practice and Territoriality: Examining Islamabad and New Delhi*, thesis submitted to Middle East Technical University,   <http://etd.lib.metu.edu.tr/upload/12619775/index.pdf>

8. Farhan Karim, *Architecture as an Appropriating Apparatus: Muslim Nationalism and Designing Presidential Complex of Islamabad, Pakistan*,   <https://architecture.mit.edu/history-theory-and-criticism/lecture/architecture-appropriating-apparatus-muslim-nationalism-and>

9. Emad El-Din Shahin, *The Oxford Handbook of Islam and Politics* (London: Oxford University Press, 2016), https://books.google.com/books?id=wUcSDAAAQBAJ&pg=PA293&dq=use%2Bof+islamic%2Bsymbols+source&hl=en&sa=X&ved=0ahUKEwjI_bXawJnbAhVMx1kKHQ2FC CgQ6AEIODAC#v=onepage&q=use%2Bof%20islamic%2Bsymbols%20source&f=false

10. Rizwan Hussain, 'Pakistan', In *The Oxford Encyclopedia of the Islamic World*, Oxford Islamic Studies Online, <http://www.oxfordislamicstudies.com/article/opr/t236/e0616>

11. Ibid

12. Syed Irfan Ashraf, *Behind the Conspiracy Theories*, Dawn, 23 July 2013, <https://www.dawn.com/news/1031299>

13. NTI.org, accessed May 22, 2018. < http://www.nti.org/>

14. Pakistan Today, 25 March 2012 'Militarisation of Society' Editorial, Militarisation of Society, <https://www.pakistantoday.com.pk/2012/03/25/militarisation-of-society/>

15. Ibid.

16. Qadeer Tanoli, 31 January 2016, 'Fewer Jobs for Pakistanis in Middle East', *The Express Tribune*, < https://tribune.com.pk/story/1037278/shrinking-prospects-fewer-jobs-for-pakistanis-in-war-hit-mideast/>

17. Pakistan Today, 25 March 2016, 'Pakistan on 8th position with $20.1 billion remittances', <https://www.pakistantoday.com.pk/2016/03/25/pakistan-on-8th-position-with-20-1-billion-remittances/>

18. Farrukh Saleem, 20 March 2016, 'Remittances Alert', *The News*. <https://www.thenews.com.pk/print/106668-Remittances-alert>

19. Denholm Barnetson, 20 August 1988, 'Zia buried on lawn of mosque', UPI Archives.
<   https://www.upi.com/Archives/1988/08/20/Zia-buried-on-lawn-of-mosque/5949588052800/>

20. Danish Hussain, 12 January 2015, 'Holy Cows? In Capital, Majority of Madrassas Operating Illegally', *The Express Tribune*, < https://tribune.com.pk/story/820454/holy-cows-in-capital-majority-of-madrassas-operating-illegally/>

21. Ibid.

20: Asim Butt's Activism Through Art

1. There is a considerable body of public art to Asim's credit: a mural done at the San Francisco Arts Commission Gallery reacting to the US 'War on Terror,' another in Mumbai, one found on the walls of The Second Floor Café, Karachi, and what he calls a 'scribble' at an *Akharra* in Lahore, and countless other ventures.

2. However, the great master Sadequain's work is largely confined to public buildings – stately and official and not always open to public at large.

3. The key examples of such endeavours are found in the capital city Islamabad, where Amin Guljee's modern sculpture greets

the ironically titled Constitutional Avenue, now closed to public for all practical purposes. Similarly, the famous Schon Circle of Karachi brought in a dislocated non-aesthetic into a cosmopolitan city, in need of far greater engagement.

4. Stuckism is an international art movement that was founded in 1999 in Britain to promote figurative painting in opposition to conceptual art. The first group of thirteen British artists has since expanded, as of March 2011, to 214 groups in forty-eight countries.